D0068155

Praise for this Book

'This is an exceptionally rich and thought-provoking work. Nyamnjoh gives us a vivid, well-researched picture of the new African media landscape, while asking probing questions about both journalistic practice and the meaning of democracy.'

James Ferguson, Department of Cultural and Social Anthropology, Stanford University

'Nyamnjoh's analysis innovatively develops a new conceptual framework in assessing studies on, and the state of, African media and how people use them. His theoretical achievement is to critique African essentialism on the one hand, while developing an indigenized critical theory on the other. He speaks from Africa, about Africa, in an engagement with Western theory, assumptions and policies. This study is a breakthrough.'

Keyan G. Tomaselli, University of KwaZulu–Natal, and president of the South African Communication Association

'Nyamnjoh's book combines the anthropologist's eyes for patterned behaviour and the journalist's nose for social criticism. The result is a delicious rendition on the complex role of communication in democracy. This should be required reading in journalism, political science and sociology.'

Charles Okigbo, Department of Communication, North Dakota State University

'Professor Francis Nyamnjoh raises the level of the debate on the media and the democratization agenda in Africa to a very high level. The book serves as an outstanding contribution and source for scholars, professionals and top-level decision-makers in the area of media and democracy in Africa. It is a "must" text for all students of mass media and development in Africa.'

Cecil Blake, Chair, Africana Studies Department, University of Pittsburgh

'A "must read". This book presents a detailed analysis of the role and place of Africa's media in its search for democratization and cultural identities. Francis Nyamnjoh is neither apologetic nor defensive about the major problems Africa faces, nor does he join the Western power-bashers. This book should be core reading for anyone with an interest in Africa.'

Professor Jan Servaes, Head of School of Journalism and Communication, University of Queensland, Australia

About this book

This major study explores the role of the mass media in promoting democracy and empowering civil society in Africa during what has come to be called the continent's second liberation struggle in the 1990s. Francis Nyamnjoh situates the African communications media in the rapidly developing context of global media change, including new forms such as the Internet. He provides a synoptic exploration for the continent as a whole of the defective nature of recent democratisation. He shows how patterns of media ownership and state control have evolved; the changing legal framework regulating the press; and the huge difficulties – of inadequate training, job insecurity and poor working conditions – under which most media workers in Africa labour. The author also explores the whole question of media ethics and professionalism in Africa, and the very important roles that radio trottoir (rumour) and political satire in the form of cartoons have played as sources of information and opinion-formation. The general analysis is supported by a very detailed unique case study of the media and democratisation in Cameroon, a country which the author sees as a microcosm of both anglophone and francophone Africa. Nyamnjoh argues that his findings are likely to be representative of the continent more widely.

The author's conclusions are startling. He is critical of the Western-derived institutional framework for multi-party democracy that overlooks the social realities of African citizens' multiple identities, and their cultural orientation to communal values. He concludes not only that African governments have done very little to encourage independent media, but that the media themselves must share some of the blame. Many journalists and the publications they work for have often been so politicised and disrespectful of the need to base reports on facts and the collection of evidence that their role in promoting democratisation has been very limited. The volume concludes by laying out some important ideas for the reform of public policy and journalistic behaviour.

About the Author

Francis B. Nyamnjoh is Associate Professor and Head of Publications and Communications with the Council for the Development of Social Science Research in Africa (CODESRIA). He has taught sociology, anthropology and communications studies at universities in Cameroon, Botswana and South Africa, and has researched and written extensively on Cameroon and Botswana, where he was awarded the Senior Arts Researcher of the Year prize for 2003. His most recent books include *Negotiating an Anglophone Identity* (Brill, 2003) and *Rights and the Politics of Recognition in Africa* (Zed Books, 2004). Dr Nyamnjoh has published widely on globalisation, citizenship, media and the politics of identity in Africa. He has also published two novels, *Mind Searching* (1991) and *The Disillusioned African* (1995), and a play, *The Convert* (2003). Additionally, he served as vice-president of the African Council for Communication Education (ACCE) from 1996 to 2003.

Africa's Media, Democracy and the Politics of Belonging

FRANCIS B. NYAMNJOH

ZED BOOKS
London & New York

UNISA PRESS
Pretoria

JA
85.2
A35
N93
2005

Africa's Media, Democracy and the Politics of Belonging was first published in 2005
by Zed Books Ltd, 7 Cynthia Street, London N1 9JF, UK,
and Room 400, 175 Fifth Avenue, New York, NY 10010, USA

www.zedbooks.co.uk

Published in South Africa by UNISA Press,
PO Box 392, Pretoria, RSA 003, www.unisa.ac/za

Copyright © Francis B. Nyamnjoh 2005

The right of Francis B. Nyamnjoh to be identified as the author
of this work has been asserted by him in accordance with the
Copyright, Designs and Patents Act, 1988

Designed and typeset in Monotype Joanna by Illuminati, Grosmont
Cover designed by Andrew Corbett
Printed and bound in Malta by Gutenberg Press Ltd

Distributed in the USA exclusively by Palgrave Macmillan,
a division of St Martin's Press, LLC, 175 Fifth Avenue, New York, NY 10010

All rights reserved

A catalogue record for this book is available from the British Library
Library of Congress Cataloging-in-Publication Data available

ISBN 1 84277 582 0 Hb
ISBN 1 84277 583 9 Pb

OLSON LIBRARY
NORTHERN MICHIGAN UNIVERSITY
MARQUETTE, MI 49855

Contents

Acknowledgements

In writing this book, I have benefited from many enriching encounters with scholars and others. I would like to thank all those who, in one way or another, have contributed to this project. In particular, I am grateful for funding from the Friedrich Ebert Stiftung and the Dutch Embassy in Cameroon, and from the Wenner-Gren Foundation for Anthropological Research, as well as for academic fellowships at St Anthony's College, Oxford (1997) and the African Studies Centre, Leiden (1998), which made it possible for me to pursue in detail my interest in media, democracy and the politics of belonging. I owe a special debt to Jeff Lever, whose copy-editing abilities have been most sensitive to the nuances and complexities of the realities the book captures. I thank Andrea Swalec for arranging the references, and Michael Ralph for helping with proofreading. Finally, I thank Henrietta and our children, for tolerating my most unholy hours of academic pursuits.

INTRODUCTION

Media, Belonging and Democratisation

in Africa

Media and Democracy

This book enters into the debate on democracy in Africa through an analysis of the role played by the media in the democratisation process of the 1990s. In popular as well as academic circles there are varying degrees of certainty about the extent to which mass media (radio, television and print) influence African audiences. Contrary to the popular understanding of the media as *magic multipliers* capable of stimulating or dulling the senses of those who receive them like a hypodermic syringe, media effects are neither direct, simple, nor immediate. The audience, by extension, is neither altogether passive nor helpless, since members of the same demographic often get different messages from the same source. In other words, what people make of particular media contents depends, *inter alia*, on where their vested interests lie, interests which are not fixed. Media effects are usually gradual and cumulative, and dependent on other, accompanying factors. With this in mind, this book examines the media in action in Africa in the 1990s, seeking to understand how the media have contributed to the continent's efforts at democratisation in a context of growing obsession with belonging.

The media, both conventional and alternative, old and new, traditional and modern, interpersonal and mass, can, in principle, facilitate popular empowerment as a societal project. If civil society is crucial for democracy, as I argue in Chapters 1, 2 and 3 below, communication is even more so, as the rest of the book evinces. For, as Philip Lee puts it, people can only participate and make their wishes known if public communication is made an integral part of political democracy. Effective democracy, he maintains, 'demands a system of constant interaction with all the people, accessibility at all levels, a public ethos which allows conflicting ideas to contend, and which provides for full participation in reaching consensus on socio-cultural, economic and political goals' (Lee 1995: 2). In order to participate meaningfully in discussions of public issues, people need both knowledge and education on how to use the information at their disposal. The media have an enormous potential to provide such knowledge and education, but the media can also be a vehicle for uncritical assumptions, beliefs, stereotypes, ideologies and orthodoxies that blunt critical awareness and make participatory democratisation difficult. Thus, only when they empower individuals and communities to scrutinise publicly and contest decisions made in their name by the most powerful members and institutions of society (Lee 1995: 2–7) can the media promote democratisation (Hyden and Leslie 2002).

However, the media do not have the same potential in every society, nor are they accessible to everyone in the same way or to the same extent. Given unequal access to wealth and power, certain communities and individuals are less privileged than others. This can make a world of difference in terms of media access, content and practice. Thus what Lee means by 'the illusion of democracy' is that even in the most privileged countries of the West, quite often, 'political rhetoric about democracy denies the possibility of inequity, inaccessibility and marginalisation' (Lee 1995: 10).

Culturally, the media are victims of an imposed hierarchy of national and world cultures, and also of the cultural industries that have opted for routinisation, standardisation and homogenisation of media content. This has occasioned the exclusion or marginalisation of entire world-views and cultures that do not guarantee profitability. African world-views and cultural values are hence doubly excluded: first by the ideology of hierarchies of cultures, and second by cultural industries more interested in profits than the promotion of creative diversity and cultural plurality. The consequence is an idea of democracy hardly informed by popular articulations of personhood and agency in Africa, and media whose professional values are not in tune with the expectations of those they purport to serve. The predicament of media practitioners in such a situation is obvious: to be of real service to liberal democracy, they must ignore alternative ideas of personhood and agency in the cultural communities of which they are a part. Similarly, attending to the interests of particular cultural groups risks contradicting the principles of liberal democracy and its emphasis on the autonomous individual. Torn between such competing and conflicting understandings of democracy, the media find it increasingly difficult to marry rhetoric with practice, and for strategic instrumentalist reasons may opt for a Jekyll and Hyde personality. Taking the latter option has meant the propagation of liberal democratic rhetoric in principle while at the same time promoting the struggles for recognition and representation of the various cultural, ethnic or sectarian groups with which they identify (see Chapter 1). The politics of belonging is thus central to understanding democracy in Africa and the role of the media in promoting it. The predicament faced by the media in this regard emphasises the need for more domesticated understandings of democracy as mediated by the quest for conviviality between individual and community interests.

Information Technologies and Democracy

Africa is in many ways marginal to current globalisation processes (Zeleza 2003), and it is quite possible to sidestep it in ongoing debates about the present and future directions of global communications technologies. Also, given the sometimes marginal impact of these technologies on African realities, it is very possible, as well, to ignore them in discussions of the media in Africa. Thanks to new technologies, global images and consumer desire, socialisation packages may be readily available and affordable to local elites in Africa, but the majority are yet to experience these technologies or to influence their content. Africa may be in the world, but few Africans are yet of the world, in this sense. While the rest of the world is significantly more advanced, and in certain cases (e.g. North America and Western Europe) there is already talk of *new media* taking over from *old media*, in Africa the so-called old media are yet to take over from the indigenous forms of communication. Africa is still infrastructurally very weak compared to the television, radio and print media already commonplace elsewhere. Silent majorities in villages and urban ghettoes are still groping in the dark, seeking footpaths and footholds in the era of satellite television, digital revolutions and the information superhighway (Nyamnjoh 1996a, 2000a; Ngwainmbi 1995). But because Africa is part of the world, and because its backwardness is less the result of choice than of circumstance, ordinary Africans are determined to be part of the technological revolutions of the modern world, even if this means accessing the information superhighway on foot, horseback, bicycles, bush taxis and second-hand cars, or relying on lifts and the generosity of the super-endowed in the latest sports and fancy cars.

This makes the African mediascape a rich and fascinating blend of traditions, influences and technologies. Coexisting in conviviality and interdependence are the most modern forms of communications technologies and indigenous media. One finds on the continent pockets of people in tune with an Internet facilitated by multimedia connectivity (Leslie 2002; Thioune 2003; Etta and Parvyn-Wamahiu 2003) – perfect examples of first-class passengers on the information superhighway staking a claim to the global village as Africans. One finds also those whose hybrid realities dictate the need to straddle the worlds of indigenous and modern media, creatively drawing on both to negotiate the communicative hurdles and hierarchies of the continent. Africa's creativity simply cannot allow for simple dichotomies or distinctions between old and new technologies, since its peoples are daily modernising the indigenous and indigenising the modern with novel outcomes. No technology seems too used to be used, just as nothing is too new to be blended with the old for even newer results. Such creativity is not only informed by cultures amenable to conviviality, interdependence and negotiation, but also by histories of deprivation, debasement and cosmopolitanism.

Given that it is not necessary to be at the same level to belong and to benefit from the fruit of technological advances, I have chosen to

introduce this discussion from the vantage point of current technological achievements and their expected benefits for Africans. Not to
discuss the new information and communications technologies (ICTs)
would be to ignore the elite few in Africa who are actively involved
with them and globally competitive, making of Africa a continent
where all types of communication technologies have their place, from
the 'Tam Tam to Internet' (Ras-Work 1998; Ngwainmbi 1995; van
Binsbergen 2004). Limited though their implantation and impact in
Africa might be, new technologies have facilitated communication and
networking in ways that threaten erosion of monolithic state control
of information and communication (Bourgault 1995: 206–25; Franda
2002: 18–26; Leslie 2002). NGOs and other development advocates
– the Canadian International Development Research Centre (IDRC) and
the Council for the Development of Social Science Research in Africa
(CODESRIA), for example (Thioune 2003; Etta and Parvyn-Wamahiu
2003) – are investing heavily in research that explains how best to
harness new ICTs in the interest of community development in Africa.
Such potential is enough for Africans to want to know more about
the new media, even if some are yet to experience the old.

In a global context it is meaningless not only to discuss in isola-
tion media and democracy in Africa but also to talk of equality and
participation when communication infrastructure is so dispropor-
tionately distributed between, as well as within, the rich and poor
areas of the North and the South (Hamelink 1995, 1996, 1999; Uche
1996; Golding and Harris 1997). Phenomenal achievements in ICTs
do not seem to be matched by greater equality for individuals and
communities globally. One example of this disparity can be found
in the development and use of the *information superhighway*. Defined
as 'the convergence of computer and communication technologies'
(Lynch 1997/98: 285), the information superhighway presupposes
the existence of a *highway* which has been widened and improved
upon to become *super*. This simply reflects a metaphorical usage that
tries to explain the possibility that all and sundry in the electronic
age can interact with each other through electronic machines which
serve as a superhighway for the transmission of messages.

The Internet, which best epitomizes the information superhighway,
is available, at a fee, to anyone with a computer, a modem and an

efficient telephone line. There is abundant literature stressing the advantages of the Internet, which has far-reaching tentacles that extend to the spheres of politics, the information economy, culture and social networks. Its proponents and enthusiasts, such as the former US vice-president Al Gore, see it as 'the essential prerequisite to sustainable development' and count on it for solutions to environmental problems, the improvement of education and health care, the creation of a global marketplace and the forging of a 'new Athenian age of democracy' (Hamelink 1996: 19). Conceivably, through the use of electronic machines, legislative power would be placed directly in the hands of the people, as laws on taxes, education, immigration, abortion, crime and other major issues could be made with the direct participation of the electorate. In the USA, for example, email has enhanced and accelerated citizen participation in politics between elections (Grossman 1994: 34). Thanks to the Internet, the Starr Report on the Clinton–Lewinsky sex scandal, voluminous as it was, was made available for instant access by millions of Internet users throughout the world. And it is thanks also to the Internet that the stalemate and post-election drama of the 2000 presidential race between Al Gore and Bush was savoured by millions in America and elsewhere.

It should be noted, however, that the rush to create an interactive electronic superhighway is to a large extent driven by commercial interests. As some have argued, if the business world is promoting the Internet, 'their motive is to create a sense of need' for their products, and 'once this perceived need is cultivated, some organizations then require a membership or annual subscription fee for the information or service that you initially accessed without cost' (Awake 1997: 8). The surge in importance of e-commerce speaks for this and has led others to wonder if the information superhighway can ever truly become as available and affordable as is fashionable to claim, when information is paid for and controlled as a commodity (Lee 1995: 2; Hamelink 1995: 16; McChesney and Nichols 2002). And if the Internet were indeed to become available and affordable, 'the question of the quality of the information' would still be raised, for an easily accessible and relatively cheap Internet could boast of little more than 'information rubbish' or 'scrap opinion'

(Becker 1996: 11). Even now already, 'there is ... an awful lot of junk, trash, and trivia' on the Internet (Hamelink 1996: 19), with unsolicited messages an increasing problem. The verdict, however, is still out. From the perspective of international and cross-cultural communication, one quickly notices how the information super-highway has linked major parts of the world. It has, to an extent, enhanced interpersonal, intergroup and international interaction, bringing the world even closer as one village to engage in 'a global conversation' (Wriston 1994: 20), accelerating the flow of exchange of products, ideas and information in unprecedented ways.

The growth of the information superhighway has revitalised debate on international news flows. While many in the West view the information superhighway as hastening the globalisation process, their counterparts in the developing world often see it as fostering media and cultural imperialism, and as globalising poverty above everything else. However, such perspectives have tended 'to limit rather than illuminate discussions', as they overstate external fac-tors and underplay internal dynamics and the creative resistance or appropriation of imported cultural products within dependent African countries (Golding and Harris 1997: 5–9), as illustrated by Mitchell Land's study of television in Côte d'Ivoire (Land 1992, 1994). It is worth noting that 'Globalisation does not necessarily or even frequently imply homogenization or Americanization', as different societies tend to be quite creative in their appropriation or consumption of the materials of modernity (Appadurai 1996: 17). Although to some it remains apparent that 'Third world nations will bear the brunt of the risk and instability associated with the exploitation of information industry technologies and markets' (Melody 1987: 26), others argue that these revolutionary media tech-nologies are rapidly shrinking the world into McLuhan's prophesied 'global village'. Jussawalla observes that 'the proliferation of global information systems and the rapid transmission of data flows across national boundaries' have rendered the nation-state meaningless and raised the prospects of the eventual creation of a global 'republic of technology' (Jussawalla 1988: 11–12). This view and optimism are shared by the G8, who, in a joint communiqué in Okinawa, Japan, in July 2000, formally declared that ICTs could empower, benefit and link people the world over, and who committed themselves to making this a global reality (*Media Development* 2000). To others, the advent of the information superhighway would mean that human rights or democratic freedoms will not be denied to people of remote places any more, since 'a global village will have global customs' (Wriston 1994: 20).

In the West the tendency is to claim that these interactive technologies offer more control over the media by consumers, allowing them to choose and consume what, when and how they want. Thus Grossman's idea that George Orwell's 'nightmare vision' of the information society presented in his novel 1984 'has been turned upside down'. For, 'Instead of "Big Brother" keeping millions of citizens under continuous electronic surveillance, millions of citizens are keeping "Big Bubba" ... under continuous electronic surveillance' (Grossman 1994: 34). Mind control of the Mussolini type has been rendered impossible by the fact that 'there are just too many pathways for news and data to find their way to us' (Wriston 1994: 18), especially as 'the original design of the Internet was to make it resistant to disruption' and censorship (Awake 1997: 11). But this is a claim denied by others (Windseck 1997; McChesney 1998, 2001; McChesney and Nichols 2002), who argue that the new technologies are conceived, designed, built and installed with the primary objective of maintaining economic, political and cultural privileges and advantage. This argument has only grown stronger with the reactionary 'global intelligence' measures adopted by the USA and other governments following the 11 September 2001 attack on the World Trade Center in New York (Todd and Bloch 2003). Thus there is a need to treat the notion of 'information society' as problematic, by investigating 'alternative options in the adoption of new technologies' and discussing various strategies for the 'social shaping' of these technologies (Lyon 1986: 585–6). For example, far from being 'a monolithic or placeless "cyberspace"', the Internet 'is numerous new technologies, used by diverse people, in diverse real-world locations', and therefore cannot be fully understood outside of how it is being harnessed and assimilated under differential political, economic, cultural and social circumstances of individuals and communities (Miller and Slater 2000: 1–25). Applied to Africa, it is regrettable that scholarly focus has been rather on what ICTs *do to* Africans, instead of what Africans *do with* ICTs through 'enculturation' (van Binsbergen 2004).

Even in the USA, where the most extravagant claims are made about the potential and reality of the Internet, research on the social background of users reveals a typical pattern: they are mostly male, young, rich and come from the ruling class of society (Becker 1996: 10). Becker considers this social background of Internet users as typical, and, drawing as well from the example of radio amateurs in the 1910s and 1920s, argues that 'technically highly-motivated young men from the upper social classes always function as the objective door-openers of a new technology market' by helping 'to conquer new and unknown markets' (Becker 1996: 10). A survey by the UN Economic Commission for Africa suggests a similar profile, with the largest number of Internet users being young, predominantly male, well-educated, having above-average incomes, English-speaking, and belonging to NGOs, the media, private companies and universities (Franda 2002: 18).

Given this pattern, others argue that detours, dislocations and disruptions would certainly result from attempts by international media giants to make even more capital out of information (Murdock 1994), or by governments to control access. The reality of information as commodity and power makes this outcome almost inevitable, as it is highly unlikely that undemocratic capitalism, as exists in the world market, would finance the global information infrastructure necessary to ensure participatory democratic communication at a global level. Instead, since the information superhighway project requires billion-dollar investments, it 'will only take off if investors are guaranteed freedom from interference and can operate without hindrance on a global market' to maximise profits (Hamelink 1996: 19).

Africa and the Information Superhighway: What Future?

No matter how unequal their effects may be, the profound technological changes taking place in the field of communication are radically transforming the lives and ways of most people and institutions in the West. This is because most already have the tools or equipment that enable them to acquire and use these technologies. But in Africa, where the basic equipment is either lacking or defective and where information is largely the preserve of the government, the information highway is still to become a reality, let alone a super one. And this, despite the optimism of some Western governments that 'the many application possibilities for new information and communication technology offer many opportunities to the developing countries, to skip over the defined steps of technical development and provide new thrust to their social and economic development' (Federal Republic of Germany 1996: 835).

With the exception of South Africa (Ras-Work 1998), Africa still resides in a world of shadows regarding the new communications technologies (Jensen 2000; Franda 2002: 7–40). The concept of an information superhighway can hardly be understood in Africa in the meantime, because the highway is yet to be travelled by enough Africans and/or Africa-based users (Okigbo 1995: 120; Jensen 2000; Leslie 2002). So far, 'African governments though using the available media and communication machinery for their own motivations, are giving lip service to the development of information and communication sectors, when it comes to the formulation of the national development plans' (OAU 1995: 2). Despite the adoption in 1989 of a common African information and communication strategy, little has been done at the level of individual countries to start implementation (OAU 1995: 5–6). Africa thus finds itself left behind, being more of an observer than a participant. Computers and telephone technologies have yet to become common in the continent where, to quote President Thabo Mbeki of South Africa, 'Over half of humankind has never dialled a phone number', with Manhattan having 'more telephone lines ... than in the whole of sub-Saharan Africa' (quoted in Lynch 1997/98: 300; see also Ras-Work 1998; Jensen 2000: 218–19; Franda 2002: 9–23). 'The cost of installing a residential telephone line ... is more than a Professor's one year salary in Nigeria', where the frustration of waiting for an installation is phenomenal, and even after installation 'the weakness is the epileptic manner with which it works!' (Uche 1999a: 199). Little wonder that 'In many African countries, it is faster and cheaper to travel than to make a telephone call' (Emeagwali, cited in Uche 1999a: 199). Although the introduction and adoption of the cellphone have done much to challenge this reality, Africa still remains the least technologically facilitated continent, despite being one of the most populated.

Indeed, as the OAU put it in 1995, 'Africa's communication and telecommunications networks and information technology remain ... most inadequate, if not appalling.' While every other region is taking advantage of the electronic revolution, 'African countries are still mere recipients and dependent on outside communication infrastructures. Telecommunication contacts and linkages among African countries are hardly available, and in most cases telephone contacts among them are made through foreign facilities' (OAU 1995: 2). Even when the technologies are to be imported, African governments have the tendency to wait until certain equipment and technologies become obsolete before importing them for less. The consequence being that, as Africans, 'We get technologies sometimes that are not adaptable to our environment and climates. We buy equipments without having the right and trained personnel to man them' (OAU 1995: 4). A sustained interest in the information superhighway by Africa must entail the domestication and standardisation of the information and telecommunications technologies, 'so that its countries become capable of easily reaching each other and exchanging experiences and training facilities' (OAU 1995: 4). This calls for a concerted and organised approach by African countries and for appropriate policies on ownership and control. As the Indian experience in this domain shows, coming up with meaningful and relevant Internet policies is far from easy, especially if a country or continent is determined to show that assumptions about Internet configurations in the USA or Europe need not necessarily be reflected in Internet developments elsewhere (McDowell and Pashupati 1998: 18–23).

Indeed, Africa's response to the emerging global information superhighway is proving to be simplistic and overly optimistic in its assumptions, objectives and timetable, in view of its lack of the basic capacity to adopt and adapt new communications technologies to local environments. In May 1996, the UN Economic Commission for Africa (ECA) adopted its Africa's Information Society Initiative (AISI), 'a broad, long-term and ambitious programme, directed at the utilisation of information and communication technologies to stimulate overall economic and social growth in Africa' (van Audenhove 1998: 76; Mukasa 1998: 8–9). But not only are these guidelines dependent on the goodwill of individual states for implementation, the leeway given private initiative leads one to question whether such 'liberalisation would indeed foster the enabling environment in which services will or can be broadly generalised' (van Audenhove 1998: 79). Countries are joining the privatisation bandwagon almost without exception, quite oblivious or regardless of the fact that private ownership does not necessarily entail better or even cheaper services, especially in a global economy where states and labour are virtually at the mercy of multinationals and their thirst for profit (Chomsky 1999). African subscribers to the new privately operated cellphone networks know this only too well and have started speaking out against poor services and exorbitant charges.

Some scholars have also criticised certain questionable assumptions in the ECA document that information and technology are neutral and the latter easily transferable, that access to information technology by Africa and Africans is necessary and sufficient to accelerate development, and that information will be free or almost free in the information society. The AISI Action Framework thus fails to 'take into account the enormous economic, infrastructural, political and social constraints, to a large extent structural, which will hamper the development of information technology and its applications and services in Africa' (van Audenhove 1998: 77–9). What is urgently needed in most countries is not so much privatisation as the constitution of an independent national regulatory authority 'to regulate the market and to introduce fair competition in certain sectors' (van Audenhove 1998: 80–81).

This picture of gloom notwithstanding, the Internet is gradually becoming an everyday tool among elites and elite institutions in Africa (Ras-Work 1998; Cochrane and Brunner 1998; Jensen 2000; Franda 2002; Leslie 2002; Thioune 2003; Etta and Parvyn-Wamahiu 2003). Even in countries where government's reaction has initially been to vacillate, the Internet is increasingly being used by universities, schools, businesses, government departments, NGOs, newspapers and individuals in major cities where telecommunications installations are less capricious. Local firms, organisations and enthusiasts have signed up with foreign agents to sell Internet services to local consumers, and Internet cafés are mushrooming in the major cities (Etta and Parvyn-Wamahiu 2003). At the *Carnivore* in Nairobi these days, carnivores who come to sample the rich variety of Kenyan wildlife are also invited to excel as *cybervores*. Current estimates indicate that Africa, with a population of 780 million, has around 500,000 Internet subscribers and about 1.5 million users. With approximately 1 million of these users based in South Africa alone and mostly white, the remaining 734 million Africans can afford only 500,000 users. 'This works out to about 1 Internet user for every 1,500 people, compared to a global average of about 1 user for every 38 people, and a North American and European average of about 1 in 4.' These figures are clearly modest by Western and world standards, but they do indicate rapid progress compared to 1996 when only 11 of Africa's 54 countries had Internet access. Today all countries are connected, at least at the level of the capital city, and the number of computers permanently connected to the Internet in Africa increased from 10,000 in early 1999 to 25,000 by January 2000 (Jensen 2000: 215). African web space is equally 'expanding rapidly, and almost all countries have some form of local or inter-nationally hosted web server, unofficially or officially representing the country with varying degrees of comprehensiveness', although in general these websites are underused (Jensen 2000: 217).

An African Optical Network (Africa ONE) Internet project is being developed with the aim of encircling the continent with fibreoptic lines that would revolutionise telecommunications (Mukasa 1998; Uche 1999a: 194). Under current structural adjustment programmes, some countries have privatised while others have earmarked for restructuring and privatisation all or some of their telecommuni-cations facilities (van Audenhove 1998: 81; Ras-Work 1998). Should this liberalisation continue, the lack of appropriate regulatory bodies notwithstanding, private investors are likely to extend and improve upon the telecommunications services, and owning a telephone or being connected to the Internet would cease to be a luxury only the most affluent members of society can afford. At the moment, acquiring Internet technology 'is still a dream for the majority of

Africans who do not live in the capital cities and are not part of the elite' (Jensen 2000: 218). It is thus possible that in the near or distant future, thanks to liberalisation and modernisation of existing telecommunications infrastructure and also to the increasing popularity of cellphones (estimated at 5 million in South Africa and 400,000 in the rest of Africa by mid-2000 (Franda 2002: 14)), it would no longer be cheaper to travel than to make a phone call in Africa. Yet, knowing the way African governments operate in defence of mediocrity and vested interests, one should hesitate to reject entirely pessimistic claims that 'Far more than half of the world's population will never use a telephone, not to speak of a PC, a modem or the Internet' (Becker 1996: 12), or that the prospects for rapid change in the telecommunications sector in Africa are dim because of the debt crisis and declining terms of trade for export (van Audenhove 1998: 80).

Politically and socially, the Internet, once fully developed and widely installed, could indeed offer Africans many avenues to address current predicaments and promote good governance (Berger 1998; Jensen 2000; Leslie 2002). For, as Becker rightly points out, far from merely being 'just a step towards the Information Superhighway', the Internet 'is also the hope of many NGOs worldwide, of scientists and community initiatives, of trade unions and critical journalists, of alternative movements and counter-movements, who wish to avail themselves of an independent, inexpensive, non-state-controlled, open communication network' (Becker 1996: 10). Thus, various branches of civil society in different parts of Africa, journalists and media organisations included, might potentially neutralise government control over media, through websites and discussion groups. Working through such networks and in solidarity, these arms of civil society could use the Internet to bypass the repression of uncaring regimes and bring their interests and predicaments to the attention of Africans in the diaspora and to the international community. Even as part of the global grip of the commercial media moguls, which Africa is bound to become eventually (Ronning 1994: 4), the Internet could serve as a formidable tool for consumer mobilisation towards exacting greater accountability and cultural relevance for media products targeting African audiences in the continent and the diaspora. The increasing use in this connection of the little that is already available, by opposition forces, NGOs and various interest groups and lobbies, augurs well for the full-fledged implantation and domestication of the information superhighway in Africa. Among the greatest Internet enthusiasts are young people, who are keen not only to stay in touch with family and friends but also to enhance their knowledge of international affairs and to take advantage of new opportunities by becoming involved with people of other countries with different realities. Prominent among these enthusiasts 'are journalists and aspiring journalists who use the Internet to research and send stories, either as employees of an African news service or as freelancers' (Franda 2002: 18–19).

The paucity of information and telecommunication facilities notwithstanding, there is hope, thanks to current efforts at liberalisation and democratisation, that more and more African governments, institutions and individuals are waking up to the euphoria of the Internet. There is the possibility, distant and remote though it might seem, that some day disillusioned Africans, impoverished and disempowered, will be active and equal participants in the 'global conversations' of the 'global village' or the global 'republic of technology'.

Again, African creativity and conviviality are already bringing hope to combat the technological difficulties. In relation to neoliberalism and the globalisation of poverty, Africans have been innovative in their responses, despite their perceived passivism and victimhood. Like other anti-neoliberal forces in the world, African activists have taken advantage of the new ICTs to mobilise and strategise against the multinational corporations and their unyielding access to the resources and protection of African governments. Prominent African activists are leading members of the anti-globalisation coalition that has given the WTO a tough time in recent meetings. In general, formal and informal networks of various kinds are taking advantage of the Internet to push ahead their agendas in situations where the conventional media continue to blunt aspirations for creative diversity (Spitulnik 2002: 185–92). True, the Internet is not free from the logic of domination and appropriation typical of neoliberalism, but it clearly offers marginalised voices an opportunity for real alternatives, as Miller and Slater have demonstrated in their ethnographic study of how the Internet shapes and is shaped by individuals and communities in Trinidad (Miller and Slater 2000).

Although connectivity in Africa is lower than anywhere else in the world, local cultural values of solidarity, interconnectedness and interdependence (Nyamnjoh 2002a) make it possible for people to access the Internet and its opportunities without necessarily being directly connected. In many situations, it suffices for a single individual to be connected in order for whole groups and communities to benefit. The individual in question acts as a relay point (or communication node) linking other individuals and communities in myriad ways (Olorunnisola 2000). The same is true of other technologies such as the cellphone: diasporic Africans or migrants collectively supply a free phone to someone in a village whom they can call to give and receive messages from family and friends. In South African townships and informal settlements, for example, the cellphone has been used creatively by poor urban dwellers to stay in touch with rural relatives and through them maintain healthy communication with ancestors (Thoka 2001).

Most cellphone owners in West Africa tend to serve as points of presence that link networks for their community, with others paying or simply passing through them to make calls to relatives, friends and contacts within or outside the country. Thus, for example, although Nigerians might actually own fewer phones than most countries in the West, this has been noted to generate higher average revenue per user (ARPU) per month. The ARPU of a cellphone user in Nigeria, with a GDP per capita of US$363, is US$91, which is five times that of South Africa, with six times Nigeria's GDP per capita, and almost twice the USA's, with close to a thousand times Nigeria's GDP per capita. For a country with a low level of economic activity relative to G8 countries, Nigeria has a high level of minutes of use (MOU) of 200, compared to France (154), Germany (88), Japan (149), Italy (118), Canada (249), UK (120) and the USA (364) (Merrill Lynch 2002). The statistics could be explained by Nigerians receiving more calls than they make, and also by the reality of single-owner/multi-user (SOMU) communities. This suggests that the economic and social value (ESV) of a cellphone in countries like Nigeria with a higher volume of SOMU communities is much higher than the ESV of a cellphone for countries with single-owner/single-user (SOSU) communities. Contrary to popular opinion, sociality, interdependence and conviviality are not always inimical to profitability.

Because the *tam tam* remains relevant, even as the Internet and the cellphone are adopted (Ngwainmbi 1995; Ras-Work 1998; Spitulnik 2002; van Binsbergen 2004), Africans are able to make the best of all worlds in a context where surviving has long ceased to be a matter of course. Ordinary Africans have refused to celebrate victimhood, as we see in Chapter 7, which discusses rumour and political cartoons as alternative media under repressive regimes. All of these creative responses imply that it is hardly the end of the story to acknowledge disempowerment and marginalisation in Africa, for in process, however clandestine, are countervailing forces in the service of hope.

Media, Belonging and Democratisation in Africa

It is against this background of a global scene marked by rapid advances in information and communications technology on the one hand, and the inequalities they occasion or reinforce on the other, that this book analyses the role of the media in promoting democracy in Africa in the 1990s. The book engages critically with conventional ideas of liberal democracy which focus on individuals as 'citizens', in relation to a continent where individuals and communities, for various political, economic and cultural reasons, may be forced or may willingly offer to be 'subjects' or to straddle the worlds of liberties and subjections.

Ethnicity and an obsession with belonging remain active forces on the African political scene. A basic assumption of this study is that rights articulated in abstraction do not amount to much. For one thing, political, cultural, historical and, above all, economic realities, determine what form and meaning the discussion and articulation of citizenship and rights assume in any given context. Having rights is something individuals and groups may be entitled to in principle, but who actually enjoys rights does not merely depend on what individuals and groups wish, or are entitled to under the law, by birth, or in the Universal Declaration of Human Rights.

Africa and the world are in an era of intensified globalisation: a process marked by accelerated flows and, quite paradoxically, accelerated closures as well. The rhetoric of free flows and boundaries dissolving seems to be countered by the intensifying reality of borders, divisions and violent strategies of exclusion. As the possibility of free and unregulated flows provokes greater mobility by disadvantaged labour in search of greener pastures, the neoliberal doctrine of globalisation becomes more rhetoric than reality for most, as global capital is privileged to the detriment of labour. This glorification of multinational capital is having untold consequences, especially in marginal sites of accumulation where devalued labour is far in excess of cautious capital. The accelerated flows of capital, goods, electronic information and migration induced by globalisation have only exacerbated insecurities, uncertainties and anxieties in locals and foreigners alike, bringing about an even greater obsession with citizenship, belonging, and the building or re-actualisation of boundaries and differences through xenophobia and related intolerances. The response almost everywhere is for states to tighten immigration regulations, and for local attitudes towards foreigners and outsiders to harden. Where migrants are welcome, interest tends to be limited to those with skills or capital to invest in the local economy, and when unskilled migrants are reluctantly accepted, they have to be ready to go for the menial jobs for which even the most destitute nationals would seldom settle. Skilled or unskilled, immigrants tend to be exploited and treated as slave labour, sleepwalkers or zombies, to be purged of entitlements and humanity with impunity. This is as true of Africa as it is of the rest of the world, and invites scholarly attention on the growing importance of boundaries in a world pregnant with rhetoric on free flows and boundless opportunities for individuals and communities without discrimination.

In Africa, as elsewhere, there is a growing obsession with belonging, along with new questions concerning conventional assumptions about nationality and citizenship. This is as true of how nationals and citizens perceive and behave towards one another as it is of how they behave towards immigrants, migrants and/or foreigners.

Even countries where ethnic citizenship and belonging had almost disappeared in favour of a single political and legal citizenship, there has, in recent years, been a resurgence of identity politics and overt tensions over belonging, as various groups seek equity, better representation and greater access to national resources and opportunities. In such situations, while every national can claim to be a citizen legally, some see themselves or are seen by others as less authentically so. The growing importance of identity politics and more exclusionary ideas of citizenship are paralleled by increased awareness and distinction between 'locals', 'nationals', 'citizens' or 'autochthons' on the one hand, and 'foreigners', 'immigrants', 'outsiders' or 'strangers' on the other, with emphasis on opportunities, economic entitlements, cultural recognition and political representation (Geschiere and Gugler 1998; Geschiere and Nyamnjoh 2000; Werbner and Gaitskell 2002). Customary African values, policies of inclusion and a mainstream philosophy of life, agency and responsibility that privilege *wealth-in-people* over *wealth-in-things* (Guyer 1993; Ramose 1999) are under pressure within the struggles and politics of entitlements in an era of sharp downturns and accelerated flows of opportunity-seeking capital and migrants. The situation is complex and the choices often unclear for the various actors involved, the media included.

To understand the concrete realities of democratisation and how the media relate with this as a process within contexts of growing obsession with belonging, the book uses ethnographic accounts from Cameroon, a country I have studied in detail since the 1980s. The state, the media and their relationship in Cameroon are particularly interesting and informative towards understanding media, belonging and democratisation in Africa. Cameroon is the only country in Africa with a dual colonial heritage of French and English cultures of democracy and media traditions, drawing from both in different ways to edify its postcolonial structures and practices. Not only has the past decade of democratisation evidenced tensions between the English- (anglophone) and French- (francophone) speaking communities (Konings and Nyamnjoh 2003), it has also marked an overwhelming reluctance by the francophone-dominated state to concede to anglophone values of democracy and media freedom. Cameroon has one of the worst records of election rigging, political manipulation and media repression in Africa. Cameroon is also interesting as *Africa in miniature* in that it represents the continent's diversity in major indigenous populations, religions and cultural traditions, and it is an excellent laboratory for the study of ethnicity and the politics of belonging that have coloured liberal democracy and polarised the media in many countries (see Chapter 8).

A basic assumption throughout the book is that the media reflect and also shape African societies marked by continuities, interconnections, convivialities and creative marriages of differences that are not always adequately stressed. Competing for the attention of the media are liberal democracy and popular ideas of democracy informed by African notions of personhood and agency. If the media are sensitive to these apparent contradictions, as they are expected to be, their content should reflect ongoing efforts to negotiate conviviality between competing traditions, influences and expectations. Equally, how well they are seen to excel in their role as mediators would depend on the indicators of democracy used, and also on how sensitive to the predicaments of ordinary Africans those indicators are.

However, liberal democratic rhetoric has dominated the struggle for democracy in Africa (Abrahamsen 2000). Within this framework, if the political and legal cultures of the larger society are not democratic, it is highly unlikely that the media will be any different or that they will have the political and legal freedom to endorse or pursue any democratic agenda. The media can only play an effective role, in this regard, if the law and its application are democratic. The book also discusses media ethics and professionalism among media institutions and practitioners, the assumption being that conducive political and legal environments, important as they may be for press freedom, are hardly enough to guarantee liberal democracy if the media operate oblivious of the need to be ethical and professional in their approach to journalism. For the conventional mass media to be meaningful in the process of empowerment of civil society in Africa within the current liberal democratic framework, they, as institutions, must acquire and live the virtue of tolerance.

The basic question thus addressed in the book is that of the contribution of the media to democratisation in Africa. As almost all states have opted for liberal democracy at least in principle, the role of the media in democratisation is considered against common assumptions made under liberal democracy (Chapter 1). To avoid being misled by declarations that do not reflect reality, the book has sought to understand both the *de jure* and the *de facto* situations of the media and liberal democracy. It has also sought, where necessary, to link statements of intent by media practitioners, politicians or administrators with actual practice. The book investigates both tolerance in society at large and the practice of journalism as a profession in Africa at the dawn of multiparty electoral democracy. It is hoped that the book makes a contribution towards a better understanding of the democratic process in Africa, and that it might serve as an impetus for greater comparative research on the media and liberal democracy both in the continent and elsewhere. Above all, the book hopes to draw attention to the strengths and weaknesses of liberal democracy and the structures and institutions it inspires and shapes in African societies, with the ultimate intention of provoking debate on how Africa could marry liberal democracy with other models of democracy informed by its historical experiences, and cultural, economic and indigenous political realities.

On its own, liberal democracy is much too parochial for Africa's sociality, negotiability, conviviality and dynamic sense of community. Since liberal democracy appears uncomfortable with salient relationships, community and creative diversity, Africans who subscribe to its rhetoric as leaders and as journalists or media practitioners find themselves reduced to a Jekyll-and-Hyde democracy: tolerant in principle but stifling in practice. Such African leaders and media practitioners, whether in government, the opposition or civil society, are forced to keep up appearances with liberal democracy in a context where people are clamouring for recognition and representation as cultural, religious and regional communities. The competing claims for their attention by internal interest groups and external forces explain the apparent contradictions, hypocrisy and double standards when their actions are appreciated exclusively from the standpoint of liberal democracy. The contribution of this book is not so much to offer structural and practical alternatives to the shortfalls of liberal democracy, but rather to draw attention to the pressing need for a democracy that refuses to celebrate success until that success is sufficiently inclusive.

The greatest shortcoming of liberal democracy is its exaggerated focus on the autonomous individual, as if there is anywhere in the world where individuals are capable of living their lives outside of communities or in the total absence of relationships with others. Losing the weight of community, solidarity and culture is not an easy feat even to the most dedicated disciples of the Barbie model. By investing so much rhetoric in the rights of the independent person, liberal democracy is left without a convincing answer pertaining to the rights of the dependant. Although in principle liberal democracy promises rights to all and sundry as individuals, not everyone who claims political rights is likely to have them, even when these are clearly articulated in constitutions and guaranteed legally. The American system, which champions liberal democracy, offers some interesting examples of how Americans, assumed to be autonomous individuals by law, find themselves bargaining away their political, cultural and economic freedoms in all sorts of ways under pressure from the consumer capitalist emphasis on profit over people.

Against this background of an extremely narrow idea of democracy, the book further argues that, if there is an illusion of democracy and participation in communication in the West, the situation is even more critical in Africa, where, in most cases, the media are the preserve of a relative few. In some countries the electronic media, both satellite and terrestrial, mean very little in language and content to the bulk of a population that is rural and has a limited understanding of the Western languages of local broadcasts. The term *mass media* in Africa is often a misnomer, given that literacy in French, English, Portuguese or Spanish serves as a criterion for accessibility and participation in the media, a privilege too remote for both rural and urban illiterates.

And in many parts of Africa, inequalities, poverty and inadequate education make the availability and affordability of media, or quality of media content, very difficult for various groups and individuals. Remote from the information superhighway or the global village and peripheral to the centralised activities of their own governments, rural inhabitants of Africa are susceptible to manipulation by reactionary and revolutionary elites alike. All sorts of statements get made in their name by literate elites with contending pretensions to know their best interests. Seldom are they invited to defend their interests or present their points of view on national issues. They are permanently eclipsed. Little wonder that *radio trottoir* (epitomised by rumour and political derision) plays such a significant role in the lives of ordinary Africans, as well as political cartoons, the force, salience and catharsis of which enable ordinary people to cope with repression (see Chapter 7).

However, although most people in Africa are still searching for a foothold on the information superhighway, there is no doubt about the liberating, mobilising and empowering *potential* of the media as a whole, and the Internet in particular. But just how such potential can be translated into reality in a world caught in the web of ever increasing circles of commodification and privatisation of knowledge on the one hand, and the globalisation of poverty on the other, remains the subject of intense debate.

The book presents a detailed and precise overview on media, belonging and democratisation in Africa in the 1990s. It discusses government problems with the newly developed 'fourth power', but in equal measure indicates the lack of comprehension by journalists and editors when it comes to defining their role in a democratic society. The book also highlights that, along with a functional legal framework and adequate professional training, an institutional framework based on interest groups is necessary to improve standards of professionalism and to develop a code of ethics. There is still too much politics and opinion but too little journalism in the media in most African countries. In this way, inadequate, outmoded and defective media technologies are like the final nail in the coffin of a characteristically narrow and undemocratic communication structure.

Repression and what I have termed *face-powder democracy* are largely responsible for the weakness and/or camouflage of the media and other arms of civil society in Africa. With its focus on democracy, this book starts with a brief but critical discussion of civil society and ethnicity in African politics, and how they have influenced the democratic process in the 1990s. This is intended to provide a framework for understanding the discussion of how the media have, in their role as promoters of democracy, shaped and been shaped by political developments and debates.

Observers of African affairs have borne witness that enfranchisement does not necessarily lead to empowerment, and universal suffrage does not guarantee access to political decision-making. Political equality has been confined to the right to vote, as autocrats have chosen to ignore the right of most to be elected or to enjoy civil liberties. In certain cases, even the right to vote is not that obvious. Although statements have been made to the contrary, ordinary people and alternative social and political organisations continue to face, in practice, enormous difficulties exercising their rights. The state remains overbearing, irrelevant and exploitative with impunity.

While passive participation might guarantee privileges for individuals and groups, only the active participation of those who have been marginalised all along would render the notion of democracy meaningful and popular with the masses. In other words, face-powder democracy must give way to a real democratic culture where ordinary Africans can do more than vote, and where democracy means more than the occasional election of leaders who excel in callous indifference to the predicaments of their people. A need exists, therefore, to provide for public control of power in Africa through public competition for power. This book takes stock of media performance against this background and explores the attitudinal and structural changes necessary in harnessing the media for more positive contributions to the institutionalisation of a culture of democracy in Africa.

In the Name of Democracy:
The Press and Its Predicaments

It is common to claim that liberal democracy and Africa are not good bedfellows, and how apt! Implementing liberal democracy in Africa has been like trying to force onto the body of a full-figured person, rich in all the cultural indicators of health with which Africans are familiar, a dress made to fit the slim, de-fleshed Hollywood consumer model of a Barbie-doll entertainment icon. But instead of blaming the tiny dress or its designer, the tradition has been to fault the popular body or the popular ideal of beauty, for emphasising too much bulk, for parading the wrong sizes, for just not being the right thing. Not often is the experience and expertise of the designer or dressmaker questioned, nor his/her audacity in assuming that the parochial cultural palates that inform his/her peculiar sense of beauty should play God in the lives of regions and cultures where different criteria of beauty and the good life obtain. This insensitivity is akin to the behaviour of a Lilliputian undertaker who would rather trim a corpse than expand his/her coffin to accommodate a man-mountain, or a carpenter whose only tool is a huge hammer and to whom every problem is a nail. The history of difficulty at implementing liberal democracy in Africa attests to this clash of values and attempts to ignore African cultural realities that might well have enriched and domesticated liberal democracy towards greater relevance. This call for domestication must not be confused, however, with the ploy by opportunistic dictatorships that

NMU LIBRARY

have often hidden behind nebulous claims of African specificities to orchestrate high-handedness and intolerance.

This chapter starts with a brief section that is critical of how civil society and ethnicity and belonging are said to relate to democracy in Africa. It examines to what extent overstressing individual rights and underplaying the rights of cultural and religious communities could well be a key problem with the current democratisation process. The future direction of democracy may well be in a marriage or coexistence between individual aspirations and community interests, since Africans continue to emphasise relationships and solidarities over the illusion of autonomy. For democracy to succeed in this context, it must recognise the fact that most Africans are primarily patriotic to their home village, to which state and country in the modern sense are only secondary. It is in acknowledging and providing for the reality of individuals who straddle different forms of identity and belonging, and who are willing or forced to be both 'citizens' and 'subjects', that democracy stands its greatest chance in Africa.

This is the point where one could differ with Mamdani's distinction (1996), as the tendency is for Africans to seek to be both 'citizen' and 'subject' for strategic political-economic and cultural reasons. Although critical of simplistic dichotomies and 'history by analogy' (Mamdani 1996: 12–13), Mamdani does not seem to have avoided the trap himself and fails to remain consistent to his idea of 'history as a process'. His world is one of neat dichotomies because he relies overmuch on the structure of the state rather than the sociological reality on the ground. One is either a citizen or a subject, but never in between – in other words, never what Ferguson (1999) refers to as the 'bushy' or 'untidy' reality in between that is at the centre of history. Mamdani's argument might be persuasive as an analytical distinction, but the reality on the ground, the sociology or anthropology of living Africans, is quite something else. We find individuals who are both citizens and subjects, who straddle the 'ethnic' and 'civic' citizenships highlighted by Mamdani, but who would not accept sacrificing either permanently. Sometimes they are more citizen than subject and sometimes more subject than citizen, but are certainly not reducible to either. They appropriate both in the most creative and fascinating ways (Nyamnjoh 2001a; Werbner 2002; Nyati-Ramahobo 2002). A democracy that focuses too narrowly on the individual and is insensitive to the centrality of group and community interests is likely to impair and frustrate the very recognition and representation it celebrates (Taylor 1994; Englund and Nyamnjoh 2004). In certain cases those seeking cultural recognition and representation are minority groupings (e.g. Botswana: see Mazonde 2002; Werbner and Gaitskell 2002). In other cases the main struggle for cultural rights is by a majority seeking redress against a state controlled by a minority which has effectively disenfranchised the majority of their cultural rights (e.g. Cameroon: see Chapter 8). Regardless of the status of those involved in 'rights talk and culture talk' (Mamdani 2000), they all are convinced of one thing: 'cultural citizenship' (Mercer 2002) is as integral to democracy as political and economic citizenship.

The chapter also situates the African media historically, and then proceeds to examine the role played by these media in stalling the democratisation process of the 1990s. By taking a closer look at how journalists and the media in different countries have articulated some of these contradictions, the chapter argues that while the media and journalists may be largely to blame for their highly unprofessional and unethical journalism in liberal democratic terms, other factors have contributed in no small way to such journalism. Evident from this discussion of the relationship between the media and democratisation in a multiparty context is the inadequate attention given to the quality of democracy needed and the quality and role of the media that should foster such democracy. Almost everywhere, liberal democratic assumptions have been made about the media and their role in democratisation and society, with little regard to the histories, cultures and sociologies of African societies.

The difficulties of the media in action must be understood not only as failures but also, and more importantly, as pointers to the very inadequacies of the liberal democratic model in Africa. If African philosophies of personhood and agency stress interdependence between the individual and the community and between communities (Nyamnjoh 2002a), and if journalists each identify with any of the many cultural communities seeking recognition and representation at local and national levels, they are bound to be torn between serving their communities and serving the 'imagined' rights-bearing, autonomous individual 'citizen' of the liberal democratic model. A democracy that stresses independence, in a situation where both the world-view and the material realities emphasise interdependence, is bound to result only in dependence. The contradictions of and multifaceted pressures on the media are a perfect reflection of such tensions and a pointer to the need for domesticated ideas of democracy in Africa.

Stalling Democratisation in Africa

Africa's democratisation along liberal lines has been a disappointment to most people (Abrahamsen 2000; Ibrahim 2003; Arrous 2003). The multipartyism projected as the solution to Africa's woes has been rather confined to competition among political elites to the exclusion of the disaffected masses (Ake 2000; Good 2002), whose role seems reduced to being called upon to defend the inordinate ambitions of those in high office, who, like chameleons, keep manipulating colours for political survival (Englund 2002a). Many factors, external and internal to the continent, have been blamed for the poor progress record. A weak civil society and ethnic belonging have been particularly highlighted among the internal factors. A critical discussion of both notions is a good starting point, not only because they help to situate the role of the media in democratisation but also in relation to the future direction of democracy in Africa.

Civil society

Much of the writing on civil society in Africa has tended to assume that its manifestation would necessarily reproduce conventional Western patterns, and that its standard democratic functions (Diamond 1994) would apply in Africa just as they have applied elsewhere. Such assumptions and the Western models that feed them are increasingly challenged (Hann and Dunn 1996; Kasfir 1998), not least for their tendency to limit civil society organisations to modernist (i.e. Western-oriented with liberal aspirations) interest groups of voluntary or uncoerced membership that bring pressure to bear on the state and government. In the particularly neoliberal settings of the West, the idea has been to minimise the power of society and social structure by 'trumpeting instead the uncompromising autonomy of the individual, rights-bearing, physically discrete, monied, market-driven, materially inviolate human subject' (Comaroff and Comaroff 1999: 3). In Africa, however, where the market is still underdeveloped and the individual is yet to find significant economic empowerment, and where the state has been very effective at co-optation and repression, it is seldom surprising that such limited (market-driven) definitions have tended to conclude that civil society is either weak or nonexistent.

However, limiting civil society to the conventional indicators of its existence misses the point, as it assumes that people will necessarily shut up, stay still and sacrifice their interests in the face of repression. Real life points to the contrary, that people normally seek alternative channels, sometimes in subtle and masked ways, for fulfilling their aspirations and protecting their interests in such situations. Hence the need to look beyond formal organisations in seeking civil society (Monga 1995, 1996: 145–62; Berman 1998: 339–40), especially in contexts where strong and strongly differentiated states are still to become a reality (Chabal and Daloz 1999: 21). Therefore, what one finds at the forefront of the struggle for tolerance, betterment or sheer survival in Africa have not necessarily been political parties and trade unions, but often informal networks and ethnic, regional, or cultural lobbies, including the critical alternative media, within which collective concerns, anxieties and dreams are discussed and played out.

This implies that we, as scholars and analysts of Africa, may not always find civil society where we are used to looking for it. We must provide theoretical space for the possibility of civil society in Africa taking other forms. Limiting ourselves to a simplistic opposition between 'modern' and 'traditional' forms of social organisation and human association (Chabal 1992: 87–97) might only idealise, exclude or obfuscate the social reality we are supposed to be analysing scientifically. Theorizing civil society in general requires asking some critical questions about the concept itself (Young 1994; Monga 1996; Hann and Dunn 1996; Kasfir 1998; Chabal and Daloz 1999; Comaroff and Comaroff 1999). It also requires a break with the tradition of simplistic assumptions that has often permitted the West to use Africa as a pretext for its own subjectivities, its self-imagination and its perversions (Mbembe 2001: 3–9).

These considerations are important if we are to avoid 'tacitly' taking civil society to mean 'a Eurocentric index of accomplishment' to which Africa's difference becomes a deviation or a deficit to be corrected at all cost (Comaroff and Comaroff 1999: 17). In Africa such theorising ought to emphasise networking and creative domestication of Western modes (Bayart 1986, 1993). This focus should check the application of misleading labels, and draw attention to the various pressures exerted on the state and private corporate entities by various groups in various ways for various reasons of empowerment. As people increasingly distrust states, markets and NGOs to accommodate their needs, they will continue to explore other avenues to fulfil their expectations (Hamelink 1999: 8).

In certain cases and situations, functions usually served by civil society as voluntary organisations in the West have been performed by non-voluntary groups and lobbies such as ethnic elite associations and development unions, often under unelected leadership (Nyamnjoh and Rowlands 1998; Nyamnjoh 2003). Walking the corridors of power and resources seeking political and economic empowerment and representation for their regions or peoples as cultural units, such ethnic associations or their representatives have often been more active and fruitful in the name of ordinary citizens and subjects than most formal voluntary associations in many an African country. A major characteristic of Africa's second liberation struggles since the 1980s has been a growing obsession with belonging and the questioning of traditional assumptions about nationality and citizenship. In Botswana, where ethnicity and belonging had almost become masked issues as the state sought nationhood and consensus through dominant Tswana values and liberal democratic institutions (Durham 1999), there has, since the mid-1980s, been a resurgence of identity politics and overt tensions over belonging (Mazonde 2002; Werbner and Gaitskell 2002). While every Botswana national can legally claim to be a citizen within the framework of the modern nation-state, some (minority groups in the main) are perceived by others, among the majority Tswana groups especially, as less authentic nationals or citizens. Without rights to paramount chiefs of their own and to representation in the national House of Chiefs as ethnic groups in their own right, these minorities increasingly see themselves as more subjects than citizens. There is a growing importance of identity politics and more exclusionary ideas of nationality and citizenship, as minority claims for greater cultural recognition and plurality are countered by majoritarian efforts to maintain the status quo of an inherited colonial hierarchy of ethnic groupings. In other words, minority clamours for recognition and representation are countered by greater and sometimes aggressive reaffirmation of age-old exclusions informed by colonial registers of inequalities among the subjected (Nyamnjoh 2002b).

We must also note that even where there are signs of an emerging civil society in the form of voluntary associations, there is a tendency for these to be infiltrated by organisations that are clearly undemocratic in orientation. Thus while civil society as counter hegemony or counterweight to state power (Rueschmeyer et al. 1992: 6; Chabal 1992: 84; Chabal and Daloz 1999: 18–30) may be unproblematic in principle, the reality of organisations passing for civil society is often more complex. When and if such organisations can claim the space to articulate interests and perspectives on issues independent of or conflictual to the state, their independence may be compromised by dependencies of other kinds, not least of which are financial constraints, hidden agendas of donors and leaders, and the passivity and cynicism of those they target. Indeed, bureaucratic legitimacy under the control of an elite, technocratic leadership, could promote opportunism and state control (Good 1999, 2002), making these organisations vehicles for careerism, exploitation and regulation (Mamdani 1990: 60). The situation is compounded by the largely underdeveloped nature of most African economies, which has retarded the crystallisation of class differentiation and professional interest groups, and consequently afforded the state a pervasive and repressive presence. By the sheer fact of its monopolisation or control of avenues of accumulation and social reproduction, the state succeeds in stifling civil society of the conventional type with strategic offers of power, privilege and wealth to critical members of interest groups (see Chapter 8).

It is precisely for these reasons that civil society studies in Africa stand to gain through an extension in focus to embrace social movements that have often been repressed in the face of an authentic struggle for rights and equality – without necessarily rejecting offhand those on the see-saw of compliance and resistance fighting for privileges and advantages for various cultures, groups and regions. Civil society in Africa should therefore comprise all organisations, groups and individuals whose actions have helped or are helping 'to amplify the affirmations of social identity and the rights of citizenship, often but not always in opposition to those in power whose natural tendency is to repress such identities and rights' (Monga 1995: 364; 1996: 149). Sometimes a semblance of collaboration with the state could be a strategic survival mechanism by which otherwise marginalised groups are able to access a degree of state power and resources.

Although the tendency has been to emphasise independence from the state, this should not blind us to the possibility of cooperation as one of the ways of seeking attention and fulfilment when even contemplating independence could be suicidal. People may collaborate with the regime in varying degrees for various reasons of survival. In the face of state repression and given the need for survival in contexts of growing economic downturns, it would be naive therefore to limit indicators of civil society to their conventional forms. Instead, we must, Mbembe advises, 'watch out for the myriad ways in which ordinary people guide, deceive and actually toy with power instead of confronting it directly'. If we bear in mind the fact that repression and the quest for survival could push people to assume multiple identities, then we could put in perspective the fact that an individual or group might openly show support for the government and state, while at the same time being critical and mocking of 'official lies and the effrontery of elites'. Thus the need not to underestimate the ability of ordinary people 'to engage in baroque practices which are fundamentally ambiguous, fluid and modifiable even in instances where there are clear, written and precise rules'

(Mbembe 1992: 24–5, 2001: 128–9). This is an argument shared by Chabal and Daloz, who see in ongoing struggles for democratisation much 'less a matter of the "revenge" of civil society against the state ... than of a complementary and often mutually beneficial interaction between the two.' Thus 'Understanding politics in Africa is a matter of identifying the complexities of the "shadow boxing" that takes place between state and society ... [and] explaining the myriad ways in which political actors, within both "state" and "civil society", link up to sustain the vertical, infra-institutional and patrimonial networks which underpin politics on the continent' (Chabal and Daloz 1999: 21–2). Such interconnectedness belies accounts premised on 'the innate goodness' of 'an angelic civil society' on the one hand, and 'a veritable satanic state' on the other (Young 1994: 47).

It should also be borne in mind that independence in the Western sense of the word is a scarce commodity, especially in Africa, given how the state and civil society constantly interpenetrate or straddle one another (Chabal and Daloz 1999: 17). Even in the private sector and NGO worlds, such independence is rare, as Garland's account of undemocratic NGO relations with Bushmen in Namibia indicates (Garland 1999). All over the continent, some interest groups are known to be hostages of donors and lobbies in a way just as detrimental to popular democracy as being hostage to government or the state. When groups fighting for privileges and advantages pose as representatives of civil society simply because they claim to be independent or identify themselves under one of the labels generally taken for granted to represent civil society, we find ourselves with organisations at varying degrees of congruence with the structures of domination and repression.

It could be argued, therefore, that patterned democracy in the form of institutional structures (multiparty elections, executive, judiciary, legislative institutions, etc.) does not necessarily give rise to participatory politics (Lardner 1993; Abrahamsen 2000; Englund 2002b). It makes democracy less threatening to the ruling elite by trivialising it to the point where this elite can afford to 'enjoy democratic legitimacy without subjecting themselves to the notorious inconveniences of democratic practice' (Ake 2000: 1). Kenneth Good has argued that this is the case in Botswana, where over thirty-eight years of multiparty politics have resulted in little more than 'elite democracy' (Good 1999, 2002).

Ethnicity and belonging

Ethnicity and belonging are common currency in discourses on democracy in Africa (Russell 1999: 68–94). Both have been blamed in part for the failure by Africans to institutionalise liberal democracy. The literature is very rich in this connection, showing how the political elite has either mobilised ethnic ideology and belonging to defend power or to seek it, as Chapter 8 demonstrates in relation to Cameroon. Scholars have given various explanations for the persistence of ethnicity and belonging in African politics. Ellis, for example, argues that 'the fact that African politicians are unable to articulate any original or critical view on economic policy', given how committed to World Bank policies they virtually all are, means that 'there is little to choose in ideological terms between rival parties'. Hence political parties tend 'to compete for the same social constituencies as their rivals', and they 'find it hard to identify and represent any social or economic interest group which has been previously underrepresented, unless, of course, such a group is ethnically defined'. This would explain 'the tendency for rival parties to recruit ethnic constituencies, just as the barons of the old ruling parties tended to do' (Ellis 1994: 120–121). It also questions the status of the party and ultimately of liberal democracy as the only modes of political organisation in a modern Africa (Ake 2000: 31).

If political parties tend to appeal to ethnic loyalties rather than seek a shared ideology, and if their partisans have consistently tended to vote along regional and ethnic lines, it is perhaps time to look beyond political parties and liberal democracy as the exclusive way of organising modern politics and government in Africa. As Ake observes, the political party system of liberal societies makes little sense in African societies where the development of associational life is rudimentary and interest groups remain essentially primary groups. In such a context, it is 'very misleading to think of democratization ... as multi-party electoral competition' (Ake 2000:

31). The recognition that there is nothing inherently authoritarian about monopartyism and nothing inherently democratic about
multipartyism (Wiredu 1997), coupled with the fact that most of
Africa has failed to develop 'a trans-ethnic public arena grounded
in universalistic norms and the essential relations of social trust in
the disinterested competence and probity of millions of unknown
and unseen others' (Berman 1998: 339), ought to push analysts to
explore other models of political organisation informed by African
cultural, political and historical experiences on the one hand, and
the reality of Africa's economic dependence and light weight on
the other. In the new South Africa, some have called for politics
informed by the philosophy of ubuntu (Ramose 1999: 128–45), and
it is likely that repeated frustrations could lead to the idealisation
of the African past and the celebration of nostalgia. Yet the quest
for the missing cultural link in African democracy requires serious
negotiation and flexibility. It requires a concept of democracy that
emphasises coexistence and interdependence between the individual
and the community, between communities, and between the state
and the various cultural communities its 'citizens' are 'subjects' of.
Thus, for this quest to be creative and fruitful, African intellectuals
and political classes must desist from a view of 'African ethnicity
as an atavism' (Eyoh 1995: 50; Berman 1998: 306), and envision a
democracy that guarantees not only individual rights and freedoms,
but also the interests of communal and cultural solidarities. Wiredu's
suggestion that Africans revisit the idea of 'consensual democracy' in
the quest for a possible solution to stalling 'majoritarian democracy'
(Wiredu 1997: 308–11) deserves to be taken seriously, not to replace
liberal democracy as such, I must add, but rather to blend with it.
Referring to consensual democracy in the traditional Ashanti system,
Wiredu argues that this was 'a democracy because government was
by the consent, and subject to the control, of the people as expressed
through their representatives'. Thus while majoritarian democracy
might be based on consent without consensus, the Ashanti system
ensured that 'consent was negotiated on the principle of consensus'
(Wiredu 1997: 308–11).

Commenting along similar lines, Ake argues that the feasibility
of democracy in Africa will depend on how Africans are able to

re-create democracy to reflect notions of participation traditionally associated with the communal political culture of African societies. This is a political culture which 'demands the involvement of everyone in promoting the common good', and people participate 'not because they are individuals whose interests need to be asserted, but because they are part of an interconnected whole'. Participation is based 'not on the assumption of individuality but on the social nature of human beings', and is 'as much a matter of taking part as of ... sharing the burdens and the rewards of community membership'. It is also more than just 'the occasional opportunity to choose, affirm or dissent', in that it requires active involvement in the process of decision-making and community life in general (Ake 2000: 184).

Guided in part by this idea of consensual democracy, and by experiences in democratic consociationism and corporatism elsewhere, it is time to investigate possible alternatives that merge liberal democracy with the cultural interests of communities in a real way. Such a blend is more likely to yield positive results than the current practice whereby politicians and intellectuals 'take comfort in ancestral traditions at the same time that they stubbornly refuse to concede to the *formal* representation of the interests of cultural solidarities' (Eyoh 1995: 50), except, of course, only selectively, for reasons of political opportunism and survivalism (Konings and Nyamnjoh 2003).

A compelling argument can be made to the effect that what seems to face difficulty in Africa is undomesticated liberal democracy, not democracy in all its forms and possibilities. As Claude Ake affirms, in Africa's quest for democracy 'there is very little in the experience of the established democracies to guide it and a great deal to mislead it' (Ake 2000: 31). What liberal democracy stresses appears in many ways to contradict what other forms of social and political organisation both in Europe and in Africa have tended to emphasise. The liberal democratic rhetoric of rights, dominated by a narrow neoliberal focus on the individual, does not reflect the whole reality of personhood and agency in Africa, which is a lot more complex than provided for in liberal democratic notions of rights and empowerment (Nyamnjoh 2002a; Englund and Nyamnjoh 2004). Instead of working for a creative mix with indigenous forms of politics and government, liberal democracy has sought to replace these, posing as the one and only way of modern democratic political organisation, the right way of conducting modern politics.

The home village in Africa has retained its appeal both for those who have been disappointed by the town, and for those who have found success in the town. It seems that no one wants to stay in town permanently; even corpses are subject to competing claims for burial by kin in different rural localities (Geschiere and Gugler 1998; Nyamongo 1999). And even those who have no ties with village kin and are permanently trapped in urban spaces often reproduce the village and localist styles in subtle and fascinating ways. It appears that no one is too cosmopolitan to be local as well.

Faced with the temporality or transience of personal success in the context of African modernities, even the most achieving and cosmopolitan or diasporic of individuals hesitates to sever their rural connections entirely. The city and the 'world out there' are perceived as hunting grounds; the home village is the place to return at the end of the day. Investing in one's home village is generally seen as the best insurance policy and a sign of ultimate success, for it guarantees survival even when one has lost everything in the city, and secures and makes manifest a realisation of success through satisfying obligations and fulfilling requests. Thus, although successful urbanites may not permanently return or retire to the rural area as such, most remain in constant interaction with their home village through all sorts of ways. Some leave express instructions with kin to be buried or reburied in their home village (Geschiere and Gugler 1998; Geschiere and Nyamnjoh 2000; Englund 2002b).

The African experience in liberal democracy where ethnicity and belonging have continued to play a major role and voluntary associations have failed to take root, reveals the need for a fresh theoretical space, addressing not only individual rights and freedoms, but also the interests of communal and cultural solidarities. What liberal democracy stresses – 'the uncompromising autonomy of the individual' (Comaroff and Comaroff 1999: 3, 14) – is incompatible with the lives of people on the ground, as Charles Piot (1999) illustrates in his study of 'village modernity' in Togo. Its logic suggests dichotomies that caricature real-life situations. In real life we

find individuals who are both citizens and subjects, who straddle
the 'ethnic' and 'civic' citizenship discussed by Mamdani (1996),
but who would not accept sacrificing either permanently. They appropriate both types of citizenship in most creative and fascinating
ways. Ferguson, in this connection, talks of a 'full house' of cultural
styles, which, as a strategy of survival, combine the local and the
cosmopolitan in the same space (Ferguson 1999: 82–122), and,
if I may add, to be simultaneously and creatively drawn from by
individuals and communities as negotiators of multiple identities.
It is a survival strategy, especially given the constraining reality of
Africa being at the fringes of global consumer capitalism.

In discussions of democracy in Africa, the narrow insistence on
individual rights and freedoms even among academics has impaired
understanding of the interconnectedness of peoples, cultures and
societies through individuals as products, melting pots and creative
manipulators or jugglers of multiple identities. Discussing democracy
in Africa calls for scrutiny of the importance of cultural identity in
the lives of individuals and groups. This argument challenges reductionist views of democracy, acknowledges the fact that democracy
may take different forms, and, most particularly, that it is construed
and constructed differently in different societies, informed by history,
culture and economic factors. The way forward is in recognising
the creative ways in which Africans merge their traditions with
exogenous influences to create realities that are not reducible to
either but are enriched by both.

The implication of this argument is that how we understand
the role of journalists and the media depends on what democratic
model we draw from. Under liberal democracy where the individual
is perceived and treated as an autonomous agent, and where primary solidarities and cultural identities are discouraged in favour
of a national citizenship and culture, the media are expected to be
disinterested, objective, balanced and fair in gathering, processing
and disseminating news and information. The assumption is that
since all individuals have equal rights as citizens, there can be no
justification for bias among journalists. But under popular notions
of democracy where emphasis is on interdependence and competing
cultural solidarities are a reality, journalists and the media are under

constant internal and external pressure to promote the interests of the various groups competing for recognition and representation. The tensions and pressures are even greater in situations where states and governments purport to pursue liberal democracy in principle, while in reality they continue to be high-handed and repressive to their populations. When this happens, the media are at risk of employing double standards as well, by claiming one thing and doing the opposite, or by straddling various identity margins, without always being honest about it, especially if their very survival depends on it.

Media Ownership and Control Patterns in Africa

There are continuities in the history of the print and broadcast media in Africa that are not adequately stressed by analysts keen to measure how similar to the West or the past the media in postcolonial Africa are. The emphasis on analogies, prescription and dogma has had the effect of stressing what African states, societies and media '*are not*' but very little of what '*they actually are*' (Mbembe 2001: 9). This section draws attention to the latter, stressing that dates may in fact delude more than point to real changes in circumstances. Given a colonial past in which freedom of expression and access to the media were not guaranteed, it is hardly surprising that Africa's postcolonial mediascape is a rich and fascinating blend of traditions, influences and technologies. Coexisting in tolerance and interdependence are the most modern forms of communications technologies and the indigenous media. Journalistic styles reflect exposure to Anglo-Saxon and Latin press cultures on the one hand, and on the other show how these colonial influences have been married with African values to produce a melting pot of media cultures. One finds on the continent people in tune with online newspapers and facilitated by multimedia connectivity, just as one finds straddlers of indigenous and modern media, creatively drawing on both to negotiate themselves through the communicative hurdles and hierarchies of the continent. Africa's creativity refuses to be subjected to simple distinctions between old and new technologies, since its peoples are daily modernising the indigenous and indigenising the modern with novel outcomes.

Colonial beginnings in the print media

The first newspapers in Africa date back to 1797 in Egypt, 1800 in South Africa, 1801 in Sierra Leone, and 1826 in Liberia – where returning slaves from the Americas set up the *Liberia Herald* to celebrate the brilliance of freedom as a gift from heaven. Missionaries were also at the forefront of the first newspapers, which were often published either in the colonial language or in indigenous languages, and a major dimension of which was news and information of a religious and evangelical nature. In 1859 missionaries started Nigeria's first newspaper, *Iwe Thorin*, in the Yoruba language, and subsequently in English as well. In West Africa, only a few countries had a press before independence, with Nigeria having the largest and most diverse press thanks to its developed trading and commercial sector. Even then, it was mostly in the English colonies of the region that the press played an important role in the struggle against colonialism, providing nationalists like Nigeria's Nnamdi Azikiwe with a formidable platform to articulate their claims of independence. In the francophone colonies, much was done actively to discourage the development of a critical local press, and the few local papers that managed to be established served mainly the white settler population. This was the case in Tunisia where a large French settler population and government support favoured the French-language press over its Arabic counterpart between 1881 and independence in 1956. In general, colonial administrative control, censorship and other restrictions severely hampered the birth and growth of a vibrant press of the type remarkable in anglophone Africa. In southern, central and eastern Africa, the press was largely a European creation to serve the information, education and entertainment needs of the large settler communities, leaving the black readership at the mercy of an irrelevant content and/or in search of alternative channels of communication. The earliest paper in Egypt, *Al Waka'e*, served as an official mouthpiece of the government, which eventually succumbed to public pressure for newspapers independent of its direct control.

This concession gave birth to several revolutionary papers that played a major role in the revolution against Ottoman domination. During the subsequent British occupation of Egypt (1882–1919), the press was active in resisting and shaping public opinion against the occupation, despite British colonial repression and censorship (Mytton 1983; Bourgault 1995; Tudesq 1995).

Although technically and economically inferior to the press in the West at the time, the indigenous colonial press in Africa was a sign of both hope and despair – hope by Africans who saw in it an opportunity to dignify themselves, despair by colonialists who perceived it as a threat to power and privilege. When elite, mostly Western-educated Africans from the continent, North America or the West Indies started venturing into the press, and claiming independence from the colonial authorities, as was the case in West Africa, they met with stiff resistance by the authorities, who treated them as subversives. In Nigeria, for example, the colonial office likened Nnamdi Azikiwe's newspapers to a plague that was afflicting the whole country and disapproved of his radical assertion of independence for and pride in Africa and African values (Kurian 1982: 688). Literacy and the press may be important for modernisation, but that apparently did not include allowing the colonised 'native' to determine the content of what to read or be informed about, especially as content of the early newspapers soon became dominated by political protest against colonial officials. Hence, almost all territories instituted strict laws regulating the right of Africans to set up and operate newspapers, and aimed at stifling the spread of 'subversive' ideas. Economic measures were also imposed to make it difficult for African newspaper proprietors to import newsprint and other technical facilities. This rigid control of the press made it particularly difficult for the African elites to articulate their anti-colonial struggles via the mass media, especially as broadcasting was invariably under much tighter control by the colonialists.

Far from giving up, however, threatened African elites eager to communicate their liberation agenda among themselves and with the African masses adopted various strategies, including the following: publish and perish from the repressive axe of the colonial administration; go underground with the press and its liberation rhetoric enhanced by pamphlets, tracts, clandestine radio and word of mouth; turn to or marry with alternative channels of communication such as the grapevine, political rumour, humour, parody, irony and derision – known under various names in different regions (e.g. *radio trottoir* in francophone Africa, *radio boca a boca* in lusophone Africa, radio one battery, bush telegraph, pavement/sidewalk radio or radio mall in anglophone Africa); and use the indigenous media as substitutes or supplements to the shackled press (see Chapter 7). These strategies were as useful in the Algerian Revolution as they were in the radical nationalism of Cameroon's Union des Populations du Cameroun party, both directed against brutal French colonialism and racism. Frantz Fanon, as a member of the Services de Presse du Front de Libération Nationale in Tunis, was able to take advantage of *El Moudjahid*, whose articles were not bylined, to disseminate his revolutionary ideas on colonialism in Algeria and Africa (Fanon 1969). Thanks to such excessive control and creative responses, the press in Africa has since colonial times shared many characteristics with *radio trottoir*, including identification with certain values, beliefs and outlooks commonly held by ordinary Africans, some of which may appear bizarre and highly implausible to Western reporters and readers (Bourgault 1995: 201–5; Ellis 2000: 225–6).

Postcolonial continuities in print media ownership and control

Independence consolidated indigenous and private initiative in press ownership, but it also maintained and enhanced attempts by governments to control the press (Bourgault 1995; Hyden and Okigbo 2002). Both as paymasters and as gatekeepers of public interest, African governments have, almost without exception, kept the press in check. In Mobutu's Zaire, for example, the press was nationalised, newspaper titles indigenised, private initiative discouraged, and journalists streamlined with an arsenal of restrictions on professionalism. If the colonial press was either at the service of settler communities or victim of repressive laws, the postcolonial press from the 1960s to the 1980s was similarly either the mouthpiece of the government or subjected to draconian laws and administrative censorship. States sought to make the press partners in nation-building and develop-

ment, by harnessing its magic multiplier capacity to inform and educate citizens on government policy and action (Hachten 1993: 3–13,
51–4; Tudesq 1995). During that period, notions such as 'development communication' and 'development journalism' became part of
scholarly vocabulary and research, as even the private press was often
persuaded to tone down its watchdog role against the excesses of
the powerful and the privileged. But when both development and
nation-building proved increasingly illusive and more rhetoric than
reality, the press and other arms of civil society started clamouring
for a second liberation from leadership without responsibility. As
leaders in Africa appeared to consolidate the state to the detriment
of the nation and development, it became evident that postcolonial
governments had simply co-opted the press. The leaders had drawn
inspiration from and added on to the rich repertoire of repressive
colonial laws to keep the press and civil society in check. Such
pieces of legislation, which accentuated the difficulties of journalists
in many countries by hardening the uncooperative attitudes of many
in high office, were targeted for reform at the dawn of the second
liberation struggles.

The freedom of the press made possible by the second liberation struggles of the 1990s is largely new. The assumption since
the 1960s was to see any critical press and journalists as dangerous
troublemakers that had to be contained. Just how much of this
has changed with the struggles for democratisation in the 1990s is
discussed further below and in subsequent chapters.

Broadcasting in colonial Africa

The introduction and development of broadcasting in Africa have been
highly influenced by Western societies and models. In their capacity
as colonial and/or economic powers, Britain, France and the USA,
for example, have been very instrumental as standard-setters for the
rest of the world, Africa included. By so doing, they have not only
made broadcasting an African reality, but have equally universalised
the values, attitudes and practices identifiable with radio and television
in the West. Many researchers have argued that, from the outset, the
overruling factor in the introduction of broadcasting in Africa was

the interests of the Western powers. In almost every case, not only were the indigenous people denied the right to choose the type of broadcast system to be introduced, they were equally denied access and/or the right to determine content and use.

France and Britain, for example, set up radio stations to provide their citizens with information from home, to disseminate their cultures and values among the 'natives', or, as was the case during World War II, for propaganda purposes against the Nazis. In certain cases, the radio stations served colonial powers under occupation, by keeping communication alive and sometimes countervailing hostile broadcasts from elsewhere. Africa was little more than 'a pied-à-terre' for most of these stations, whose broadcasts were not aimed at the local audiences (Gibbons 1974: 109). Long before the colonists ever saw the need to develop broadcasting stations in their various colonies, they were already transmitting to these territories from Europe. France started broadcasting in French to its colonies in 1931, and the BBC launched the British Empire Service in English a year later, while as early as 1927 the Netherlands began making regular transmissions in Dutch to the East Indies (Washburn 1985: 38).

The aim was to consolidate their positions in the colonies by promoting the use of their languages and selling their cultures to the 'natives', as a foil to the forces of dissidence. It is partly for the same reason that the programmes in the colonial media were mainly rebroadcasts of metropolitan versions. When broadcasts in indigenous languages were introduced, the reason was not to celebrate African cultures but, rather, to reach as many people as possible with messages aimed at curbing dissidence. In this way, the nationalists, in their struggles for independence, depended heavily on the folk media (what Frank Ugboajah (1985: 32) of Nigeria has termed 'oramedia' – i.e. media that are rich in symbolism and grounded in indigenous cultures, produced and consumed by members of a group, and that reinforce the values of the group). They had little or 'no access to radio, which remained a tight government monopoly' (Head 1977: 86–7). Thus in Nigeria, for instance, when Awolowo criticised the 'MacPherson Constitution' and was accused on Nigerian Broadcasting Service 'of being unfaithful' by the British Governor-General, he was denied equal access to the radio to defend himself (Uche 1985: 22).

Broadcasting in the colonies acted as a catalyst in the process of acculturation and containment needed for colonisation to continue unopposed.

Much has been published about the broadcast systems which the newly independent states of Africa inherited from the colonists. Research shows that broadcasting in the postcolonies has followed the style, formats and practices of similar institutions in the West. But a careful reading in this area points to an aspect of this 'inheritance', 'extension and imitation', 'transfer' or 'borrowing' (Linden 1998: 48–67), which has tended to be inadequately stressed, if at all: that is, the double standard of preaching pluralism and freedom of information back home in the West but clamping down on nationalists struggling for exactly the same rights in the colonies; or enlisting a dominated people to fight against possible domination of Europe by Hitler.

Colonial administrations were far more heavy-handed than would have been tolerated back home at the metropolis. By so doing, the colonists appeared to make it clear to the leaders of the would-be independent states of Africa that governments are most vulnerable if they fail to maintain rigid control over the media, broadcasting in particular. Having thus been made to see broadcasting as a most sensitive institution, the African nationalists, once in power as a government, were likely to seek exclusive ownership and control of radio and television. Subsequently, their opponents or critics, equally keen on reaching the masses with their doctrines, would, in some cases, opt for clandestine radio stations situated within or outside the territory of their clamour for recognition and representation (van de Veur 2002: 86–93).

Perhaps because they were unaware of this unintended effect of their rigid control of broadcasting, the former colonial powers would increasingly find that their doctrine of free flow of information and political pluralism fell on deaf ears among the leaders of the newly independent states. Ironically, once out of the colonies, the Western societies began to criticise the very political and media repression and rigidity that as colonial masters they had worked so hard to validate, and had found to be particularly useful in crushing opposition to domination and exploitation.

A careful look at the literature on broadcasting in Africa reveals that everything the colonists did in the domain of radio and television was for their exclusive interests. So, just as the French and the British tended to introduce new radio stations during World War II, so too was the idea of a less centrally controlled broadcasting system, coupled with that of the free flow of information, introduced only when the pressures for independence could no longer be resisted (Golding and Elliott 1979: 42). Moreover, when threatened by the alternative political and economic organisation offered by communism at the dawn of the Cold War, the former colonial masters strove 'to maintain their preferred status [in Africa], while staving off the efforts of the Communist Bloc to gain footholds on the continent' (Head 1977: 85).

The failure to harness broadcasting in the colonies, and later in the postcolonies of Africa, has instituted a characteristic universal to broadcasting, which should normally not be the case. Only this tendency towards 'universalism' can explain why there is no difference in the professional values, programme format, style and schedules between broadcasters in Nigeria, Sweden or Ireland (Golding and Elliott 1979; Katz 1977: 113–20); or between Ethiopia and Liberia, who escaped colonisation, and the rest of Africa, who did not – despite the fact that all of these countries have economic, political, social, cultural and historical differences.

One of the contributory factors for this tendency towards universalism is the fact that most broadcasters in Africa have been, and continue to be, educated, trained and offered refresher courses in the West, where they imbibe Western media values, attitudes and professional ideologies, as well as a certain 'receptivity to the men and machines they have learned to work with' (Golding 1977: 295). This, together with cheap, standardised or McDonaldised programmes from abroad, endow broadcasting with 'a global uniformity of style and content, creating that very universality of standards preached by the "professionalizers", and in turn the audience expectations which reinforce demands for more of the same and thus the security of the market' (Golding 1977: 300). Even in local training centres in Africa, 'the texts used by Anglo-Saxon or French communications theorists serve as points of reference without any questioning of their relevance to a different framework' (Mattelart et al. 1984: 75). Here, sufficient time has not been given to making the necessary distinction between training as 'cultural exchange' and training as 'the simple transmission of technical know-how' (Mattelart et al. 1984: 71). The broadcasters have been socialised into a Western 'profession' or 'sect' whose values and practices they do not question, because these appear 'natural' or 'inherent' to broadcasting. Here, as in media and communications research, emphasis has been on mimicking rather than on creative thinking, and on prescription and dogma rather than on innovation and relevance (Eribo and Tanjong 2002). Like liberal democracy and civil society, Western notions of media culture and practice have not been domesticated to suit the needs and expectations of Africans, their communities or their world-views.

Postcolonial ownership and control patterns in broadcasting

The literature points to a tendency by African countries towards more centralised broadcast systems at independence (Bourgault 1995: 68–152; Linden 1998: 48–67; van de Veur 2002). But in view of what we have noted about the colonial situation, this tendency must not simply be seen as an abandonment of 'the element of autonomy from government control which was explicit in most models of broadcasting structures transferred from the West' (Katz and Wedell 1978: vii). To see it thus is to ignore the reality under which these states lived as colonies, which in no way was a reflection of the European situation. Instead, the option for rigid state control has to be seen as an indication of which of the two inherited models of broadcasting appealed more to the postcolonial leaders of these states. They preferred the rigid, highly centralised colonial model to the freer and more accessible metropolitan one, of which as colonies they experienced next to nothing, and which was 'transferred' just a little before or after independence, in order to fill the gap left by removal of colonial control.

In opting for state ownership and control, these governments, like their colonial predecessors, equally sought to justify why broadcasting needed to be controlled. Though the two had one reason in common – power – they tended to differ in the others. From the early days of independence until recently, it was common for African governments to claim that centralism was necessarily the better of the two models for purposes of nation-building. It was justified as less wasteful of the limited resources, and as guaranteeing the political stability badly needed for rapid development. Generally, they claimed that once their countries had become more mature and stable, they would loosen their hold over broadcasting and the other media; just as the colonists saw the importance of free and private initiative in broadcasting only when colonisation came (or was about to come) to its end. These similarities generally point to how much the postcolonial leaders had learnt from their colonial predecessors.

Just as the colonial administration was most rigid about broad-casting and less so with the print media, so too have been the governments of postcolonial Africa. Broadcasting was singled out as the media that needed to be watched at close range. This was also because radio was largely considered the most 'mass' of all the media, capable of hypodermic effects and with enormous potential to contribute to nation-building and development. In most countries from independence to the early 1990s, when the clamour for multi-party democracy became widespread in Africa, the public-service journalist was little more than a public relations (PR) man or woman for the government. He/she was committed much less to the truth and the public than to building a positive image, selling the ideas and promoting the interests of government and the ruling elite. Instead of serving as active and critical gatherers and disseminators of relevant information, such journalists were confined to feeding the public with doctored information made available to them by government. Often they took for granted (or were too powerless to question) the truth of what they were fed, which they in turn presented to the public as if it were the fruit of professional or disinterested journalism.

Under the single-party and military-regime era, it was subversive to question government policies, outlooks or options by suggest-ing alternative ways of going about nation-building and national development. There was room only for 'constructive criticism', and criticisms were thus considered only when made by those who had accepted the system, not by those who did not belong to the ruling party. Governments were hostile to the propagation of 'unconfirmed news', and such was generally anything printed or broadcast without prior authorisation and/or significantly at variance with government views and policies.

These attitudes and practices portrayed the government as omniscient and infallible, and as showing preference for one-dimensional societies. The governments' preoccupation with development media was little more than an alibi to mask a much deeper concern by the ruling elite to reaffirm and consolidate its authority, even to the detriment of the individual and group liberties it purported to defend. Thus, instead of tackling the real and substantial differences of society, successive governments tended to hide these differences, opting rather for repressive centralised states in their pursuit of the 'nation-state' mirage.

The fact that broadcasting was often part of the civil service meant that civil servants or politicians with little or no knowledge about the media were often charged with overseeing the way radio and television were operated. Professional broadcasters became subservient to these bureaucrats, who determined appointments, salary scales and promotions, and who were expected to approve every initiative beforehand, no matter how technical or how driven by the 'stopwatch culture' of the broadcasting profession. This was unduly harmful to creativity and frustrating to talented broadcasters, some of whom were known to give up entirely or were sucked in wholly by the vacuum cleaners of bureaucracy.

Since the 1990s, however, African scholars and media activists have joined the bandwagon of debates on media ownership and control, increasingly informed by and largely focused on the effects of globalisation and neoliberalism on media scenarios the world over. And governments have largely succumbed to the pressures and rhetorics advocating liberalisation, even if only cosmetically in certain cases. Almost everywhere, old patterns are giving way to new configurations at a phenomenal pace. National, state-owned, public-service media systems are yielding to commercial media characterised by increasing concentration of ownership and control through takeovers, mergers and globalism. Propelled by 'the incessant pursuit of profit', global media entrepreneurs are ready for nothing but the total 'relaxation or elimination of barriers to commercial exploitation of media and to concentrated media ownership' (McChesney 2001: 1–4). According to Robert McChesney, the trend is towards global oligopolies, and the guiding logic of the media firms is to 'get very big very quickly, or get swallowed up by someone else'. Firms, he argues, 'must become larger and diversified to reduce risk and enhance profit-making opportunities, and they must straddle the globe so as to never be outflanked by competitors'. Not only is the traditional idea of public-service radio and television fast becoming outmoded, calls by concerned countries for some ground rules to protect cultural diversity by keeping culture out of the control of the WTO have simply been greeted with the rhetoric of free flows. What is more, the corporate media are in a particularly powerful position to 'get their way with politicians', given their ability to 'use their domination of the news media in a self-serving way' (McChesney 2001: 3–9). As Thomas and Lee (1998: 2) have put it, 'Global media corporations ... enjoy an enormous leeway to negotiate and protect interests from the vantage of prior monopoly positions. Bill Gates, Rupert Murdoch and the owners of Time–Warner do not have to bend over backwards to strike deals. It is generally the case that they decide and the world follows suit.'

This implies that the global media corporations are not all about 'unregulated flows' of the world's cultural diversity. They perpetuate a 'deeply and starkly inegalitarian' process (Golding and Harris 1997: 7) that favours a privileged minority as it compounds the impoverishment of the majority through closures and containment. The objective of the corporate media operators is to control not only global markets but also global consciousness, by encouraging 'the emergence of a small number of monopoly concerns which command a disproportionate share' of the global market (Thomas and Lee 1994; Murdock 1994; McChesney 1998, 2001). As Murdock argues, 'the new media mogul empires' are 'empires of image and of the imagination' in that 'They mobilise a proliferating array of communications technologies to deliver a plurality of cultural products across a widening range of geographical territories and social spaces, and are directed from the centre by proprietors who rule their domains with shifting mixtures of autocracy, paternalism and charisma' (Murdock 1994: 3). The tendency is to mistake plurality for diversity, oblivious of the possibility that an appearance of plenty could well conceal a poverty of perspectives (Murdock 1994: 5). Democracy is doubly endangered by concentrated ownership and control that limits media voices, restricts diversity and increases the power of media barons over viewers, readers and listeners (BusinessWeek 2004: 36–42; Thomas and Nain 2004). Thanks to 'the marriage of media content (news, films, TV shows) with media distribution (TV or radio networks, internet services and the like)', media giants are able to 'use their sales power to batter their way into living rooms' around the globe (Economist 2004a: 9).

This leaves ordinary consumers at the mercy of the McDonaldised, standardised or routinised news, information and entertainment burgers served to them in the interest of profit by the global corporate media. Because the global media system 'advances corporate and commercial interests and values and denigrates or ignores that which cannot be incorporated into its mission', content becomes uniform, regardless of the nationality of shareholders and regardless of where the corporate headquarters is located. This is hardly surprising since what is wanted are passive, depoliticised, unthinking consumers more prone 'to take orders than to make waves' by questioning the 'light escapist entertainment' menu presented them (McChesney 1998: 7). In this regard, the basic split is not between nation-states, but between the rich and the poor, across and within national borders (McChesney 1998: 6; 2001: 13). However, the fact remains that the investors, advertisers and affluent consumers whose interests the global media represent are located more in the developed world than in Africa, where only an elite minority are involved in any serious way.

In most of Africa the threats to a free, open and participatory media system and society are as much from repressive governments as from the interests of rich nations, international financial institutions and communications multinationals. Given the weakness of African states in relation to the latter collection of interests, and given their peripheral position in the global economy and politics, the only real authority or semblance of power affordable to African governments is towards their own populations. What neoliberalism wants of them, as governments, are national and regional policies in tune with the profitability expectations of capital, and policies that minimise countervailing traditions, customs and expectations. Once they have guaranteed global capital stability, security and protection from labour and its needs, African governments need not do more than embrace the rhetoric of liberal democracy and the tokenism of its freedoms. And once they have opened up passively to the unregulated flow of global news and entertainment media, they can control local political media content unpoliced by the gendarmes of free flow. Often it is understood, though not openly stated, that they need not go beyond paying lip service to liberal democracy, since no one seriously believes that it is possible for African states or governments to be tolerant to both the demands of global capital and to the exigencies of their own citizens (Abrahamsen 2000).

Nowhere is this partnership and collusion better illustrated than in the relationship between African governments and the World Bank and IMF. Both institutions have preferred the rhetoric of 'uncritical and idealized models of liberal democracy, the market and civil society' (Berman 1998: 307) to the reality of even an imperfect democracy. Keen to see their neoliberal projects through, the World Bank and the IMF have readily provided support for acquiescing states and governments in order to neutralise opposition to their unpopular structural adjustment conditionalities. In this way, instead of helping bring about democracy the way its proponents would like to think and make believe, structural adjustment has had highly repressive and authoritarian political consequences; exogenously induced, it has had to repress popular opinion and rely on authoritarian regimes for its implementation, making it difficult to be seen as contributing to democratisation. On the contrary, its negative economic, social and political effects are believed to have been responsible for popular appeals for political reform (Mkandawire and Olukoshi 1995; Abrahamsen 2000). In Kenya, for example, the hardship brought about by the World Bank and IMF in the 1980s and early 1990s gave birth to popular songs of protest by ordinary people seeking to free themselves from 'dominant illusions' through the nostalgic re-creation of 'exemplary heroes and leaders' as embodiments of popular values and public virtues. The songs showed the inner lives of the Kenyan workers 'as impoverished, dominated by exacting physical work, hateful discipline and other constraints'. They also expressed the concern of their Kenyan composers with 'dignity, self-esteem and the ability to live a life autonomous from that dictated by the market economy and those who are dominant in it' (Gecau 1997: 154–71).

If globalisation and neoliberalism create opportunities, to some these opportunities come as paradise, but to most they come as hell. The rhetoric might be one of a bazaar to which all are invited, but the reality is that few benefit or are given clear-cut choices. One can therefore not afford to be insensitive to the hierarchies of inequalities that make of globalisation less a process of flows than closures, compression than inflation, enhancement than depletion for most in Africa. Mindful of this, it should surprise few that the mediascape in Africa in the age of intensified globalisation speaks more of continuity than change and more of exclusion than inclusion, as is further substantiated below and in subsequent chapters.

Press Freedom and Democratisation in Africa in the 1990s

The current democratic process in Africa has brought with it not only multipartyism but also a sort of media pluralism (Hyden et al. 2002). In almost every country, the number of private newspapers increased dramatically with the clamour for more representative forms of democracy in the early 1990s. In 2005, fifteen years into the second liberation struggles, most countries have opened up the airwaves as well. The fact that African governments largely resisted private initiative in broadcasting since independence, and waited till the pro-democracy clamours of the 1990s even to contemplate weakening their monopoly, is but a logical continuation of their colonial heritage. Commercial or non-state-owned radios, like Africa No. 1 of Gabon, Radio SYD in Gambia, Radio ELWA in Liberia and Trans-World Radio in Swaziland, were for some time rare intrusions in a continuum of state dominance (Tudesq 1992; Bourgault 1995: 68–152). It is therefore of significance that the clamour for democracy in the 1990s led some governments to concede to demands by international broadcasters such as the BBC, RFI and Africa No.1, as well as by private investors, to set up FM transmitters and provide satellite television services within their territories (Bourgault 1995; Campbell 1996: 18–20; Bouhafa 1997: 4–5; Fardon and Furniss 2000; van de Veur 2002: 93–8), targeting their citizens – an unthinkable concession before then.

More and more countries are opening up to satellite television, with little indication of any large-scale efforts by governments to regulate its reception, even though satellite television is known to threaten public broadcasting by 'pulling away audiences and available advertising funds' (Paterson 1998: 574–5). Digital, flexible, global and quality broadcasting is now a reality, thanks to satellites hovering above the continent. West Africa has experienced a boom in private, local and commercial radio stations, with over seventy-two new stations in less than five years by 1996. In Burkina Faso and Mali, where there has been a real explosion, the majority of these stations are rural (Sangho 1996: 72–3; Bouhafa 1997).

Most of these stations are nonprofit organisations of a public-service character, and most prefer to stick to music, sports and other 'innocent' content in order to avoid interference and possible closure by nervous governments. South Africa, Uganda, Rwanda, Burundi, Zambia, Namibia, Senegal and Botswana are other leading examples of private involvement in broadcasting (Bourgault 1995; Kandjii 2000; Fako and Nyamnjoh 2000; Phiri and Powers 2001; van de Veur 2002). Malawi launched its first national television station in January 1999 (Chimombo 2000) and Botswana did the same in July 2000 (Fako and Nyamnjoh 2000). On their part, Lesotho and Swaziland have recently mobilised a South African commercial broadcaster, M-net, to provide a pseudo-national television system, and have also allowed private radio stations (Bereng 2001; Mogekwu 2001). Zimbabwe is the exception in the region, as government is yet to liberalise broadcasting or tolerate a critical private press (Manhando-Makore 2001; Nyahunzvi 2001).

South Africa in particular, with democratic intentions and equity in mind, has not only reformed the South African Broadcasting Corporation (SABC) that served as the mouthpiece of apartheid into the early 1990s (Teer-Tomaselli and Tomaselli 1996; Barnett 1998;

Graybill 2000; Tomaselli 2002) but has also opened up to satellite television greatly. The subscription satellite television service M-net, operational since 1986 and owned by a consortium of South African newspaper publishers, has rapidly spread its tentacles throughout the continent, and together with Multi-Choice (a subscriber management company whose Digital Satellite Television, DSTV, offers over twenty-three satellite television channels and forty-eight audio channels) and Canal Horizon of France virtually dominate the scene of satellite entertainment television (Paterson 1998; Teer-Tomaselli 2001). These providers specialise in routinised, standardised or McDonaldised international sport and entertainment, which they serve to every subscriber on the continent, regardless of region, nationality or cultural preferences, an approach that has occasioned renewed criticisms of Western cultural imperialism through South African media (Rwomire 1992; Bereng 2001). As Teer-Tomaselli (2001) notes, apart from increasing its local programming content and bringing a bit of the rainbow composition of South Africa to reflect on its on-air presentations, M-net has done little to alter its positioning in the new South Africa. It is hoped that increased local production and programme exchange through such organisations as the Union of National Radio and Television of Africa (URTNA) would correct the dependence on cheap, imported programmes and sports of little direct relevance to Africa.

South Africa has equally witnessed an explosion in community radio stations, with more than 100 licences granted, of which 'some 80 stations were actually on the air on a daily basis' in 1998 (van Kessel 1998: 12–13). It is estimated that there will be over 200 community radio stations in the near future. Although, according to veteran community broadcaster Zane Ibrahim of Bush Radio Cape Town, a proliferation of stations is not necessarily a good thing, as those likely to benefit most 'are the "consultants" and the many new broadcast equipment supply companies', who are more likely to be 'laughing all the way to the bank' than serving any community interest. He is equally critical of government involvement with community radio, as such involvement can only be detrimental to 'communities not overly friendly with the ruling party of the day' (Ibrahim 1999: 15).

Although the media have seen themselves, and have been seen, as key players in the democratic process (Hyden et al. 2002), research on media and elections suggests that the media have not performed this role properly. There is little evidence that the media have undertaken systematic voter education during campaigns, nor explained the voting process to the voters. These shortcomings may be due to bias, but also to lack of professionalism (Lush 1998: 47–50; Chiumbu 1997: 113–41) and other factors discussed below. But, placed in perspective, such shortcomings are hardly surprising, given that the task for the media has been rendered extra difficult, if not impossible, by the failure almost everywhere to give democracy an 'identity' relevant to the experiences and marginalised value systems of ordinary people (Zhuwarara et al. 1997).

If the private press and private radio stations of Africa are often independent and critical of government, they have not always succeeded in displaying a similar attitude vis-à-vis the opposition or other pressure groups and lobbies (ethnic, religious and regional). Thus, instead of seeking to curb intolerance, fanaticism or extremism of all kinds in accordance with the logic of liberal democracy, some of these media have actually fuelled them. Examples abound of newspapers in Senegal (Ndao 1996), Mali (Sangho 1996), Niger (Senghor 1996: 1), Côte d'Ivoire (Bahi 1998; Tudesq 1997; UNJCI 1997: 29–75) Kenya (Charo and Makali 1998; Rutten 1998), Madagascar (Randrianja 1998), and Cameroon (Nyamnjoh 1996b; Monga 2000) that have served as mouthpieces for divisive forces, often reproducing calls to murder, destruction and hatred, and generally keeping everyone fearful of a Rwanda-type situation, where Radio Mille Collines proved what the media can do to spur ethnic cleansing. In Mali, for example, the press exacerbated ethnic tensions and conflicts in the north, encouraged striking students to paralyse the educational system for three years, and sections of it allowed themselves to be manipulated by 'certain leaders of the opposition ... in order to attempt to make the country ungovernable' (Sangho 1996: 70–71).

In Kenya, the ethnic violence that occurred in Laikipia and Njoro in January and February 1998 exposed the press as keener to promote 'hate journalism' through exaggeration and politicisation of ethnic tensions than accurate and responsible journalism. While the tendency was for the private press critical of government to portray the Kalenjin (President Moi's ethnic group) 'as the villains in the clashes' and the other ethnic groups, the Kikuyu especially, as innocent victims, the state-owned Kenya Broadcasting Corporation and pro-government print media focused on the Kalenjin as victims. As a whole, the press 'settled on politics as the cause' and whipped up ethnic or political emotions, often without bothering 'to venture into the battlefront' (Charo and Makali 1998: 1–2).

In South Africa the tendency is for newsrooms to reproduce 'prior metanarratives of social schisms, even when those narratives may be radically inappropriate and counter to available evidence' (Fordred 1999: iv, 215–20). It is often a case of much talking without listening and of an exaggerated sense of self-righteousness on the part of most journalists, who often do not hesitate to sacrifice truth for 'a good story'. This tendency of 'twisting or falsifying the supposed news to fit a journalist's opinion about where the truth really lies' is not exclusive to Africa. It is also 'typical of much of modern British journalism', as demonstrated by Lord Hutton's recent inquiry into a BBC report which accused the government of having deliberately 'sexed up' an intelligence-based dossier on Iraq's weapons of mass destruction, in order to justify going to war (The Economist 2004b: 11, 31–3). However, the tendency among African journalists and media to serve ethnic, religious and regional interests is also indicative of their predicament as professionals and institutions expected to fulfil liberal democratic functions in a context where people are clamouring, as well, for recognition and representation as cultural, religious and regional communities. Such competing claims for their attention explain the apparent contradictions, hypocrisy and double standards when their actions are appreciated from the standpoint of liberal democracy.

The competing claims for their attention also explain other shortcomings associated with them throughout the 1990s. African journalists (both official and private) have, for instance, been accused of professional impropriety, not only by governments and other prominent political actors but also by the general public and even by fellow professionals at home and abroad (Kasoma 1997a, 1997b, 1999; Tanjong and Ngwa 2002). A veteran journalist summed up this new trend of journalism in Sierra Leone thus: 'Cheap propaganda, rather than reporting issues as they affect the common man, has become the preoccupation of most of our journalists. Most of them are today partisan and, as such, have fixed ideas that hardly accommodate the views of others' (Sesay 1998: 267–8).

In Nigeria, instead of uniting to 'challenge legislation designed to license the media and emasculate them in other ways' and to 'speak with one voice against the annulment of the 1993 presidential elections', the press chose to sacrifice professionalism for ethnic, religious, regional and clientelist interests (Dare 1998: 15). The ethical shortcomings of the press in Mali have been well summed up by Sangho as 'lack of professionalism, client–patron relationship, disseminating unverified news or partisan news, attacks on the honour and dignity of citizens, incitement to revolt against public authority, abuse and libel' (Sangho 1996: 86). These accusations levelled against the press in Mali are just as true of the rest of West Africa (Blay-Amihere and Alabi 1996; Karikari 1996a). The press has been accused of 'journalistic hooliganism', of 'observing a conniving silence' over certain happenings, while being 'irresponsible and reckless' in reporting others; thus bringing their states 'to the brink of civil war'. The private press has been accused of being light, frivolous and full of shortcomings, and of using invective to gain cheap publicity. Fellow journalists in the official media have accused the critical private press of selecting for insults, defamation and scandals only public authorities or individuals sympathetic to the government – thus giving the impression that members of the opposition are beyond blemish. In Togo, the great majority of the private newspapers that mushroomed in Lomé between 1990 and 1991 'were hostile to President Eyadéma and sympathetic to the work of the National Conference' and the opposition in general (Ellis 1993: 462).

This tendency, coupled with the fact of a weak opposition in most countries, has offered repressive governments the easy option of branding as oppositional all critical media, and blaming on the opposition any embarrassing reports by the media instead of addressing the issues raised (Ronning 1994: 18). Similarly, the private press in particular, by taking upon itself a highly oppositional political role, has often allowed itself to be 'used as pawns in the

dirty game of politics', and has eased the destruction of its professional credibility with sensationalism and suspicious advocacy. It has
also given governments an easy excuse to seek to withdraw past
concessions on freedom of expression and democratisation (Kasoma
1997a: 298–307). The result is that newspapers are often irregular in
publication, 'appearing and disappearing with such speed that it is
often difficult for an outsider to follow their progress or to establish
who owns or runs which paper' (Ellis 2000: 224).

The press has been called all sorts of names, from 'cocktail',
'bread-and-butter', 'cheque-book', 'yellow', 'attack–collect', 'brown-
envelope' or 'survival' journalism on the one hand; to 'guerrilla
journalism', 'le journalisme de combat', 'liberation journalism', 'journalisme
insurrectionnel', 'jungle journalism', 'junk journalism' or 'gutter journalism' on the other. The private press is seen as leaning too overtly
towards commentary and opinion. Although it could be argued, in
certain cases, that journalists probably focus on commentary and
opinion because these are much less perishable than the news which
they cannot come out with in time because of financial problems,
censorship and staff shortages, the fact remains that such opinion and
commentary have often been presented as if these were the news.
The press has also been accused of sensationalism, of frightening
rather than reassuring its readership, of seeking to confront indecent
governments with indecent language, and of being unprofessional
and unethical in their representation of events, individuals and
groups. This should not be the case, and nothing in the profession
justifies the use of indecent language, sensationalism or unethical
practices (Kunczik 1999). As Kasoma observes of The Post of Zambia,
which constantly referred to President Chiluba as 'childish', 'im-
mature', 'criminal', 'forger', 'fool', 'scoundrel', 'crook', 'bandit' and
so on', journalists must distinguish 'between being critical of a
head of state and insulting them' (Kasoma 1997a: 301). Indeed,
many newspapers in Africa are 'simply smear sheets churning out
badly-sourced and one-sided gossip which they present as news'
(Kasoma 1999: 449).

The private press has equally been libellous, and the volume of
court cases and letters to the editors complaining against defamation
and falsehood are there, in every country, as proof not only of the

state using the courts to stifle the press but also of the press being libellous (Blay-Amihere and Alabi 1996; Karikari 1996a; Ngah 1998). The most recurrent criticism of the private press in this regard is the tendency to rush into publication after hearing only one side of a story, and most often very distortedly.

For a fee, editors and proprietors have allowed their newspapers to be used by some individuals or interest groups to blackmail other institutions, individuals or interest groups (Sangho 1996). In Kenya, for example, a 'Gutter Club', comprising The Dispatch, Exposure, Weekly Sun, Compass, Crossfire, The Post, The Post on Sunday, Dunia, Kenya Confidential and others, has established itself with a regular menu of extortion, corruption and harlotry (Makali 1998: 1–3; Rutten 1998: 3–18). According to Makali, the 'Gutter' press does not hesitate to kill stories for bribes, sell entire print runs to corrupt people anxious to cover their tracks, use intimidation to extort money from prominent politicians and businessmen, or allow their pages to be used by traders and politicians 'to teach their rivals a lesson'. In Nairobi in particular, publishers, editors and conmen have established a syndicate 'to squeeze money out of gullible and corrupt people'. The conmen act as links between the scribes and their victims and are usually close to the victims, who are often politicians and corrupt tycoons. They give information to the publishers on dirty deals involving their 'friends' and then pretend to advise the latter 'that so-and-so has damaging information about you and it is only safe that you buy him'. When the tycoons get into the trap, the go-betweens share the loot with the publishers (Makali 1998: 3).

In most countries, journalists are ordinarily perceived as mouth-pieces for competing political pressure groups. This is true of West Africa (Karikari 1996a; Blay-Amihere and Alabi 1996) and also of southern African countries such as Malawi (Minnie 1999: 13), where it is common knowledge even among journalists themselves 'that certain writers or newspapers are the unofficial mouthpieces of particular interests or politicians or are simply open to hire in the form of bribery by any faction, occasionally for the defamation of their rivals' (Ellis 2000: 225). The pressures on them to please those for whom they work or with whom they belong are such that they cannot report fairly on all sides of an issue in the most attentive and self-critical manner, suppressing personal prejudices and sticking to the facts. The private press pushes everyone else to the wall with its half-truths or blatant lies, claiming infallibility. Although very hostile to negative criticism of their manière de faire, the private press journalists do not hesitate to judge, instruct, moralise and condemn others. Headlines like 'Kill this Man' on the front page of The Messenger by the editor-in-chief himself, referring to the governor of the South West Province in Cameroon, are common currency and refresh memories of the atrocities in Rwanda.

As Diana Senghor puts it, various media have, in the name of freedom and the right to inform, abused certain human rights, and it is hardly surprising that between 1992 and 1996 hundreds of legal actions were instituted in the region against the press, mostly on charges of undermining the dignity and respect of the government and important officials (libel, sedition, etc.) (Senghor 1996: 1). In Ghana, many cases of ethical violations against social responsibility and public interest, professional integrity, respect for human rights, and the search for truth have been well documented by Koomson (1996: 42–58). Some of these have resulted in legal suits 'brought against publishers, editors and reporters of the private press by ministers of state and parliamentarians', and some media practitioners have served prison terms for libel (Arthur 1997: 12). This is a development true of the rest of Africa (Kasoma 1996, 1997a), where 'bemused citizens have watched with mixed feelings: some in utter disbelief as the 'liberated' press makes all kinds of allegations against their leaders; others have hailed the muckraking journalists as heroes whose shocking 'revelations' and attacks on those in power they hope would bring some sanity into African politics'; and 'flabbergasted politicians ... have vowed to do everything in their power to restrict press freedom once again' (Kasoma 1996: 100–101). Ellis reports that in Zambia The Post faced over a hundred actions for civil libel from members of government and others between 1991 and 1996, and that it was also subjected to 'legal action under more unusual legislation, some of it dating from the colonial period' (Ellis 2000: 224).

In Benin, where the press had by the end of 1993 attracted forty legal proceedings, libel alone accounted for about seventy convictions between 1990 and 1996 (Quenum 1996: 10–11; Palmer 1997: 253–8). In Côte d'Ivoire, there were forty-seven libel suits against the press by individuals before 1994, and twenty suits of 'insult on the President of the Republic, or insults on the Head of State of a foreign country' were initiated against the press by the public prosecutor between 1992 and 1994 (Toure 1996: 25–6, 34–5; Tudesq 1997: 298–300). For Senegal, Ndao (1996: 121–38) discusses in detail cases of libel against individuals and public personalities, the use of forgeries and sensationalism by the press (e.g. Le Témoin, Le Soleil, Le Cafard Libéré, Promotion, Carrefour Républicain, SOPI), how the courts have dealt with these, and perceptions by journalists and the public of these breaches. For Mali, Sangho (1996: 72–87) provides an interesting and well-documented account of breaches to professional ethics by broadcast and print media from 1992 to 1994, and also of how these breaches are perceived by journalists themselves and by lawyers. Soola documents interesting cases of pro-government partisan journalism by the Daily Times and the state-owned government-controlled broadcast media, as well as cases of violation of professional ethics by the Daily Times, the New Nigerian and Nigerian Tribune on the one hand, and state and private broadcast media on the other (Soola 1996: 104–19).

These examples of complaints against certain kinds of journalistic practice imply that Africans aspiring for liberal democracy have little interest in newspapers which can bend over backwards in favour of the government, the opposition or lobbies of various kinds. They want the press to be honest, fair and accurate in reporting. Not only is the public aware that the journalists are partisan and self-interested; they are also concerned by the fact that it is difficult if not impossible to find journalists who go for the truth and who treat it with the respect and distance that a news story deserves. Not only are their opinions 'informed and influenced' by the cultural, religious, regional and political groupings to which they belong; they do not succeed in rising above such opinions as the canons of journalism under liberal democracy would suggest (Feldmann et al. 1998: 8; S. and M. Chimombo 1996: 26–33).

Some scholars are keen to stress that the situation is not totally bleak throughout the continent, similar though it might be in many regards (Hyden and Okigbo 2002; Ogundimu 2002). The private press in Botswana, which consists of seven weeklies, has been thought of as offering a noteworthy exception (Zaffiro 1993, 2000; Fako and Nyamnjoh 2000). Zaffiro maintains that this press enjoys a degree of tolerance from government that is rare in Africa, and that it has earned credibility for its critical and investigative journalism, especially following its reporting of the 'Botswana Housing Corporation scandal' and the 'Newslink Africa' affair (Zaffiro 1993: 19–23). On his part, Good acknowledges the achievements of Botswana's private press, but equally discusses legislation and action by government aimed at muffling it in ways not dissimilar to the rest of Africa (Good 1994: 503–16, 1999: 51–5). It must also be noted that, while the private press is eager to uncover scandals among the ruling elite, it has been criticised in the ruling Botswana Democratic Party (BDP) circles. It has been suggested that the press was sympathetic to the opposition, and was so unprofessional that it would rather not print, than print anything that showed the BDP in a positive light, a sentiment similar to that shared by the opposition parties vis-à-vis the state radio. What all critics of the media in Botswana seem to agree on is the low level of professionalism and ethical standards among journalists, many of whom have few credentials other than a school leaving certificate, or a university degree in anything but journalism (Fako and Nyamnjoh 2000: 39).

While the picture painted above is typical of sub-Saharan Africa (Bourgault 1995; Ngugi 1995; Uche 1999b; M'Bayo et al. 2000), the situation in post-apartheid South Africa, where the conventional media were until recently in the service of black disempowerment and dehumanisation (Graybill 2000), deserves a special comment. For many years in South Africa, press ownership was dominated by the Argus Group, Times Media Ltd, Nasionale Pers and Perskor, who 'together owned more than 90% of the market of daily and weekly newspapers and half of the magazine market'. This made the media a preponderantly white-controlled business. Although the end of apartheid has led to some degree of black ownership and partnership in the media, this has not necessarily 'made the newspapers more representative of South African society'. As van Kessel observes, 'it is unmistakably true that South Africa's print media are of little relevance to the majority of its population', and that the 'presence of more black faces in board rooms and news rooms' has not resulted in more or better coverage of black reality. The fact that newspapers are yet 'to develop a more comprehensive news formula' that takes into account black interests has occasioned a decline in overall penetration among blacks, who, unlike whites, coloured and Indians, tend to rely on radio and television for news coverage (van Kessel 1998: 4–10; see also Tomaselli 2002).

Although there is little evidence yet of the new black owners of newspapers imposing a political agenda on their papers (Gooch 1997; van Kessel 1998), concern has been raised about the fact that these 'black press barons are a highly politicised breed'. The 'grip of political correctness' on many papers has resulted in: (i) ANC supporters often finding it difficult to criticise their party, while others are reluctant to appear disloyal towards the experiment with a new society; (ii) journalists, 'reluctant to publicise the successes of the new government out of fear to appear subservient', focusing on daily incidents and trivia, while 'government complains with some justification that it finds it difficult to get its policy across to the public'. In the face of this situation, van Kessel sees 'an obvious need for a new kind of journalism, which feels confident both to explore the exciting experiments in South African society and to criticise its failings' (van Kessel 1998: 4–10). Tensions occasioned by ANC government concerns about, and the Human Rights Commission's (HRC) inquiry into, 'racism in the media' and the 'racialized and stereotypical portrayal of blacks' (Pityana 2000; Glaser 2000; Jacobs 2000: 5; Graybill 2000: 229–30; Rhodes Journalism Review 2000; Berger 2001) are indicative of how much bridge-building remains to be done. As Jane Duncan puts it, although much has changed within an extremely short space of time in South African media and society, much seems to have stayed the same. The rhetoric of transformation does not seem to match the realities and expectations, as the media continue to 'talk left, act right' (Duncan 2000).

These concerns are echoed by Barnett (1998) and Tomaselli (2002), who discuss, among other things, surging state control and the declining influence of the Independent Broadcasting Authority, and also by Mamphela Ramphele, former vice-chancellor of the University of Cape Town, who feels that 'misguided loyalties and a culture of silence are putting South Africa's democracy at risk', as 'the new ruling elite, left to their whims' and 'concentrating absolute powers' have the potential to be just as bad as the apartheid authorities they have replaced (Ramphele 1999). While the fear of being labelled racist blunts the critical sting of the white-controlled press, the ANC government reinforces the syndrome through repeated accusations of racism and bias against this press. However, as Ebrahim Harvey argues, while there may be truth in these accusations, they are also 'an opportunistic invention to rationalise, divert attention and conceal ... [the] ambitious class interests' of the ruling black elite and 'their middle class hangers-on in other institutions' (Harvey 2000: 22; see also Glaser 2000).

To What Extent Are Journalists and the Media to Blame?

However, to blame all of these shortcomings on the media and their practitioners would be to overlook other factors that make it difficult for even the most committed professionals to excel ethically in the African context. In many countries, journalists have realised that were they to practise journalism according to the rule book, publishing only verified facts, shunning rumour and respecting ethical prescriptions, corruption would wreak havoc with impunity in their societies (Rying 1994; Hyden and Okigbo 2002; Ogundimu 2002). As Rying notes of francophone Africa, having chosen 'ad hominem repudiation of embezzlement and scandals' as a journalistic genre, most newspapers, because of the scarcity of credible news sources, 'swing between rumour and information', knowing that any attempt to respect 'ethics' or 'the golden rules of investigative journalism' would mean a tacit endorsement of 'pernicious corruption in the society' (Rying 1994: 19). In Sierra Leone the New Tablet defied a ban by the Armed Forces Revolutionary Council (AFRC) with the argument that 'an illegitimate regime ... had no right to declare a paper illegitimate' (Sesay 1998: 267).

   In certain countries, the difficulties of journalists are accentuated by the uncooperative attitudes of many in high office. Decades of dictatorship seem to have instituted a perennial fear in officials, even the most highly placed, of the administrative axe from above. The overcentralised systems wherein most Africans operate make experts in various domains unable to give information to the journalist. The government proclaims democracy and freedom of information but does not hesitate to sanction even a cabinet minister who makes an uncleared statement on a burning issue. This makes access to government-held information particularly difficult for the journalists of the private press. Some governments, by practice, have usually not invited journalists of the private press to official ceremonies at the presidential palace and other seats of government or as parts of government missions within or abroad. So these journalists write about the government as outsiders because they are usually chased away from sources of evidence (Eribo and Tanjong 2002).

Among factors that make it difficult for the above-highlighted professional shortcomings to be blamed entirely on journalists and the media, are the following elements.

Culture of one-dimensionalism

In Africa, the freedom of the press made possible by current efforts at democratisation is something largely new (Ziegler and Asante 1992; Land 1992; Tudesq 1995; Bourgault 1995; Hyden et al. 2002), a sort of reawakening after what Hachten has described as a 'false start' in his examination of the failure to develop of the African press since independence (Hachten 1993: 3–13, 51–4). French-inspired legislation for francophone Africa (Chindji 1996; Fombad 1999a) and British-inspired libel, sedition and official secrets acts for anglophone or Commonwealth Africa (Mnangagwa 1996: 113–18; Feltoe 1996: 138–47; Ziegler and Asante 1992: 102–13; Gariyo 1993; Berger 1998; Martin 1999; Kupe 1999: 6–7) have traditionally stressed control and containment more than freedom. It is still very common to charge journalists simply for making statements that bring any state official into disrepute, as documented cases in Togo, Côte d'Ivoire, Cameroon, Zambia, Zimbabwe, Nigeria, Kenya, Sierra Leone, Malawi, Namibia, Central African Republic, Swaziland, and other countries show (Lwanda 1993: 270; Fritz 1996: 81–4; Ogbondah 1997: 285–6;

Russell 1999: 58–66; MISA 1999; Mogekwu 2001). The Media Institute of Southern Africa (MISA), the Panos Institute, Friedrich Ebert Stiftung and other monitors of censorship, harassment and attacks on journalists and media institutions, have been very active in their documentation in this connection. MISA, for example, has regularly published its reports in this area under the title *So This Is Democracy? State of the Media in Southern Africa.*

In Côte d'Ivoire, for example, 99 per cent of all journalists sanctioned since 1990 were sanctioned for offences against the head of state (Mbougueng 1998: 24). Ellis details two telling cases brought against the Zambian *Post* by the Chiluba government:

> In the case of *The People* v. *Bright Mwape and Fred M'membe*, senior editors of the *Post* were charged in 1994 with insulting President Frederick Chiluba by reporting that a deputy minister had referred to him as 'a twit'.... In another case, the same two defendants and *Post* columnist Lucy Banda Sichone were found guilty in February 1996 of contempt of Parliament by the Standing Orders Committee of the Zambian National Assembly – which is not a court of law – for publishing articles that criticised a parliamentary speech made by the vice president. The speaker of the National Assembly then directed the inspector-general of police to arrest the three. Mwape and M'membe were jailed for a period, but released by order of the Lusaka High Court on March 27, 1998. The government has appealed this decision. (Ellis 2000: 224)

In March 1999, the *Post* published a front-page article that warned of the Zambian army's vulnerability to a possible attack from Angola and raised critical issues of national security. The government cracked down, and the entire *Post* staff were charged with espionage and endangering national security. The state-owned *Times of Zambia* sided with the government, accusing the *Post* of overstepping its limits, of aiding the enemy with intent to dismantle and disgrace the nation, and of behaving outside the perimeters of journalism. But for the editor of the *Post*, Fred M'membe, this was only the latest episode in a catalogue of government hostilities since his paper was launched in July 1991. 'Our journalists have been arrested and detained several times over the past eight years. But none of this frightens us.... Eight years of hardship and struggle, of unyielding tenacity and experience, are not worthless' (*Rhodes Journalism Review* 1999: 10).

In Swaziland in 1999, *Times of Swaziland* (a critical and privately owned paper) journalist and editor Bheki Makhubu was heavily criticised, lost the support of management and his job, and was arrested and charged with criminal defamation for daring to tell the truth about the girl and future bride the Swazi king had chosen for himself at the Reed Dance. Bheki Makhubu had put the girl, Senteni Masango, under the searchlight. He had reported that 'the young girl was a high school drop-out, a truant and generally a "naughty girl"', and noted that the girl lacked discipline and had been expelled from two schools in two years. The story raised a lot of dust in the nation, and was condemned by many traditionalists and loyalists as 'being in bad taste and serving only to damage the girl's reputation and that of the royal household'. Others saw it as 'a way of getting at the king', while some felt the media had no business making such revelations, no matter how true. The *Swazi Observer*, the only other paper in the country, is owned by the Tibiyo Trust, which is headed by the king (Mogekwu 2001: 20–21).

On Botswana, Good argues that the existence and occasional utilisation of laws on sedition, defamation and contempt 'encourages self-censorship on the part of publishers, editors, journalists and others'. He presents concrete cases of newspapers and journalists victimised by the law (Good 1994: 503–16, 1999: 51–5). To discourage journalists from scrutinising the ruling elite and their activities, news concerning the Botswana Democratic Party (BDF) tends to be tied to state security, and the media may be accused of undermining national security by publishing 'sensitive' information (Good 1999: 52–3).

Equally frowned upon are journalists asking national or foreign dignitaries questions that are perceived as embarrassing by government. In Uganda, for example, three journalists were charged 'with defaming a foreign dignitary contrary to section 51 of the Penal Code because they had dared ask the then visiting Zambian Head of State, President Kaunda, three provocative questions at a press conference at State House, Entebbe, on 29 January, 1990'. And because one of those involved, Abdi Hassan, was a local BBC correspondent, the Ministry of Information and Broadcasting 'deregistered all correspondents to foreign media organisations and asked them to

re-apply after laying down new rules' (Gariyo 1993: 40–41). 'In
many other cases, journalists who anger or embarrass a government
may be subject to unlawful physical intimidation or worse'; and
the remarkable rise in the number of journalists killed in Africa in
recent years, with thirteen journalists reportedly murdered in 1999
alone (Ellis 2000: 224), is not unconnected with increased press
freedom. In November 2000 in Mozambique, Carlos Cardoso, a
renowned investigative journalist, who successfully created and ran
a highly influential faxed daily newspaper, Metical, 'was shot dead in
a hail of machine-gunfire outside of his office'. He was known to
ask too many questions about sensitive matters, the latest of which
being the embezzlement of millions of pounds at the Mozambique
Commercial Bank. His killing was thought to have been commissioned by senior officials and businessmen who feared exposure (see
www.misanet.org; Fauvet and Mosse 2003: 1–5, 312–38).

Thus, before 1990, media in Africa were effectively controlled
either with draconian laws or by simply making them part of the
civil service. In the case of the public media, governments have
ensured that journalists think of themselves more as part of the
central administration than as a separate institution or profession.
Like other civil servants, state journalists were and still are employed
by the government, appointed to positions of responsibility by the
president or minister, and given titles that are identical to titles
elsewhere in the civil service. As such, they are expected to pay
allegiance to the government by respecting the canons of the civil
service rather than those of journalism.

The integration of the public media into the civil service permits
the government to impose certain restrictions on state-employed
journalists that hinder the effective practice of their profession. Not
only is the civil service insufficiently remunerating; the practice of
journalism in the state-owned media is constantly impaired by political and administrative barriers deliberately set up by government,
or simply the inevitable consequences of excessive centralisation
and bureaucratisation.

Thus state-employed journalists find it difficult to reconcile the
government's expectations with their professional beliefs, or with
the expectations of the public; a predicament which has forced

many practitioners either to quit the profession entirely or to opt for a Jekyll-and-Hyde personality. Taking the latter option has meant the propagation and defence of party and government policies, stances, and action in public, while at the same time criticising or condemning these in private among trusted colleagues, friends and relations. For others it has meant publishing critical allegations against the government in the private press under pen names. By assuming the role of paymaster for all state employees, governments have procured themselves an effective weapon for exacting loyalty and subservience from state-employed journalists.

The legal framework regulating the press

An examination of most legal frameworks in Africa reveals a craving to control that leaves little doubt about how the lawmakers see journalists as potential troublemakers who must be policed. In francophone Africa, the tendency is for new laws to grant freedom in principle while providing, often by administrative nexus, the curtailment of press freedom in practice (SDLP/UJAO 1994). Thus in Burundi the November 1992 press law, which was drawn up without consultation with the Association Burundaise des Journalistes and in spite of government's catchphrase of the need for dialogue, grants journalists a right to protect their sources, yet says they may be forced to relinquish that right by a competent judge. The law provides for a national communication council but gives government the leeway to appoint its members and remote-control its activities. And by retaining administrative censorship, it cancels out any impression of freedom that a surface reading of its text might give (Ntiyanogeye 1994: 131–3). This tendency for government to take away with one hand what it is giving with the other, in matters of freedom, is well exemplified in Cameroon, our case study (Fombad 1999a, 1999b). And, although strongest in francophone Africa, this use of 'derogable and clawback measures' by the state to limit the right of expression and press freedom is common throughout the continent, as Ogbondah's examination of constitutional provisions regulating freedom of expression in sub-Saharan Africa shows

(Ogbondah 1997: 281–3, 2002). Lush, who describes the lip service paid by African governments to the 1991 Windhoek Declaration on Promoting an Independent and Pluralistic African Press as 'a pledge of convenience', discusses how Southern African governments (Zambian, Malawian, Tanzanian, Namibian, Zimbabwean and Mozambiquan) have continued to use 'out-moded legislation inherited from their one-party and colonial predecessors' to criminalise dissent and numb the critical instincts of the press (Lush 1998). The Botswana office of the Media Institute for Southern Africa's *So This Is Democracy* has tempered the exceptionality of Botswana with a 62-page inventory of media-unfriendly laws and practices in the country (Balule and Maripe 2000).

Even the Nigerian press, often presented as the most vibrant and critical, has to struggle with a battery of laws which the Nigerian Union of Journalists (NUJ) 'considers to be inimical to journalism or media practice in general and a disincentive to the development of the profession'. Oloyede discusses eleven different cases of detention of journalists under the State Security Decree No. 2 of 1984, showing how the said decree was used over the years 'to deter the publication of views and opinions opposed to the policies and actions of the Federal Military Government or those the government would not like expressed' (Oloyede 1996: 55–71), or 'any statement which brought any state official into disrepute' (Soyinka 1996: 10). In addition to the laws are obstacles such as 'the renewal of the licence to operate', 'the right of the authorities to close down any medium at will' (of which Oloyede (1996: 81–90) documents eighteen instances between 1968 and 1995), the forfeiture of the deposit made on application in case of refusal of registration (Anyakora and Potiskum 1996: 103–5), and 'the denial of foreign exchange to certain publishing houses … often critical of the government' – thus leading 'to the purchase of newsprint through third and fourth parties' at exorbitant and often unaffordable costs (Ogbondah 1997: 290). Such repressive laws and practices are to blame for the rise of the 'underground press' that 'practices junk or gutter journalism' yet cannot be disciplined by the Nigeria Press Council since they are not registered journalists and publications with the NUJ (Anyakora and Potiskum 1996: 103–5).

Although certain aspects of draconian press laws of the one-party era have generally been replaced by new provisions that are relatively more tolerant of oppositional views and of criticisms in other countries (Ogbondah 1997, 2002), often the selective application of the law, together with the use of extra-legal measures, have been to the detriment of the critical private press, and have made it very difficult for this press to have the professional independence it needs. In many countries we notice a situation similar to that of Sierra Leone, where 'the laws of libel, sedition, treason and preventive detention are used to control, cow or silence the mass media, while various press licensing rules and other regulations are instituted from time to time' (Cole 1995: 60). In 1993, the control was made even tougher when the minister of information and broadcasting issued the NPRC Decree No. 6 compelling all thirty newspapers to register afresh within four weeks. To make matters worse, the registration fee was raised beyond affordability for most, and other conditions were imposed with the intention of exclusion (Cole 1995: 50–51).

Such control, Cole rightly remarks, occasions self-censorship on the part of journalists, what Ronning has termed 'internalised assumptions of what is expected of the media' that have proved far more restrictive to critical journalism than any pressure by political powers in many African countries (Ronning 1994: 8). Editors and publishers in Sierra Leone, Cole argues, 'refuse to publish if they think they will be persecuted' (Cole 1995: 60); a practice which, as Nyahunzvi has noted in Zimbabwe, tends to filter down to the rank and file, creating a situation whereby 'reporters would rather be their own censors than be censored by someone else', seeing, as they do, little 'point in pursuing a story which will be so emasculated that the final version bears no resemblance whatsoever to the original' (Nyahunzvi 1996: 162). 'These developments have led to a crisis of credibility of the mass media in Sierra Leone. Whenever stories break which portray the government in a bad light, people tend to rely on the BBC and other foreign media for the truth' (Cole 1995: 60), a tendency also true of Nigeria (Soola 1996: 111), Côte d'Ivoire (Tudesq 1997: 300), Zimbabwe, Zambia, Malawi (Lush 1998: 44; Chimombo 2000: 10), and other countries in Africa. Indeed, 'the access that foreign journalists have to the corridors of power in many African capitals is the envy of their African counterparts – and yet another indication of the imbalance of credibility on the continent' (Onadipe 1998: 263). It also raises questions of an epistemological nature about reportage on Africa, for consumption not only by European and North American audiences but also by Africans, based on Western representations that do not exclude preconceptions, prejudices and misinformation (Franklin and Love 1998); a concern well illustrated by Niranjan Karnik's critical examination of coverage of events in Rwanda by the *New York Times*, from 1989 to 1994 (Karnik 1998).

Thus, as Mayer has observed of the West, and this is applicable to Africa just as well, to be able to perform the vital role as defenders of liberal democracy and as watchdogs for the community, 'journalists as individual persons need a framework of laws and collective agreements which concretely and in detail guarantee the conditions to fulfil their task and to work under reasonable terms' (Mayer 1993: 56). Only as a body united in values and aspirations can journalists 'ensure that exceptions to the right to information are kept at a minimum and cannot be misused to hide information of public interest' (Mayer 1993: 58). United thus, African journalists would be able not only to establish traditions of dealing with libel and other shortcomings but also to ensure that legal costs are not unduly inflated to paralyse the press (Karikari 1996a; Blay-Amihere and Alabi 1996). It is not unthinkable in a situation where the judiciary is far from independent, courageous and assertive (Ogbondah 1997: 288) for the courts to collude with government to stifle the press with exceedingly high legal costs.

Job insecurity, poor salaries and poor working conditions

Lack of job security, poor salaries and poor working conditions are equally a constraint. Newspaper publishers have capitalised on the helplessness of some job-seekers, who have not been guaranteed regular salaries. This has inevitably led to 'prostitution' by journalists or to what one may term a hand-to-mouth journalism, if not a journalism of misery. Any bit of money can lure a journalist to write anything, including blackmail, as was the case in Zaire under Mobutu (Nlandu-Tsasa 1997: 75–93). In Côte d'Ivoire, lack of resources, excessive costs of production, a 50 per cent fall in advertisement revenue, and a regular unsold rate of over 80 per cent for most papers (Mbougueng 1998: 25), have generally pushed journalists 'to trample on the rules of their code of ethics' (Toure 1996: 30–31) by pursuing '*gombos* – tips which they openly ask for from politicians and businessmen' (Mbougueng 1998: 25). The same is true of Mobutu's Zaire, where, because of the collapse of state structures and generalised kleptocracy (Russell 1999: 9–40), journalists abandoned all professional ethics, and allowed the *coupe* or *coupage* (bribe or motivation fee) to determine not only what news story was covered but the very quality and placement of that coverage.

Wages are generally low even in the official media. According to Cole, professional journalists in Sierra Leone find that 'if they work outside the media, they would get better emolument, quicker promotion, more serious attention to their training needs, better personal security, less chances of their being persecuted, and better recognition and status. Consequently, many of the experienced journalists have left the profession for more financially lucrative jobs either overseas or in other employment in the country' (Cole 1995: 64). In the new South Africa, where 'there is tremendous lack of qualified black professionals', the newspaper industry is rapidly losing its 'limited pool of professional black journalists' to government, corporate business and television, 'all of which offer better remuneration and higher status' (van Kessel 1998: 8). In general, poor salaries throughout the continent have made 'the profession less attractive to highly-qualified people', and 'media workers susceptible to compromise, bribery and corruption' (Lush 1998: 53).

Financial difficulties, lack of personnel and specialisation

The next type of constraint pertains to financial difficulties that have compounded the problems of news gathering and news production and made papers even less credible as they stretch and strain to make possible every single edition. In Sierra Leone, visiting a newsroom in Freetown 'is like visiting a museum. Reporters are pounding old typewriters, copy is being prepared for Linotype operators and there is a marked absence of wordprocessors, let alone computers. The newspapers simply do not generate enough revenue to be able to afford them' (Cole 1995: 62).

An obvious consequence of this situation, which is equally true of Guinea (Lootvoet and Ecoutin 1993: 154–5), Cameroon (Boh 1997), Zimbabwe (Nyahunzvi 1996: 163) and other countries, is superficiality, lack of research and background in most of the stories. There is simply no means to encourage specialised reporting. Everyone can write on anything, from sports to politics through economics and culture. But, as some veteran journalists have argued, a journalist cannot be good in everything, and being 'a jack of all trades' is bound to result in superficiality. The 'overwhelming number of generalist reporters and very few specialists' has occasioned 'shallow and inadequate coverage and analysis of events, especially on socio-economic issues' and tended 'to distance the mass media from the society they are supposed to serve' (Cole 1995: 64).

Another result of poor finances is the dearth of personnel, trained and experienced or not. Most newspapers have a skeleton staff, and some are virtually a one-person affair, who may be publisher, editor and reporter all in one (Sangho 1996: 79–80; Lootvoet and Ecoutin 1993: 154–5). 'One wonders how they sometimes manage to produce a newspaper' (Nyahunzvi 1996: 163). It is hardly surprising that few newspapers can afford to go out for news gathering and investigative journalism. Often they rely on documents (which few can afford to verify) to be fed them by a neighbour's or *téléboutique's* fax machine, and to wordprocess or typeset them they have to search for an affordable typist with a computer that can do the job. In Côte d'Ivoire (Mbougueng 1998: 25), the high death or hibernation toll among newspapers is clear proof of these difficulties, as few can boast sufficient finances to pay for competent staff, quality processing and printing, and efficient delivery to vendors (Lootvoet and Ecoutin 1993: 155).

One of the reasons for poor finances is the ease with which, in financial terms, it is possible to start a publication in most countries. In Kenya, for example, 'with as little as six thousand shillings ... you can print 1000 copies of an 8-page A4-size newsletter and make your presence felt on the street', and how you stay will 'depend on which side of the political divide you are or the weight of your godfather' (Makali 1998: 2).

Ignorance of the market

A militant and unprofessional approach to journalism has meant that journalists are animated more by their assumptions, prejudices or stereotypes of the public and public interest than by any real knowledge of their audiences as sovereign consumers of media products. Public interest as a dynamic and complex reality has eluded them. Few newspaper proprietors have bothered to study the market before launching their products. Far from seeking to educate themselves on what the public wants, media proprietors and practitioners have often assumed that the public needs education and information, and they have arrogated to themselves the role of fulfilling these needs. It is hardly surprising, therefore, that many of them have failed in their attempt to please the public or to succeed in business (Kasoma 1999: 448–50). They have not understood that their papers can only become profitable businesses if they reconcile themselves to the fact 'that the most important people on a newspaper are not the owners, the editors, the journalists or the staff as a whole – the most important people are the readers who pay their money to buy the paper' (Garside 1993: 71). This fact calls for modesty on the part of journalists, who 'may write the most wonderful stories in the world but if there are too few readers willing or able to buy the product, business will fail and the quality of content will be lost' (Garside 1993: 69). The demise of the alternative press in South Africa could serve as a good lesson in this regard. Cultivated in 'the 1980s as organs of the anti-apartheid struggle' and funded largely by donors, most of this press was forced to close down for failure 'to make the transition from a heavily politicised "struggle" culture to the more market-oriented environment of the 1990s', after donor funding had dried up (van Kessel 1998: 10–11).

Admitting the sovereignty of the reader or viewer is all the more urgent since, in many countries, commercial advertising revenue does not account for much in the running of the media (Lush

1998: 54–5; Kasoma 1999: 448–9). If the official media succeed in attracting some revenue from advertising, this is usually from government and parastatals or from private business entrepreneurs keen to impress the government. In certain cases, newspapers depend almost entirely on low sales, and when businesses do advertise, or politicians offer sponsorship, they virtually call the tune. In countries like Mozambique and Botswana, the private press is taxed for its production equipment and advertising, while the government-controlled media are exempt from such taxes (Lush 1998: 55). In some countries where government's grip on national life is still pervasive, with practically every business transaction requiring one form or another of governmental approval, private media operators invariably find themselves doing business with government, thus rendering themselves even more vulnerable (Dare 1998: 15; Lush 1998: 55). Being critical of government could lead to 'directives ordering all government ministries and parastatal companies not to advertise' in a given paper, as was the case in Lesotho in August 1996 against the MoAfrika, because of its 'negative stance' towards the government (Lush 1998: 55). On 30 April 2001 a Government of Botswana directive called on all government ministries, departments, parastatals and private companies in which government was a shareholder to 'with immediate effect … cease advertising in the Guardian newspaper and the Sun Group of papers.' Although the government cited economic considerations, its decision was most likely motivated by repeated critical coverage by these papers. In Malawi, the Independent, for being 'too critical of Mr Muluzi's government', lost advertising from a chain of garages, its main advertiser, when the manager decided to transfer their business to 'another paper without a day's notice'. Questioned, the editor, David Nthengwe, explained the paper's dilemma: 'The difficulty is that you have to fight between survival and objectivity. Companies warn unless we tone down our line they will leave us. What can we do?' (Russell 1999: 62–4).

If industry and commerce behave as though advertising were doing publishers a favour, this is due largely to the very unprofessional approach to journalism of which the press is guilty, but also to the fear on the part of businessmen of drastic government sanctions on anyone keen on investing in the private press or media. Increased professionalism would most likely lead to high circulation and more advertising, and consequently more revenue for the publishers to invest in new technology. It could also act as an incentive to big business to invest in the media industry, which has still to attract 'the really big players in the international media scene'. So far, although 'the adoption of an open market economy and liberal democracy is already attracting ... investment in the media industry' in certain countries (Ogbondah 1997: 280), Africa as a whole is yet to become 'a viable market for the really strongly commercialised international media' (Ronning 1994: 4). Unlike in Central Europe where the media have been able to attract substantial foreign investment in the current democratic transition, the media in Africa have continued to work under serious financial difficulties, with thinly developed consumer markets and a chronic shortage in advertisement revenues (Campbell 1996: 2–3).

The international community and the underdog syndrome

The Western tendency to assume that the press would necessarily work in the direction of liberal democracy if it were free of government control is rather simplistic. Not only does this ignore the ability of the opposition, businesses and other lobbies in society to manipulate the press, it also overlooks the fact that, just like in Europe and North America (as the history of the press shows), media proprietors and practitioners in Africa might be attracted to journalism for reasons other than to promote liberal democracy. Since 1990, it has sufficed for papers to cry foul, for Western governments, human rights associations and press freedom watchdogs (e.g. Reporters Sans Frontières of Paris, Committee to Protect Journalists of New York) to inundate the African states concerned with appeals, threats and accusations of muzzling freedom of expression and a democratic press. 'In Zambia in 1996, for example, a number of donor countries, which included the USA, Britain and Japan, reduced their aid to the country after expressing unhappiness over the Chiluba government's souring relations with the independent press' (Kasoma 1997a: 299). It has hardly occurred to them that the media practitioners might be using liberal democracy simply as a smokescreen behind which to articulate hidden ethnic, regional and sectarian agendas, while presenting themselves as victims of repressive laws and authoritarian governments. Not even an admission by MISA, which has monitored and assisted the media since its creation in 1992, that 'little Frankensteins have been born under the guise of so-called "free and independent" media' (Minnie 1999: 12–13), has called for more critical international attitudes towards the press in Africa. It is with this in mind that Kasoma has pointed to the international community as one of the factors to blame for the journalism of excesses in Africa. He argues that the support given to 'the muckraking journalists to carry on with their "good work" of uncovering the dirty work of the people in government' by western donor countries and agencies has worsened unprofessionalism among journalists in Africa. He regrets the fact that the West has tended to content itself with 'allegations made by the press … in the name of democracy and freedom of the press' rather than seeking the truth of such allegations. Yet, 'making allegations against politicians, based on the flimsiest hearsay and suspicion that there is dirt under the political carpet is not the same as actually exposing the dirt' (Kasoma 1996: 101). If the West has often succeeded in imposing its bitter pill, SAP, on African regimes desirous of staying economically afloat, it should predicate more of its assistance to the African media on evidence of professionalism and sign fewer blank cheques than it has done in the past. Far from simply endorsing simplistic rhetoric on democracy from the media and journalists working in Africa, the international community ought to expect greater evidence of commitment on the part of the media to the principles and practices of liberal democracy.

The call for a more responsible and professional approach to journalism has come not only from politicians and concerned segments of the public but also from fellow journalists. Thus, the above discussion of the media and democratisation is hardly complete without a critical focus on issues of ethics, training and professionalism. Could a more professional and ethical approach to journalism have strengthened the case of African journalists and made the media's contribution to the liberal democratic process more positive and constructive? The next chapter examines various efforts by governments, journalists, media institutions and interested organisations to address ethical concerns and professional issues in the practice of journalism in different countries of Africa, under the reality or illusion of liberal democracy.

2

Media Ethics, Professionalism and Training

in Africa

From the evidence in Chapter 1 it is clear that the practice of journalism in many African countries in the 1990s left much to be desired. Even though the media operated within a particularly difficult legal, economic and political environment, some of the constraints to a professional and financially viable press are obviously internal to the institution itself. In strictly liberal democratic terms, it is possible that some of the shortcomings dealt with in Chapter 1 would have been avoided had the press kept a professional distance from their regional and ethnic origins or political affiliations, or had they simply been open and clear about their biases. This chapter discusses the ethical problem further, seeking to understand its nature, manifestation and causes. It also discusses efforts by journalists and media associations at creating awareness and promoting higher ethical and professional standards.

The Question of Ethics

Lush has argued that: 'For the media to demand accountability, it too must be accountable, just as in the same vein, for the media to be pluralistic, it must reflect the diversity of the societies in which it operates' (Lush 1998: 52). This calls for journalism that enjoys public trust and respect; such journalism comes about by no other means than through a rigorous commitment to ethics and professionalism. Among the attributes of ethical and professional journalism in Africa, Joe Kadhi has identified and discussed freedom of the press, independence, accuracy, impartiality, fair play, decency, responsibility and respect for human rights and gender equality (Kadhi 1999). Yet these attributes have been found most wanting in African journalism in the 1990s.

In Sierra Leone after the military coup that brought the AFRC to power, journalists who wrote in favour of the coup 'were branded "junta journalists", while those who professed to defend democracy were labelled "Kabbah journalists"' (Sesay 1998: 267). It was as if being a journalist in the public interest was simply inconceivable (Khan 1998; Gordon 2004). Screaming, sensational, confrontational headlines devoid of any real content or substance were all too typical. This situation is similar to Angola's, where 'there is little tradition of independence and impartiality within the ... media'. Here journalists are under sustained pressure to be either for or against the government (MPLA) or opposition (UNITA) (MISA 1994: 2–12). In Mali, as elsewhere, it is common for readers to be 'trapped' by 'bugle-call headlines on the front pages' into buying a paper just to 'realize that there is nothing in the body of the article that merits that headline' (Sangho 1996: 81). As Bruce Cohen observes of Malawi, and this is true of other countries, 'Most newspapers ... are not interested in mundane matters of fact, evidence, rebuttal or attribution. They find far more satisfaction in using their pages as a rough canvas for raging brush strokes of rancid insult and wild propaganda, signing their vitriol "a reliable source"' (quoted in Lush 1998: 50).

Whether coincidentally or not, the most critical private papers happen to be owned by persons who share the same ethnic/regional origins as the most prominent opposition leaders (if not by the latter themselves). The papers most conciliatory to government also are in the hands of persons from the same ethnic group or region as the president or other members of government. This is true of Sierra Leone, Mali, Benin, Côte d'Ivoire, Nigeria, Cameroon and many other countries in the West African subregion (Karikari 1996a; Blay-Amihere and Alabi 1996; Gordon 2004). In southern Africa it is particularly true of Malawi, where most of the so-called independent papers that were established just before the 1994 elections 'are privately owned by opposition parties, the state, government ministers or other politicians in their personal capacities', with the sole aim of smearing political rivals (Minnie 1999: 13).

Commenting on the situation in the whole continent, Kasoma (1996: 99) acknowledges that the 'independent tabloids' in particular 'have spared no one in their muckraking journalistic exploits, libelling, invading privacy and generally carrying out a type of reportage ... that can best be described as "vendetta journalism"'. This journalism often uses abusive language, chooses not to approach a source for a comment on a story that incriminates him/her, selectively chooses facts that paint a bad picture of the source, uses sarcasm in reporting sources a journalist hates or dislikes (Kasoma 1996: 99–100; 1997b: 141–55). In general, Kasoma observes that newspapers are full of exaggerations, base their reports on flimsy hearsay, make headlines cry wolf, quote sources out of context, deny a fair hearing for people against whom allegations are made, are very biased in reporting, publish smear-campaign columns based more on the emotions of the writers than on reasoned opinions, and are guilty of illogically written editorials and more (1997a: 299–300).

The same writer is critical of the widespread tendency among African reporters to attribute information to unnamed sources, under the pretext that they are protecting them. Indeed, Kasoma believes 'it is time African journalists started telling their sources that if they are prepared to make serious allegations against other people, they should be brave enough to prove their allegations publicly.' This will free the press from being 'haunted by the people they malign', especially those in positions of influence who can make them pay dearly for basing 'their stories on anonymous or dubious sources' (Kasoma 1997a: 304–5). Kasoma argues that, 'Driven by selfish motives of profit maximisation or political expediency, the African press has increasingly become the accuser, the jury and the judge all rolled up in one as it pounces on one victim after another in the name of press freedom and democracy' (1996: 95).

Journalists themselves have not been very enthusiastic about accepting their common calling. They do not hesitate to exaggerate the differences between the trained and the untrained, those who work for the official media and those in the private press. The splits, squabbles and instability witnessed among newspaper proprietors and journalists in most countries over the past ten years mean that the press has been more preoccupied with internal wrangles than with a concerted effort to pool resources to fight for better laws and on behalf of persecuted journalists.

It is thanks largely to external pressure and encouragement that professional associations and unions have been created at national and regional levels. There is, for example, the West African Journalists' Association (WAJA), which 'functions as an umbrella organisation for sixteen countries' (Feldmann et al. 1998: 16) and is supposed to publish alerts and take action after unjust accusations of journalists (Vogt 1997; Karikari 1996a; Blay-Amihere and Alabi 1997; WAJA 1996). The Media Institute of Southern Africa (MISA) was created in 1992 'to promote and defend press freedom and take appropriate steps where such freedoms are violated and to seek to remove obstacles and impediments to the free flow of information' (Ronning 1994: 1). In the words of one of its officials, MISA has been 'the flagbearer of the Windhoek Declaration in the SADC region' and has based its regional programme on the practical recommendations of that Declaration. Examples of its achievements have included: developing cooperation between private newspapers, developing NGO codes of ethics for journalists, supporting the creation of regional press enterprise, monitoring attacks on journalists and media institutions, creating a data bank for private media institutions, identifying legal and economic constraints to free and independent media, and training of journalists and managers of the media (Minnie 1999: 12).

However, the creation of unions and associations has not minimised the squabbles and divisions among journalists; nor has it led to a satisfactory knowledge of the basics of journalism and ethics. In almost every country, many journalists still ignore the contents of their own press code (Kadhi 1999). For two years Francis Kasoma, in his capacity as president of the Press Association of Zambia (PAZA), tried in vain to rally together Zambian journalists. 'The majority remained either non-members or non-active members of the association. The few journalists who rallied behind PAZA were very good at talking, making all sorts of demands, but did little or nothing to propagate the aims of the association' (Kasoma 1996: 111). Things got worse when journalists of the private press broke away to form the Zambia Independent Media Association (ZIMA), 'claiming that PAZA was dominated by journalists from government media'. Since then, the two bodies have spent more time quarrelling with each other than seeking to enforce the practice of responsible journalism (Kasoma 1997a: 306). In general, the idea of media self-regulation, endorsed in principle throughout the continent, has in practice only created more divisions among media institutions and practitioners.

Some analysts have blamed the lack of cohesion and team spirit among African journalists on the quest for stardom, pursued less with effort and style than with a readiness to sacrifice fellow journalists. In Cameroon, for example, Asunkan, a veteran broadcaster, argued in 1993 that if the Ministry of Communication had tried in the past to draw up and impose a code of ethics on the journalists, this was only to fill the gap that the journalists themselves had created by not coming up with one. To him 'the journalists in Cameroon ... are scattered as sheep on a hill.' They were 'a divided and divergent body' because of the quest for stardom and because of excessive individualism and the lack of modesty and continuity. He decried the fact that 'there are no elders' in the profession, as the young are not prepared to learn from the old hands, who may or may not be prepared to teach (Asunkan 1993).

In Sierra Leone as well, 'the absence of written rules and regulations before February 1993 as to the qualifications of an editor' together with 'the prestige and perks which went with this position encouraged many young people interested in journalism to become editors overnight irrespective of qualification and experience' (Cole 1995: 52–61). In the new South Africa, 'the need for affirmative action appointments in top echelons has led to rapid promotions, leaving newsrooms drained of qualified journalists'. This, in turn, 'has resulted in a juniorization of newsrooms: the vast majority of journalists working for newspapers are under 30. Lacking training and adequate working experience, they are nevertheless burdened with heavy responsibilities' (van Kessel 1998: 8–9). In Zimbabwe, the '"Kicking up stairs" of young, inexperienced reporters shows very clearly in the final product' (Nyahunzvi 1996: 163). Little wonder, therefore, that 'a quick glance at the content, style, diction and quality of the papers shows that the standard of most of them has been dismally low. Except for a few, most of the editors lack professional training and experience' (Cole 1995: 52–61).

Thus, infighting and the quest for stardom have compounded the ethical dilemmas of media in Africa. While journalists of the government media are fighting one another for administrative positions and sinecures, those of the private press are battling for survival through blackmail and slander, commonly referred to as 'cheque-book', 'yellow', 'attack–collect' or 'brown envelope' journalism (Khan 1998: 594–5). The presence of unions and associations with written codes promising to respect ethical ideals and foster professionalism does not seem to be making much of a difference.

While the press is certainly to blame for most of the excesses we are likely to read about of journalism in Africa, it would be wrong to ignore the circumstances under which the press is called upon to practice. Indeed, an ethic or code of conduct has meaning only if it derives from a context that is conducive to its implementation or practice. A code of conduct that treats truth as a virtue, denounces corruption, and encourages honesty or fair play would have a difficult time getting implemented in a society that condones dishonesty, and overlooks corruption. The point here is that the media are, in many ways, a reflection of their society. If the politics and culture of the larger society are essentially dishonest and corrupt (or unethical), it is unlikely that the media will be any different. Nor is it likely that they will have the political, legal and moral empowerment to practice a journalism of tolerance, fairness, accuracy and credibility, especially if simultaneously struggling against financial difficulties. Hence, in considering journalistic ethics and their violations, we must take into account 'the moral integrity of the journalist, his sincerity or otherwise, his technical skill and creativity, his education and training, as well as the demands of civil society, and the prevailing moral standards of the political and social elites who wield both power and wealth' (Karikari 1996: 145).

Professional ethics in journalism is therefore a concept which, like a seed, might thrive or perish, depending on whether it falls on fertile soil, or not. African journalists might be trained locally, but they are made to understand that journalism adheres to universal canons, among which are a set of ethical values. Local schools of training have seldom considered including courses on ethics (Boyomo and Nyamnjoh 1996; Kadhi 1999), let alone having these adapted to the ethical concerns of the wider society (Kasoma 1994, 1996; Moemeka 1997). Of course, governments have always tended to stress that local schools and journalists must take into account the African context as a developing continent. But this has been intended more to serve political exigencies than to promote a certain African ethic or world-view. In addition, financial hardship leads many African journalists to seek positions as stringers for the major Western media. To be accepted, they have to think, see and write as Westerners do. Their principles are informed by Western epistemological assumptions about truth and practice, even if the reality on the ground should entail a more contextually appropriate system of meanings (Nyamnjoh and Jua 2002).

It is hardly surprising, therefore, that when asked about journalism or its ethics, African journalists would immediately reproduce what they have gathered from books on the matter. Most codes of ethics and professional values adopted in the continent are heavily inspired by Western codes or Western-derived international codes, and dwell on ethical issues of relevance to Western concerns in the main (Blin 1993; SDLP/UJAO 1995; Kunczik 1999). The Benin press code, for example, 'was inspired by the Charter of the professional duties of French journalists' (Quenum 1996: 21). The journalists admit that their activities are governed by 'norms that are universally recognised'. Indeed, among the professional values borrowed from the West in their code of ethics, they see none to be 'incompatible with the conceptions of ethics in Benin'. If there is any disagreement at all, it might come from the 'conscience clause', which 'clashes somewhat with the culture and psychology of the land'. For social and family reasons, Beninois journalists would tend to be conciliatory and measured, and therefore, 'not … push things that far in anti-establishment activity, in making claims or engaging in confrontation with employers' (Quenum 1996: 21–2). The Ivorian code is similarly inspired, and Ivorian journalists identify with and are expected to respect such principles as accuracy of facts, integrity, fairness, balanced treatment of information and credibility.

The Nigerian Union of Journalists (NUJ), whose membership in 1993 was 15,000, has achieved much in 'negotiating for good conditions of service for journalists' and was able, with moral and material support from the then military regime, to establish an International Institute for Journalism Training and Retraining in Abuja. Other regulatory bodies for the media include the Nigeria Press Council created in December 1992, the National Broadcasting Commission, and the National Media Commission for policing the watchdog (Anyakora and Potiskum 1996: 102–6). Malian journalists have created, *inter alia*, an association for the promotion of professionalism in the media, a national commission for the issuing of press cards, and an association of press editors (Sangho 1996: 80–82). In Ghana, the Ghana Journalists Association (GJA), with 'a formidable force of 700 members', 'has been at the forefront of the search for the freedom of the press and democracy'. A National Media Commission (NMC) has been 'set up by constitutional provisions to promote press freedom and high journalistic standards' and, hopefully, to 'insulate the state-owned media from government interference and control by removing the right of government to appoint and dismiss editors and members of governing bodies of public corporation managing the media' (Arthur 1997: 13; Koomson 1996: 58–62). Organisations such as the Panos Institute, FES, NIZA and MISA have been at the forefront of the design, adoption and enforcement of professional codes of ethics, with Western codes generally taken for granted. The Cameroonian code of ethics, which is about the most recent in West and Central Africa, was designed following an initiative aimed at uniting journalists by the FES Cameroon, consisting of making available to the Union of Cameroon Journalists (UJC) various Western and international codes. Mimicry is the name of the game so far as the African codes are concerned.

However, having a code of ethics is not synonymous with being ethical in practice; nor does it 'necessarily lead to the development of an ethical conscience' (Karikari 1996b: 150). As Onadipe puts it, professional independence in Africa is generally an uphill task, and journalists 'invariably get caught up in the eye of the storm' of the 'cataclysmic events swirling around them' (Onadipe 1998: 262). In Angola, for example, where the public was 'polarised by the war' and journalists 'threatened and branded in the streets', the pressure was such that the majority of journalists opted for 'self-censorship in the interest of self-preservation' (MISA 1994: 2).

The existence of local training schools (since the late 1950s for anglophone Africa and late 1960s for francophone Africa) does not seem to have brought about the appropriate indigenisation of the imported 'universal canons' of journalism. Those who run such schools believe that these norms are and should be the same everywhere. The West might have different priorities from Africa, but its basic assumptions about journalism are shared almost un-questioningly by African journalists. What governments are more interested in obtaining from local journalism is political control and not the inculcation of an African ethic, real or imagined. Little wonder therefore that the major training schools in Ghana, Nigeria, Senegal, Cameroon, Zimbabwe, Uganda, Kenya and elsewhere are state-owned and government-controlled.

Although trained in the same national institute (ESSTIC), the anglophone and francophone journalists of the official media in Cameroon have not developed a common style of reporting or present-ing news. The anglophones continue to be inspired by Anglo-Saxon media traditions, while the francophones have remained French or 'Latin' in style. All journalists interviewed recognise this and have an explanation for it. According to Howard, when Senegalese, Ivorian and francophone Cameroonian journalists talk of themselves as having been socialised into the 'Latin' system of journalism, they are referring 'to the tendency to wait for events to happen before they are reported', as opposed to the 'Anglo-Saxon' style of 'investigative reporting à la Watergate' (Howard 1980: 6). Writing about RFI and French broadcasting in general, Gaillard (1986: 66) complains about the chilly sobriety (la froide sobriété) of the BBC style, which does not appeal to the Latin audience. While the francophone journalist wants to attract the audience, the anglophone journalist is more inclined to go for the facts and to avoid opinions.

Whether intended or not, the effect is the perpetuation of French and Anglo–Saxon media cultures. For just the fact that journalists speak English as distinct from French as a first language already puts them in a specific perspective. Their own view of the world is very different, and they selectively refer only to those sources or practices that would consolidate that perspective. The differences in colonial heritage are blamed for the lack of common local style. But the very fact that such differences have persisted even within individual and bilingual states like Cameroon is an indication of the lack of cohesive and enforceable cultural policies capable of providing local alternatives to inherited colonial values.

Francis Kasoma believes that this situation constitutes the greatest tragedy concerning journalism in Africa today, where journalists 'refuse to listen to any suggestions that journalism can have African ethical roots and still maintain its global validity and appeal' (Kasoma 1996: 95). He calls for a move away from money- and power-centred journalism to a society-centred journalism that is grounded on traditional African communal values and that draws from what he has termed 'Afriethics'. He shares the view that journalism should be practised according to the ethical tenets of the society of origin of the journalist and agrees with those who have 'bemoaned the lack of Africanness in African journalism'.

Kasoma argues that in the African tradition from which he would like journalists to draw in ethical matters, the need for common good for the community is greater than any other concern or interest. 'The basis of morality in African society is the fulfilment of obligations to kinsfolk, both living and dead. It is believed that some of the departed and the spirits keep watch over people to make sure that they observe the moral laws and are punished when they break them' (Kasoma 1996: 107–8).

This emphasis on social and communal relationships with the living and the dead has, Kasoma argues, resulted in morals aimed at keeping the society or community alive and in harmony (Kasoma 1996: 108). Organising their profession around African ethical values would entail a number of things. First, journalists must make the basis of morality in their practice 'the fulfilment of obligations to society and to the journalistic corps' by seeking to solve communal problems rather than create them. Second, they must 'develop a deep sense of right and wrong so that they are able to feel guilty for behaving unethically and try and correct colleagues who falter in their journalistic performance'. Third, 'there is need for dialogue among media people so that the practice of mass communication becomes a democratic and participatory one drawing its strength from the African cultural heritage'. Fourth, journalism must be seen as 'a communal profession in which the wrongs of an individual journalist have a capacity to tarnish the image of every one who practises it'. Fifth, 'the ethicality of the individual acts of the journalist should be first and foremost measured against whether or not they serve the wider community and the journalism profession. If they do not, there is every likelihood that they are unethical'. Sixth, 'erring journalists or media houses should, in the true African spirit, be counselled by the other journalists to behave well and not be immediately condemned as misfits in the 'family' of African journalism'. Seventh, the journalists must cultivate a deep sense of solidarity and oneness of voice. Only in this way can African journalism 'put its house in order' (Kasoma 1996: 109–11).

However, the communalistic values and ethics which Kasoma presents, and which Moemeka (1997) shares, are based more on a romantic reconstruction of the precolonial and a frozen view of harmony in rural Africa. Appealing as this ethic might be, there is little evidence of its impact on life in contemporary Africa where major decisions are taken by cultural hybrids or creoles in the cities who are more in tune with Western and cosmopolitan influences than mainstream Africa. Moemeka recognises this when he laments the erosion of and challenge to this ethic mainly by the young in their quest for 'personal freedom' (Moemeka 1997: 186).

The implication of this is that being African is not a static or frozen state of existence, but a dynamic identity that keeps redefining itself with new experiences and contacts with other peoples and cultures. What we should therefore advocate is the creative adoption of global influences and the rehabilitation of the best elements of mainstream cultures of Africa that are victims of marginalisation and unfair competition. It is true that African journalists have not been creative in their adoption of ethical codes and have tended to mimic the West most of the time, but ignoring Western influences altogether is hardly a solution, given the hybridity of contemporary African identities.

Although it is not within the scope of this chapter to propose ethical alternatives, Kasoma's Afriethic stands a better chance of endorsement if advocating the recognition and valorisation of African mainstream values and ethics does not imply the exclusion of the cultural influences that have reshaped African identities since the colonial period (Werbner 1996). Obviously, two of the major tests that an Africentric ethic would have to pass are: (i) to convince journalists of the wisdom of elders, who, in the eyes of many youths today, are to blame for Africa's predicaments; and (ii) provide guarantees that the quest for communal harmony would not be used as a recipe for intolerance against outsiders and competing voices, or, as Moemeka himself puts it, to 'stifle individual initiative and ... create a culture of dependence' (Moemeka 1997: 186).

This calls for a negotiated idea of Africanness and ethics informed by the issue of domesticated democracy discussed in Chapter 1. Domesticated democracy informed by popular values and world-views would provide a good foundation for an ethics of journalism that is more in tune with the predicaments of Africans as members of communities. As Kasoma and Moemeka have noted, it is traditionally African to see and treat the individual as a child of the community, as someone allowed to pursue his or her needs, but not greed. The individual's creativity, abilities and powers must be harnessed in order to be acknowledged. Agency, as I have argued elsewhere (Nyamnjoh 2002a), has meaning only as domesticated agency, by which is meant agency that stresses negotiation, interconnectedness and harmony between individual interests and group expectations. In other words, with domesticated agency, the freedom to pursue individual or group goals exists within a socially predetermined framework that emphasizes coexistence with collective interests while simultaneously allowing for individual creativity and self-fulfilment.

Through domesticated agency, the collectivity shares the responsibility of success and the consequences of failure with the active and creative individual, thereby easing the pressure on individuals to prove themselves in a world of ever-diminishing opportunities. Domesticated agency does not deny individuals the freedom to associate or to be self-reliant or independent, but rather puts a premium on interdependence as insurance against the risk of dependence, where people face the impermanence of independent success. Achievement is devoid of meaning if not pursued within, as part of, and on behalf of a group of people who recognize that achievement. For only by making their successes collective can individuals make their failures a collective concern as well. Such domestication emphasizes negotiation, concession and coexistence over maximization of pursuits by individuals or by particular groups in contexts of plurality and diversity. Appreciation should be reserved and room created for excellence, especially for individuals who demonstrate how ready they are to engage with collective interests. No ethics predicated narrowly on the individual as an autonomous agent would be adequate in most African contexts. The problem with existing codes has been precisely the failure to recognise this fact and to take on board popular ideas of personhood and agency (Nyamnjoh 2002a).

That African journalism is in ethical crisis is evidenced by how much debate and literature in this domain have increased since the 1990s. Papers published on journalism training have emphasised media ethics (de Beer 1995), and training schools like ESSTIC of Yaounde which have long ignored ethics have created space for this in the curricula (Boyomo and Nyamnjoh 1996). Training seminars and workshops have been organised on and around journalism ethics in Africa, with the Friedrich Ebert Stiftung, the Panos Institute, NIZA and MISA taking the lead to encourage the creation of regional and national journalism associations with codes of ethics to govern their activities (Vogt 1997; Karikari 1996b: 143; Kadhi 1999; Minnie 1999). In 1994, the African Council for Communication Education (ACCE) published a special volume on *Journalism Ethics in Africa* that addressed a range of themes, including: the need for journalism ethics and ethical reasoning; aversion to deontology in African journalism; indecency in news reporting; the protection of journalists; ethics in news gathering, news selection and processing; and ethics in photojournalism (Kasoma 1994). In almost every conference organised by the ACCE in the 1990s a special session was reserved for journalism ethics in Africa. In February 1996, the Panos Institute and the Ghana Journalists' Association organised a regional seminar on ethics in journalism and subsequently published a rich survey of ethical practices in seven West African Countries

(Karikari 1996a). For over two years the United States University–Africa in Kenya conducted discussions on ethics, the main points of which included freedom of the press, independence, impartiality, fair play, decency, accuracy and responsibility (Kadhi 1999: 82). In September 1999, over one hundred journalists, media practitioners and researchers from Africa and from elsewhere gathered in Accra, Ghana, 'to discuss wider issues about Ethics, journalism practice and journalism training in Africa with the principal aim of defining skills and institutional capacity to strengthen quality of media professionalism in African countries'. This was followed by the publication of a book rich in country case studies, the creation of an Ethics Media website in Africa, and the setting up of an email 'Ethics Network News' linking users in Africa and the rest of the world (Ukpabi 2001: 12).

On Training and Professionalism

Much of the bad journalism in Africa today has been blamed on the lack of professional training for most journalists (Kasoma 1999: 451–8), a factor which, according to Onadipe (1998: 263), has affected 'the capabilities of the messenger, the nature of the message and how it is received' and has made quality, prestige and credibility suffer. Although journalists of the official media have, generally speaking, benefited more from formal training in schools of journalism, they do not seem, judging from their output, to be much better off professionally than their counterparts in the private press who have had little or no formal training in most cases. In certain situations, the official journalists are no less in need of training and education than are their counterparts in the private press. This has led journalists of the private press to argue that in the current context of multipartyism and democratisation, it is precisely the official journalists who have more to learn about the profession. The view is very strong among journalists of the private press that although trained formally in recognised schools of journalism, journalists of the official media have operated in a context that does not allow for excellence and that has indeed stifled any professional competencies they may have acquired at training school.

This controversy notwithstanding, in thinking of how current shortcomings can be corrected, it is important to distinguish between the formally trained journalists who have not had the opportunity to implement what they learned at school and those who join the profession without any training or basic journalistic knowledge. While the latter need to be introduced to the techniques and principles of news gathering, news writing and news presentation, those who have had formal training without practical experience need refresher courses to keep themselves abreast of technological developments and with cases of journalistic excellence in the continent and elsewhere. In sum, African journalists all need to be conversant with new technologies in information gathering, processing and dissemination (Ochieng 1992: 81–165) and to understand the ethical implications of using these technologies (Pratt 1994). Some of the training schools may not be well equipped to make this correction, given that over the years economic difficulties, lack of resources and dilapidated equipment have rendered these institutions increasingly theoretical in approach. New, more commercially oriented schools do not seem to offer better prospects in much of Africa. South Africa offers a noteworthy exception. Not only does it boast several technikons (vocational colleges) and university departments that offer courses in journalism and media production, it is also a leader in relevant and new technology in information and communications. The Department of Journalism and Media Studies at Rhodes University is a good example in this connection, bringing together media trainers and media industry in innovative and unprecedented ways. Today it offers courses to both regular and occasional students in conventional journalism, specialised reporting and the latest domain of New Media (multimedia learning, education and design).

Francophone Africa seems to have lagged behind in the opening of mass communication training schools. Whereas Ghana, Zambia, Kenya and Nigeria were running journalism schools in the late 1950s and early 1960s, it was not until 1965 that the 'Centre d'Études des Sciences et Techniques de l'Information' (CESTI) of Dakar was opened. It was only in 1970 that Cameroon, Gabon, Central African Republic, Rwanda, Chad and Togo jointly set up L'École Supérieure Internationale de Journalisme de Yaoundé (ESIJY). In 1973, Zaire opened its Institut des Sciences et Techniques de l'Information (ISTI) in Kinshasa, followed in 1977 by Niger with its own institute. In 1978, it was the turn of Congo to set up the Department of Mass Communication (DMC) in the Faculty of Letters and Social Sciences of Université Marien Ngouabi. However, whereas training at ESIJY and CESTI was geared essentially towards journalism, ISTI and DMC also train students in public relations and, in the case of DMC, in documentation as well.

Today, journalism training schools and departments of mass communication have mushroomed all over Africa, especially with the easing of regulation of private initiative in this and other areas of national life in many countries. Nigeria alone has some 45 such institutes (Anyakora and Pokiskum 1996: 103). In Uganda, Makerere University was the first in East Africa to offer training in journalism and media studies at undergraduate level in 1988. In 1998 the programme was made an autonomous department of mass communication, and it has received students from Burundi, Democratic Republic of Congo, Kenya, Rwanda and Tanzania. In Mozambique, Instituto Superior Politecnico e Universiterio (ISPU), a private tertiary institution, was created in 1998 and produced its first eleven graduates in journalism and public relations in 2000. The University of Zimbabwe has offered a postgraduate programme in journalism and media studies, with the assistance of the University of Oslo in Norway, since 1993. The Zimbabwean Open University (ZOU), created in 1999 to provide distance education, also provides journalism and media studies at undergraduate level. In South Africa, the Graduate Programme in Cultural and Media Studies (CMS) has provided an outlet for Africans seeking graduate studies at M.A. and Ph.D. levels since 1984. In some countries, however, governments have been slow at seeing the need for formal schools of journalism. Sierra Leone is a case in point, where 'the old British tradition that a journalist is born and not made has had a profound influence on the government media executives with regard to training in journalism' (Cole 1995: 63). Journalism training is still not a priority in the education and training programmes of some governments; nor is it perceived as an independent academic discipline at some universities.

The problem of journalism and communication training has often been posed in terms of choice between formal school training and training on the job. In most countries where these two systems co-exist, however, the school system has not been able to impose itself as the only one that can turn out qualified and competent professionals, since many renowned journalists have often never been in any training school or centre. There is no consensus view on who qualifies as a journalist. While some legal definitions tend to recognize as a journalist any person who 'on the basis of his intellectual faculties, his training and talents … is recognized as being fit to carry out research and process information intended for mass communication' (e.g. Cameroon; see SOPECAM 1991: 38), others are more prone to go along with the ILO concept, which spells out that a journalist is someone who earns most of his/her living from journalistic activity. These differences notwithstanding, everyone seems agreed that training of some sort, formal or informal, is indispensable for good or professional journalism (Kasoma 1999).

Kunczik (1988: 236) argues that the practice of journalism in the context of a developing country should aim not at giving the very latest information, which in most cases means sacrificing careful research and background drawing; it should rather give sense to and orientate reporting about themes important to the development of society in the long run. Also, the language used by journalists must be accessible to as many readers as possible so that content can be followed without difficulty. The simple rule is that if one has something to say one must say it in the language of those whom one is addressing. One must also avoid the manipulation of language aimed at taking advantage of the reader. Many journalists in Africa today do not master the language, with the result that they present news and reports that look like outright lies.

There is also the need for African journalists to understand that in a plural or heterogeneous society it is normal to have or expect other perspectives. As Kunczik (1988: 235–6) puts it, 'Journalism training must impart technical competence but should not lead to homogenisation of perspectives or to impoverishment and constriction of world views.' The journalist must not be aggressive and negative but critically distant and fair. He must avoid sensationalism and the deliberate falsification of facts. Journalists must also avoid scapegoatism – that is, giving the impression that there is an individual, a group (ethnic, linguistic, religious, political, etc.) or a section of society that is responsible for all the problems in that society. The fact must be stressed that in reality these norms are extremely difficult, if not impossible, to realise, and that they call for extra effort from journalists on a daily basis.

The training programmes must be tailored more and more towards the *real* (as opposed to the imagined or the imposed) needs of African states as developing countries in search of basic freedoms and betterment for the majority of their peoples. For, as Kunczik rightly maintains, development journalism, which most African states have endorsed, 'needs strong, courageous, socially engaged people willing to make sacrifices and able to stand conflicts, because development journalism is irreconcilable with servile government-say-so journalism' (Kunczik 1988: 233). Our journalists must be trained to serve as the conscience of the nation, which means that their 'training must intensively address the issues of professional ethics'. For 'a purely technical craft training of journalists which does not promote awareness of the ethical dimension can lead to stabilisation of overtly unjust structures of rule. The then technically improved journalism can be used to manipulate the population and for government propaganda' (Kunczik 1988: 234).

In conclusion, it goes without saying that professionalism, training and ethics are cardinal to journalism, and that in Africa the bulk of journalists are not well equipped in this regard. Thanks to local initiatives supported by Western NGOs and institutions, journalists have created associations and unions, and adopted codes of conduct, in a bid to improve upon their situation and profession. But this is far from solving the ethical crisis in African journalism, as (i) adopting codes of conduct has not necessarily resulted in better professional standards; (ii) the codes adopted have shown little creativity on the part of African journalists, in terms of reflecting the concerns and interests of the majority of Africans; and (iii) the debates on and around ethics have done little to embrace the idea of African identity as a dynamic and hybrid reality. For a viable and meaningful ethic of journalism to come about in Africa, there is clearly the need for a conscious effort, one that draws not only from the experiences and concerns of journalists and politicians but also from those of the wider society, especially the silent majorities who are still in touch with the often marginalised mainstream cultures and values of Africa. Being professional and ethical is a sure way for the media to regain public trust and respect, and to contribute meaningfully to democratisation, however defined. For the media cannot expect accountability when they themselves are not accountable, nor expect tolerance when they themselves are not tolerant.

3

Multiparty Politics in Cameroon

In Chapter 1 we noted how, almost everywhere in Africa, the quest for democratisation has been disappointing. There has been a tendency to interpret this concept narrowly, as synonymous with multiparty electoral competition, yet even this low-intensity democracy has not enjoyed great success on the continent. Cameroon offers a good case study where even such limited democratisation has been faced with phenomenal hurdles from a reluctant state. While the ultimate aspiration in Africa might be participatory democracy, the current, often uncritically endorsed, liberal democratic option has yet to gain more than lip service from the political elite. The Cameroonian history of multiparty electoral democracy in the 1990s offers an excellent illustration of this experience.

A Brief Political History of Cameroon

The name 'Cameroon' is said to have come about when Portuguese sailors discovered a countless number of prawns (*camaroes*) as they sailed into the estuary of the River Wouri *circa* 1472. However, although it turned out that 'what the Portuguese saw were crayfish, not prawns' (Le Vine 1964: 288), the name Cameroon has been maintained. As with many institutions imposed by Europeans during colonialism, the leaders of postcolonial Cameroon failed to question a name that resulted from misperception and misrepresentation.

A brief political history of Cameroon is necessary to clarify certain misconceptions. Many outsiders know of Cameroon as a former colony of France, but are quite ignorant of Britain's involvement with the territory. The French heritage might be preponderant – partly because of the greater proportion of francophone Cameroonians, but largely because of the effects of France's colonial policy of assimilation – but the Cameroonian constitution officially recognises both the French and the English legacies. Consequently, it is to be identified neither exclusively with francophone nor with anglophone Africa, but with both.

The political history of Cameroon is often treated as if it originated with the German occupation in the nineteenth century. Sufficient significance is not given to the fact that before it became a German protectorate in 1884 Cameroon consisted of organised states and kingdoms ruled by monarchs who had as much right to their crowns or positions as did their European counterparts. As far back as 1472, these monarchs 'signed treaties of amity and of commerce on terms of equality with the representatives of kings and rulers of other nations'. Even with the advent of Europeans, they continued to negotiate on an equal footing. Thus in 1826 King Bille Losenge of Bimbia signed a treaty with a representative of Queen Victoria to abolish the slave trade. In 1856 King Manga Bell of Douala and Captain Walker of the British firm of Messrs Horsfall signed a commercial agreement. The future German governor, Dr Nachtigal, himself started off by signing a commercial treaty (Kale 1967: 1–3). It was not until the Berlin Conference in 1884 agreed on the Balkanisation of Africa that Cameroon was proclaimed a German protectorate.

Colonisation means domination and exploitation. If Germany declared Cameroon a protectorate, it was not because the territory had no record of self-rule. Rather, it was because Germany, like the rest of Europe, was too powerful and too expansionist to respect Africa's right to self-determination. The overriding factor was not the welfare of Cameroonians but German prestige, trade and plantations (Rudin 1938: 222–96; Chilver and Roschenthaler 2001). German administrators are remembered for 'the barbaric depths' to which they 'descended in bringing civilization to the "primitives"' (Joseph 1977: 21). The period under Germany was marked by warfare, as 'the natives' fought against conquest and subjugation 'to the white man's rule' (Rudin 1938: 414). Thirty years after the occupation, Germany fought and lost both World War I and its colonies in Africa. The latter became 'mandated territories' of the League of Nations, which assigned them 'under mandate' to the victorious powers.

The Cameroonian territory was arbitrarily divided between Britain and France, with the former having one-sixth and the latter five-sixths of the whole. The argument in favour of the mandate was that the former German colonies were 'not yet able to stand by themselves under the strenuous conditions of the modern world' (Kale 1967: 7–8). The fact that Africa had not asked to be made part of Europe's 'modern world' was of course ignored.

There is little doubt that most of 'the present ambiguity and ambivalence towards local authorities' (Rowlands and Warnier 1988: 120–21; Nyamnjoh 2003), in Cameroon and Africa at large, were created during colonialism and subsequently inherited by the 'modern' leaders at independence. The history of colonialism was one of fundamental structural and institutional changes, which were not reversed at independence. Hitherto key institutions were either deprived of their powers, or adapted to serve as instruments of colonialism. Thus, though kings (called 'chiefs' by the colonists and by the postcolonial 'modern' leaders) and their councils often escaped total extinction, they were supposed to act as 'reliable intermediaries' (Bridges 1933: 107). As Lloyd (1965: 73) remarked, though the colonial native administration preserved vestiges of the traditional administrative process, the precolonial policymaking process evaporated as rulers took their lead more from the administrative officer than from the indigenous 'political elite'.

French and English administrators, like their German predecessors, acknowledged that different ethnic groups had enjoyed an organised form of government. But, conditioned by European notions about Africa, they remained surprised that 'these pagan natives' had been able to develop such complex social structures. In his first administrative report on Bum in the Bamenda Grassfields, a British colonial officer described Bum as a

> powerful, self-contained and independent kingdom, with a complete social structure and an effective system of administration, fully competent to

safeguard its own interests and to oppose any interference from without.... It may be that other clan organisations are as complete but it is doubted if the organisation of any native community surpasses that in existence at Bum before the advent of Europeans. (Pollock 1927: 24–5, 36)

The interference with such a 'complete' organisation, therefore, was not seen as an effort to raise it up to that of 'any native community', but rather to remodel it along colonial lines. In other words, from an entirely 'native' standpoint, Bum social organisation might have been complete, but it still had to be changed because colonial officials considered it inferior to that of European states. Equally complete though the Bum judicial system was, the same colonial official advocated its replacement because there was 'no authority nor Government approval for the continuation or execution of the decisions arrived at or judgement given' (Pollock 1927: 54). Only those without a proper understanding of colonialism would wonder why a judgement rendered by a Bum judicial apparatus to the Bum people needed the approval of the British authorities.

The colonial powers rejected those local institutions which conflicted with their administration, retaining only those compatible with colonial rule. Bridges (1933: 23) recommended that the Bum king be allowed to 'continue to constitute the Native Authority' because, having a 'hereditary position', he was well placed 'to receive and issue executive orders; and to exact the willing obedience of all'. The king was therefore recognised as an auxiliary. Nevertheless, he could not command the same authority, because the colonists had failed to recognise the *Kwefon* – the body of councillors that governed with him and had acted as a check against any abuse of power. The *Kwefon*, which had legitimated the king's authority in pre-colonial Bum, was replaced by a 'Native Authority', which quite lacked the social legitimacy the king needed to exact obedience from his subjects. It was a situation that placed the king at perpetual loggerheads with his councillors and people, and led to numerous conflicts of values. Hitherto used to living under the joint leadership of the king and the *Kwefon*, the Bum people suddenly found themselves forced to choose between the two (Nyamnjoh 1985: 100–21). Other states in British Cameroon went through similar experiences (Nkwi and Warnier 1982; Rowlands and Warnier 1988: 120–21; Awasom 2003).

As Lord Raglan remarked, essentially democratic political institutions were replaced all over British Africa by despots who were guaranteed by the colonial government 'against any fear of deposition by their subjects' (Kale 1967: 9–10).

Elsewhere in French Cameroon the situation was much the same (Balandier 1963; Gardinier 1963; Le Vine 1964). France created 'warrant chiefs' in acephalous societies in the southern half of the territory. In areas with kingdoms such as the North and the Bamileke region, it tried to turn their kings into auxiliaries of the central administration. Where it met with resistance, France was quick to depose the kings in question and replace them with leaders of its own. Under this system, many kings 'lost their prerogatives', including the sultans of Bamun and Ngaoundere. The policy everywhere was the introduction of 'a French created system of local control' through 'a gradual erosion of the power of indigenous political authority' (Le Vine 1964: 91–8).

Like Britain, France ran into problems of legitimacy with its appointed 'chiefs' and *conseils de notables*, who, although imbued with authority and backed by the central administration, were not accepted by the people. This legal system 'encouraged differential treatment' of Cameroonians 'according to a cultural rather than a legal yardstick' (Le Vine 1964: 91–104), thus laying the foundation for the distinction between 'citizen' and 'subject' that came to characterise the bifurcated state (Mamdani 1996). It is evident that the 'chieftaincy reforms' carried out by the French (Le Vine 1964: 97–8) were adopted with very little alteration by the post-colonial state (Nkwi 1979; Nyamnjoh 1985; Awasom 2003). Traditional political elites of today are as dependent on the state and central government as they were under France and Britain, even when they are seemingly included in the national and regional political processes (Geschiere and Nyamnjoh 1998; Nyamnjoh 2002a; Nyamnjoh 2003).

At the end of World War II, Cameroon became a trusteeship of the United Nations, but remained under British and French control. From the outset Britain had decided against an independent administration for British Cameroon. It divided the territory into the Southern and Northern Cameroons, which it respectively administered as integral parts of Northern and Eastern Nigeria (Ardener 1962; Kale 1967).

According to Kale, its administration of the territory prior to World War II was 'haphazard and full of misgivings'. 'There was an apparent lack of administrative interest', which he thinks was due to 'the fear that Germany might suddenly demand a return of her former African possessions'. For this reason, Britain might have thought it 'preposterous spending, and possibly wasting, British tax-payers' money and talent on what was not, strictly speaking, a developing British country' (1967: 12–13). In Whitehall, Cameroon was often regarded 'as somewhat of a colonial liability', and administered all the way from Lagos, with hope of its 'eventual integration with Nigeria'. It had neither a separate budget, nor separate public accounts; all its government revenues were treated as part of a common fund (Le Vine 1964: 194–201).

France, on the other hand, administered French Cameroon as an independent entity, giving it full benefit of its policies of paternal 'association' and 'assimilation' (Ardener 1962; Gardinier 1963; Le Vine 1964; Joseph 1977). However, the winds of change that blew across the continent in the 1950s and early 1960s did not leave Britain and France unaffected, reluctant though they were to grant independence. Many political parties developed, some of which agitated for independence and for the reunification of the Cameroons. Prominent among them were, from anglophone Southern Cameroon, the Kamerun National Congress (KNC), the Kamerun People's Party (KPP) and the Kamerun National Democratic Party (KNDP). In French Cameroon, there were the Union des Populations du Cameroun (UPC), the Démocrates Camerounais (DC) and the Union Camerounaise (UC).

These parties were modelled after European ones. The idea was for the territory's leaders to learn 'the essentials of political and parliamentary life' (Le Vine 1964: 142). At first, metropolitan parties simply created branches in Cameroon, with French parties and organisations such as SFIO, RPF, MRP, RDA and CGT each having local branches (Le Vine 1964: 145). It is no wonder, then, that for a long time parties remained 'the playground of the political elite' with programmes 'created elsewhere and clumsily adapted to Camerounian conditions'. Party politics 'struck little popular response' and 'enthusiasm' before the creation of UPC, 'The only true nationalist party with a dynamic organization, an ideological commitment, and a militant leadership'. After independence, with the UPC in disarray, the existing parties, which 'behaved much more like local interest groups than organisations conscious of broader national obligations', could do little to stop the collapse of multipartyism. It has been argued that had the UPC not 'dissipated its vitality in a premature attempt to seize power', it would have 'grown into an all-Cameroun movement' (Le Vine 1964: 221–3) and might have effectively challenged the creation of a one-party state. There is evidence that the UPC was already working in this general direction when its affiliates and sympathisers created the One Kamerun party to promote the ideology of the UPC in anglophone Cameroon (Ntumazah 2001).

In January 1960, French Cameroon became independent, with Ahidjo as its first president and in accordance with the terms of the limited autonomy granted all French colonies by the Loi Cadre of 1956. So limited was the autonomy that France retained jurisdiction over almost every sphere of importance, including finance, diplomatic representation, commercial law, external commerce, penal code and external defence (Le Vine, 1964: 162). Dissatisfied with French involvement, and with the way France had manipulated things in order to maintain its influence, the UPC was determined to continue its fight against 'French imperialists' and their 'puppets' in government, even after it was forced to go underground (Ardener 1962: 347–8; Le Vine 1964: 145–61; Joseph 1977: 239–350; Bayart 1980: 159).

After independence, UPC leaders continued to mobilise support and to contest Ahidjo's legitimacy, but committed backing from the French authorities, together with ruthless repression by Ahidjo, eventually crushed their resistance (Medard 1978: 40). With Um Nyobe assassinated by French forces in 1958 and Dr Moumié killed by French agents in 1960, the rest of the UPC leadership were forced to continue their guerrilla warfare, flee the country, or betray the party and its ideals by making a pact with Ahidjo. France, together with Mbida, Ahidjo and other enemies of the UPC, exploited the fact that the latter received support from revolutionary governments around the world, some of which were communist, to accuse it of communism. UPC determination to continue with the struggle for genuine independence, even from the underground and in exile, led to various attempts to reinvent itself, earliest among which was the creation of the One Kamerun party by Ndeh Ntumazah of the Bamenda Grassfields (Ntumazah 2001).

Proof of the legitimacy of its cause is the fact that even those who were so violently against the UPC ended up borrowing from its manifesto, albeit halfheartedly. By opting for 'cooperation with France in an atmosphere of reciprocal cordiality and confidence' (Le Vine 1964: 167), Ahidjo was seen by the French as the moderate they needed to guarantee France's postcolonial position. The first constitution of the Republic of Cameroun 'bore a remarkable similarity to that of the French Fifth Republic', despite the historical and political differences of the two countries (Le Vine 1964: 224–7). This was an indication as to how far Ahidjo was ready to go in his 'cooperation' with France. It was therefore unrealistic to think that France, which had fought so hard to resist the radical independence advocated by the UPC, would agree to the kind of autonomy needed for authentic nation-building in Cameroon.

With Nigeria and French Cameroon both independent, there was a pressing need to define the future of British Cameroon. Under the auspices of the UNO, a plebiscite was conducted in the territory in February 1961. Due to what was largely seen at the time as the result of manipulation of votes by Britain, the Northern Cameroons voted to become part of Nigeria. On its part, the Southern Cameroons opted for a federation with La République du Cameroun, despite the voices which advocated a union with Nigeria. In spite of a 'popular' disinclination for an 'early reunification after secession from Nigeria' (Ardener 1967: 302), the UN never gave the people that option; the only choice was between Nigeria and French Cameroon (Ardener 1962, 1967; Le Vine 1964: 206–14). Also, the boundaries of the reunified territory 'were not willed by those who wished for reunification', but were imposed on them. Consequently, these boundaries were much narrower than they would have been 'if a simple reconstruction of German Kamerun had been achieved' (Ardener 1967: 288). Some have argued that from a legal point of view, Cameroon was never colonised by France and Britain. This is an argument that fails to take account of the fact that Europe's scramble for Africa was itself illegal, both under their individual constitutions and in the eyes of the African states whose say was ignored.

Following a conference at Foumban in July 1961 between Foncha (KNDP) and Ahidjo (UC), the unified territory became known as the Federal Republic of Cameroon, comprising two states – West and East Cameroon – each with its own prime minister and assembly. Ahidjo became the federal president but soon began to think the idea of a federation expensive and wasteful. He started scheming for a single unified party. In 1962 he suppressed East Cameroonian multipartyism and in 1966 merged the UC with West Cameroonian parties to form the Cameroon National Union (CNU). By 1972 reunification had been achieved through a combination of political intrigue and manipulation (Medard 1978: 41; Bayart 1985: 109–38; Konings and Nyamnjoh 1997, 2003). In May of that year, the federation was replaced by a United Republic which was to last until two years after Ahidjo's resignation in November 1982. This change, which the authorities termed 'The Peaceful Revolution', also involved the division of the country into seven administrative units known as provinces, namely: Littoral, Central-South, East, North, West, North-West and South-West.

Like his counterparts elsewhere in Africa, Ahidjo spent more than twenty years consolidating his supremacy as president and as chairman of the party, maximizing his personal powers and centralising government (Medard 1978; Etonga 1980; Bayart 1980; Bayart 1985: 141–82). Having initially been forced to adopt a federal constitution in order to facilitate reunification with Southern Cameroon, Ahidjo was to gear his politics towards increased centralisation aimed at assimilating anglophone Cameroon and at weakening all opposition, including the authority of the traditional political elite. He succeeded so well in this quest that he virtually dominated all public and political institutions. He held executive power as head of government and state, controlled legislative power as chairman of the party, and subdued the judiciary through direct appointments. In this way, he was able to impose his authority over the party, government, parliament and administration. As Medard observed, 'President Ahidjo is an absolute monarch: not only does he concentrate all powers of a very centralised and authoritarian state, but in a certain way the state is him' (Medard 1978: 40–42).

In November 1982, Ahidjo resigned and was constitutionally succeeded as president by Paul Biya, who promised to build a more democratic society. In 1984 President Biya carried out a series of constitutional changes, which embodied, inter alia, the creation of three new provinces: South, Adamawa and Far North. There was also a change of name from United Republic of Cameroon to Republic of Cameroon. This move attracted criticism from certain anglophone academics who saw it as an attempt to influence history in favour of the French heritage. The critics argued that the only neutral and acceptable change of names would have been a return to the German Kamerun, when the country was one to all Kamerunians. As Kofele-Kale (1980) has argued, Cameroonians look up to the German era not because Germany left behind any sense of 'Kamerunianness' as such, but rather because it provided the framework for the future concretisation of what Ardener (1962) termed the 'Kamerun Idea', the idea of a people united by the common feeling of facing the same challenges under German colonialism.

The so-called 'modern political institutions' of today have more in common with those of the colonial state and Europe than with the institutions of pre-colonial Cameroon. Although at independence Ahidjo promised to 'draw the basic principles of African democracy' from 'our traditional chieftainship' (Ahidjo 1964: 31–3), the role traditional rulers were eventually asked to play remained as peripheral, ambiguous and ambivalent as under France and Britain. The various kings were only seen as useful if they could serve as instruments for the implementation of government policies among their people, policies elaborated centrally by the 'new elite'.

To this end the government took a series of steps. These included an invitation in 1966 to rally round the unified party, establishing criteria for the award of a 'Certificate of Official Recognition by the Government' in 1967, a presidential warning to all chiefs who were seen to be reluctant to change in 1969, and a decree in 1977 defining their role within the new 'nation-state' (Nkwi 1979: 111–15; Nyamnjoh 1985: 102–5). Thus, while the precolonial autonomy of Cameroonian societies has not been restored, the kings remain mere auxiliaries of the government, subservient to their Divisional Administrative Officers (DO or Prefet). This makes it possible for the central government to be able to draw from kings as 'vote banks' without having to credit them even with the illusion of real power and active participation in decision-making (Fisiy 1995). As Nkwi argues,

> While the state guarantees the protection of chiefs and the defence of their rights while they are in office, it also lays down sanctions for those chiefs who fail to live up to the laws of the nation-state. They can be made destitute or thrown out of their traditional office by government. They must carry out their traditional duties within the limits of the laws of the state. Their powers have been completely eroded and they can only survive if they recognize and function according to the dictates of the new political elite. (Nkwi 1979: 115)

From these observations, it is clear that despite the variety of forms of political organisation in precolonial Cameroon, the new leaders did nothing to challenge the alternative systems grafted onto the country by France and Britain. In the postcolony, just as in colonial Cameroon, the power of the traditional kings is undermined by the central authorities, while that of the 'warrant chief' has to be constantly propped up by demonstrations of force against the local populations. The state is hardly in gear with village communities (Rowlands and Warnier 1988: 120; Fisiy 1995; Geschiere 1997; Geschiere and Nyamnjoh 1998; Monga 2000; Socpa 2002). In the name of political unity, the various ethnic groups have seen their local and sectional loyalties and interests suppressed and have been forced into a relationship of dependence on 'a highly centralized' government (Bayart 1980). For the same reason, ordinary Cameroonians have felt increasingly powerless. This remains the reality, despite the mounting rhetoric and propaganda on how successful Ahidjo was and Biya has been in the pursuit of nation-building, development and democracy.

Politics in the 1990s

Cameroon experienced a brief period of multipartyism both before and shortly after independence. The single party instituted in 1966 reigned for twenty-five years, with only a brief change in appellation in 1985 when the Cameroon People's Democratic Movement (CPDM) replaced the Cameroon National Union (CNU) to consolidate President Biya's accession to power in November 1982. During this period, the state's impatience with alternatives was remarkable. The party and government monitored and incriminated Marxist-Leninists, UPCists (Mukong 1985; Ntumazah 2001) and anyone, even the clergy, with sympathies the power elite did not share.[1]

For twenty-five years Cameroonians were forced to live a system where the centre of power was identified with the centre of truth. What transpired in such a system was, to paraphrase Václav Havel (Vladislav 1986: 39), a conspiracy of silence, a total abdication of reason, conscience and responsibility. Despite government declarations to the contrary, Cameroonians, especially those who had differences with the state, needed to 'go underground or into exile or desert their families to be able to express their opinions' (CPDM 1985: 35). The dual ideologies of national unity and national development were used to stifle initiative and creativity. Its critics thus silenced, the state could argue that all was well and that Cameroon was a veritable island of peace and quiet in an Africa of turbulence.

It is such thinking that the stalwarts of the single party used to explain away the 'obstinate' launching by John Fru Ndi of the Social Democratic Front (SDF) in Bamenda on 26 May 1990. The one-party logic demanded that accusations, whether true or false, be levelled against John Fru Ndi and everything SDF. Thus the allegations that John Fru Ndi owed the defunct Cameroon Bank FCFA 400 million, that certain anglophone students at the University of Yaounde had sung the Nigerian national anthem, that 10,000 Nigerians had marched in Bamenda during the launch, and that John Fru Ndi himself had escaped to Nigeria following the death of six people at the launching of his party. Indeed, the whole initiative was presented not only as limited to Bamenda and the North West province but also as being 'essentially of a tribal character', in which all the people who took part or sympathised with the launching were branded as 'victims of a manipulation' (Ngniman 1993: 24–64; Takougang and Krieger 1998: 103–10) by someone (John Fru Ndi) who was low in morals and who was not creditworthy.[2]

However, pressured from every direction, President Biya used the first extraordinary congress of the CPDM (dubbed the Congress of Freedom and Democracy) to urge militants to 'be prepared to face possible competition' and to be tolerant. But he also urged them to, 'in all circumstances, maintain a winning spirit',[3] a statement whose full meaning would only subsequently be revealed through a stubborn and consistent disregard of the verdict of the ballot at elections (Boulaga 1997a; Takougang 1997; Mehler 1997; Takougang and Krieger 1998; Fonchingong 1998; Nyamnjoh 2002c; Socpa 2002; Takougang 2003; Gros and Mentan 2003).

The decision to open up was not made because the CPDM was lacking in democratic achievements, President Biya argued. He highlighted the contributions made by him and his party to the advancement of democracy. The CPDM, 'born out of the call for freedom and democracy by the Cameroonian people after 20 years of an authoritarian regime', 'did not wait for democracy to be kindled in the countries of Eastern Europe as a universal principle ... to realize that it is the sole medium of apprenticeship in freedom and development'. However, given that democracy is a process, Biya promised to continue their 'onward march towards a modern democracy' but 'at our pace, according to our means and by taking into account our country's specificities'.[4] Again, the emphasis on '*at our pace*' would largely account for why every subsequent initiative at accelerated democracy would be dismissed by Biya and his party as a ploy by irresponsible 'purveyors of illusions' (Mono Ndjana 1997a; Konings and Nyamnjoh 2003).

As promised, President Biya convened parliament in November 1990 to discuss measures aimed at liberalising the country. This resulted in a series of decrees on 'rights and freedoms' promulgated in December 1990.[5] Among these was law no. 90/05[6] of 19 December 1990 authorising multipartyism, a law criticised for placing the decision to authorise the legal existence of political parties in the hands of the minister of territorial administration (MINAT), himself a member of the CPDM. By acting as both umpire and player, the CPDM was in a position to redefine or bend the rules of the game of multiparty democracy in Cameroon (Monga 1992: 13–24; Gobata 1993). That notwithstanding, by the time of the first multiparty legislative elections in March 1992, the country had 68 political parties. Of these parties 32 were officially claimed to have participated in the elections, following which four parties gained representation in the 180-seat parliament: the CPDM (88), l'Union Nationale pour la Démocratie et le Progrès (UNDP) (68), UPC (18), and Mouvement pour la Défense de la République (MDR) (6). The elections were boycotted by SDF because of the electoral code, which it described as 'obnoxious' and as having 'set in place an organised racket for rigging any elections',[7] despite the offer by President Biya of FCFA 500 million to parties willing to participate. The CPDM proceeded to form a government with MDR, a party that was to regain the ranks of the opposition after the 1997 legislation elections, when the CPDM negotiated a new alliance with the UNDP, a much bigger party. More parties were created and authorised before and after the early and highly controversial presidential elections of 11 October 1992, to the point that today Cameroon has over a hundred registered political parties.

The multiplicity of parties, most of which had no existence outside the personality of their founders, can be explained partly by the government's interest in dissipating real democratic opposition. But adding to the problem was the fact that, in a plural society like Cameroon, it was difficult for any one political party, founded along ethnic, linguistic or religious lines, to cater for every group's interest (see Chapter 8). That the existence of most of these parties means little in terms of representation has been repeatedly evidenced in elections. For example, 37 opposition parties contested the January 1996 municipal elections. Of this total, only 8 of the parties won at least one council of the 336 council areas, and 'only six of them got at least (to the nearest) one percent of the 9,886 seats that were contested.... The SDF with 21 percent and the UNDP with 10 percent of the seats are the only opposition parties with a following in more than one province though in only four and three provinces respectively.' Similarly, of the 43 opposition parties that took part in the parliamentary elections of May 1997, only 6 of them won at least one seat: SDF 43, UNDP 12 and UDC 5, with UPC, MDR and MLJC winning a seat each. The CPDM won 116 seats, according to the official figures of an election thought to have been 'thoroughly rigged' (Fonchingong 1998: 125–7). The outcome of the 2002 legislative elections was little different: the CPDM won 149, the SDF 21, the UNDP 1, CDU 5 and UPC 3 seats (Takougang 2003).

The first signs of cracks in a united front of opposition parties appeared when four parties headed by leaders from the same Beti ethnic group as President Biya dissociated themselves from the Yaounde Plan of Action of 15 June 1991. The results of the 1 March 1992 parliamentary elections, the 11 October 1992 presidential elections and subsequent elections in 1996, 1997 and 2002 showed that Cameroonians were voting along ethnic and regional lines, and endorsing national leaders primarily through their ethnic and regional elites (Fonchingong 1998: 126–7; Nyamnjoh 1999; Monga 2000; Socpa 2002; Takougang 2003), a phenomenon that is consistent with the rest of Africa in general perhaps, but that analysts of democracy have tended to treat as a problem with Africa rather than as a problem with liberal democracy (Chapter 1). Voting along ethnic and regional lines emphasises that Africans might be more comfortable with a democracy in tune with their social background and their predicaments under the global economy.

Today Cameroonians have multipartyism, but the one-party logic persists. Those who do not share the same political platform with 'us', cannot be right. They must be dishonest, traitorous and unpatriotic. How can they afford not to see things like we do? (Mono Ndjana 1997a; Zognong 1997; Onomo 1997; Nyamnjoh 1999; Monga 2000). In this way, after the presidential elections of October 1992, the CPDM, in order to consolidate what Ngniman (1993) has termed 'parcelled democracy', succeeded in having every party in parliament represented in government. The result was the end of a real parliamentary opposition. One of the consequences was that for five years after the 1992 parliamentary elections, the real opposition in a multiparty Cameroon with a multiparty assembly was to be found outside parliament (Takougang and Krieger 1998; Gros and Mentan 2003).

The radical opposition itself has not proved to be above the one-party logic. During the period of 'ghost towns' or *villes mortes*, members of the public were forced to buy opposition party cards, sometimes at very exorbitant prices. Innocent persons were also forced to buy 'yellow', 'red' and 'green' cards purportedly issued by 'the people of Cameroon' against the enemies of democracy (Ngniman 1993: 98–9). Prominent members of the ruling CPDM were coerced to join the opposition. Those who did not do so were termed unpatriotic and traitorous and, in certain cases, suffered vandalism and intimidation. The 'ghost towns' period lasted from April 1991 to January 1992, and was marked by opposition calls, ultimatums, tracts and marches asking the public to immobilise economic activity by staying indoors, blocking streets, refusing to pay taxes and bills, and boycotting the markets and offices. The intention was to force Paul Biya and his government to hold a 'sovereign national conference'. These protests were to intensify after President Biya, in what many observers have termed his firmest and most provocative speech ever, declared on 27 June 1991 that 'the national conference is pointless in Cameroon' and that he would maintain order at all cost (Monga 1992, 1996; Takougang and Krieger 1998: 126–58). Such coercion, no matter how justified, made those in search of real democracy wonder if the opposition simply wanted to substitute one form of intolerance with another. As Zacharie Ngniman, victim of such intolerance, has observed, 'I could hardly digest their propensity to want to force me to share their way of seeing things' (Ngniman 1993: 62).

The 'ghost towns' period was decreed by the opposition. There was no campaign to inform and educate the public. Road blocks were erected, tyres burnt, shops looted, and damage done to vehicles and buildings of public and private ownership (Ngniman 1993: 84–142). It was an exercise in intimidation and violence, pillars of the very dictatorship that the opposition claimed they wanted to end, giving the impression that one form of intolerance was seeking to replace another.

Naturally, the CPDM government took advantage of the opposition's acts of intolerance to accuse it of intimidation. In his 27 June 1991 speech to parliament, Paul Biya mocked the opposition's failure to live up to democratic behaviour:

> Violence, vendetta, vandalism, terrorism risk becoming the order of the day. Intimidation, threats, illegal strikes are all used to destabilise our country. Is this what Cameroonians expect of democracy? – Cars, houses, schools

have been burnt down, shops and factories looted and plundered, citizens molested. Is this what Cameroonians expect of democracy? – Institutions are called into question. Leaders as well. Intolerance, sectarianism and tribalism have become the order of the day. Is this what Cameroonians expect of democracy? – To humiliate the people, to want to bring the government to its knees, to paralyze the country and its institutions, to jeopardize the academic year, to threaten the diplomatic missions of friendly countries. Is this what Cameroonians expect of democracy? (cited in Mono Ndjana 1997a: 27)

Speaking to his supporters on the eve of the October 1992 presidential elections, Biya accused the opposition of lacking real programmes of action and of simply wanting to gain power by changing the authors of change: 'What change is it all about? The change of change, or the change of the man who brought change?' (Mono Ndjana 1997a: 47–51). A group of intellectuals (Collectif) spear-headed by academics from the Bamileke ethnic group retorted with a publication, Le Cameroun Eclaté (1992), a follow-up to an earlier book, Changer le Cameroun: Pourquoi Pas? (1990), published at the same time that Biya and his supporters were either demonstrating against multipartyism or advocating un multipartisme réfléchi (Mendo Ze, 1990). But the drive to stay in power meant that government did not look deeper than necessary. It could of course be argued, as Boh Herbert has done, that

> vandalism, provoked by the absence of dialogue and by brutal military repression, is the people's only way of speaking loud enough to be heard above the noise generated by the firing of tear gas and gun shots. It is a desperate message from millions of peace-loving countrymen enslaved by abject poverty.[8]

The government not only blamed the opposition for all the unrest, it took no immediate political action to stop it. This brought accusations of provocation and intransigence from the opposition (Ngniman 1993: 103–42; Gobata 1993: 60–62).[9] The government failed to attend to calls for dialogue, thus leaving the disaffected with little option other than to make Cameroon ungovernable. There was, too, little evidence of any dialogue between the president and his colleagues in government (Nyamnjoh 1996b: 24); Cameroon's leader was instead repeatedly accused of maintaining a 'stunning' silence over 'burning' issues which it was his duty as head of state to resolve.[10]

The one-party logic has prevented Cameroonian multipartyism from addressing the real issue: how best to bring about participatory democracy. The momentum for change generated with the rebirth of multipartyism petered out shortly after the 1992 presidential elections. Even though the results of these elections gave a majority of votes to the opposition (the first and last of its kind), the CPDM was still able to woo the Mouvement pour la Défense de la République (MDR) and Union des Populations Camerounaises (UPC) to join it in government. The CPDM was to be further comforted by a crisis within the Union Nationale pour la Démocratie et le Progrès (UNDP) party when two key members (Ahmadou Mustapha and Issa Tchiroma) accepted ministerial positions in the government formed after the October 1992 presidential elections, which Paul Biya won with 40 per cent. The opposition candidates thus together scored a total of 60 per cent, showing that even according to official statistics the majority of the electorate wanted a change of president. The opposition, which had failed to present a consensus candidate, made some critical noises about the level of rigging, as did the international community. Yet this yielded little dividend, for the protests were neither organised nor sustained. Subsequent elections since then have made little difference, and the opposition parties, one after another, have displayed the same contradictions, the same disinclination to go beyond rhetoric in matters of democracy within their parties and in their constituencies, and the same craving for power without vision (Nyamnjoh 1999, 2002c).

Opposition parties have thus created the impression that they are more concerned with their sectional interests than national well-being (Sindjoun 2004). It is like the war of the bellies, where the quarrel of the opposition is more with 'the eaters' than with 'the eating'. Those of them who have managed to get themselves involved in government have quickly fallen prey to the comforts of chaos. Opposition to malpractice in high office comes across more and more as a mere political gimmick. Even the most radical and populist of them – Fru Ndi of the SDF, for example – have not sought to go beyond what Celestin Monga has termed 'slogans in line with populist illusions' (C. Monga 1995: 371, 1996: 150).[11] The opposition has failed to inspire popular hope by its actions in intra- and inter-party differences, in its councils, or in the way it has comported itself in parliament (Ngwane 1997).

After the 1996 municipal elections, which the opposition won in a significant number of key urban councils, the government was able to gain effective control of these councils by imposing CPDM government delegates with powers to manage council projects and finances. Again, the opposition did little to correct the situation, limiting themselves to critical press releases and newspaper condemnation of government action and unjust laws. The same can be said of opposition reaction after the May 1997 parliamentary elections, in which official results claimed the CPDM won by 116 seats as against 64 for the opposition (Fonchingong 1998: 126), and of the June 2002 legislative elections, which the CPDM won by 149 seats as opposed to 31 for the opposition (Takougang 2003; Nyamnjoh 2002c). The opposition cried foul, but came short of any meaningful action to reverse the official results. Finally, in October 1997 Cameroonians again witnessed another presidential election, which Paul Biya won with 92 per cent of the vote (3,167,820 votes of 3,433,081 allegedly cast). While the three major opposition parties in parliament (SDF, UNDP, UDC) boycotted the elections for want of an independent electoral commission, President Biya hailed the 'essentially democratic' nature of the electoral system in place (Ndongo 1997: 51–2). Again, little came of threats by these parties to disrupt the elections with an 'active boycott', apart, of course, from the claim that 80 per cent of the electorate had stayed away from the polls. And so, as the popular comedian Tchop Tchop put it in his satirical sketch on election protest and political prostitution in Cameroon, 'les chiens aboient; la caravane passe' ('complain as you may, we do our thing') (Tchop Tchop 1997).

And how true this remains! Cameroonians today, fifteen years later, find themselves asking for the same freedoms they had demanded at the start of the current clamour for democratisation. At the parliamentary session of November 2000, the opposition parties (SDF, UDC, UPC–K, MDR, MLDC) asked for an independent electoral commission. The ruling CPDM and UNDP, its partner in government, turned this proposal down. The government instead offered a National Electoral Observatory (NEO), the members of which were to be appointed by President Biya himself. The opposition parliamentarians boycotted the debate on the bill that modified the electoral law to provide for the NEO. But, as in the past, this action did not deter the government. Although the NEO was intended in principle 'to contribute to the observance of the electoral law in order to ensure regular, impartial, objective, transparent and fair elections', most people suspected that the reality of elections under the NEO will be everything but free and fair. As The Herald noted in an editorial on the prospects for democratisation in 2001, 'the fact that the NEO does not have the power to organise elections makes it a far cry from the demands of the opposition and the people who have been too used to electoral malpractices.' When President Biya announced postponement of the June 2002 elections and sacked the minister in charge, it became evident that the NEO was never really in charge. As expected, the confusion, drama, violence and controversy of the elections yielded a landslide victory of 149 (of a total of 180) seats in parliament for the CPDM, reducing every other party to a dying regional flicker, and imposing the CPDM as the only national party.

There has indeed been little dialogue or fair play in Cameroon's multiparty electoral democracy, even by African standards. While the first multiparty legislative elections were conducted according to a one-party electoral law, the presidential election of 1992 and subsequent elections in 1996 and 1997 were conducted under new but highly controversial electoral laws (Tolen 1997). According to section 8 of Electoral Law No. 92/010 of 17 September 1992, for example, candidates for presidential elections must be 'Cameroonian citizens by birth and show proof of having resided in Cameroon for an uninterrupted period of at least 12 (twelve) months.' In general, one has to prove a continuous stay of at least six months in a given locality to qualify to vote there, and to stand for elections in that locality one must be an indigene or a 'long-staying resident'. An elaborate set of rules and stipulations determine who is to vote where, as the ruling CPDM has tended, for its own political survival, to give a semblance of protecting 'ethnic citizens' from being outvoted by 'ethnic strangers'. Other 'requirements' not explicitly formulated in the law are invoked to disqualify opposition candidates by MINAT, which, as noted above, is both player and umpire.

During the consecutive presidential, legislative and local elections of the 1990s and 2002, MINAT devised additional preconditions and diversionary tactics for determining who is allowed to stand as a candidate or to vote at all. In practice, therefore, the complicated electoral laws provide the government with precious opportunities to manipulate the electoral roll in its favour, while making matters extremely difficult for the opposition and their supporters. For instance, it is not uncommon for opposition supporters to be told in the city where they live that they have to vote in their home area (their village of origin, even when they were born in the city), but once there they are informed by the local authorities that they have to vote where they live (in the city). In this way many voters never make it to the polling station on election day. At every election, the newspapers are full of stories about opposition lists that have been disqualified by MINAT, either for failure to 'reflect the sociological components' of the locality or for including candidates that did not 'quite belong' in the area concerned (Geschiere and Nyamnjoh 2000; Socpa 2002; Gros and Mentan 2003).

As long as free and fair multiparty elections imply a risk of losing power, the CPDM and President Biya will continue, so their actions and vacillations indicate, to ignore the wishes of ordinary Cameroonians. To do this effectively, they will have to continue doing what they do best, namely stating one thing and doing something rather different. They do so by disallowing Cameroonians in the diaspora from participating in elections at home. They complicate the process of obtaining national identity and electoral cards that qualify one to vote or to be voted for. Electoral cards from those least likely to vote for the CPDM are withheld, and polling stations are located in the homes of people loyal to the CPDM. Traditional chiefs, bureaucrats, intellectuals, journalists, the jobless, businessmen and women are co-opted to facilitate illegitimate victories for the CPDM. Election violence is used to justify irregularities. Tailor-made electoral constituencies favour CPDM strongholds to the detriment of the opposition. They have also ensured that the National Elections Observatory is the CPDM in everything but name, and that it neither barks nor bites. Within the ranks of the opposition itself, the CPDM has encouraged carpet crossing, dissension, scandals, and various crises in its favour, with tempting offers to key individuals and communities.

How Biya and the CPDM have so skilfully deflated opposition politics in Cameroon continues to astonish most analysts and ordinary Cameroonians. Yet it is not only civil servants or opposition parties that have failed to assert themselves against government's diversionary tactics. The anglophone community, through the Teachers Association of Cameroon (TAC), the Confederation of Anglophone Parent-Teachers Association of Cameroon (CAPTAC) and the churches, fought very hard to have an independent examinations board granted them in 1993 (Nyamnjoh 1996d), but they have done little to consolidate this victory (Konings and Nyamnjoh 2003). The GCE board thus lost its autonomy to the Ministry of Education, which was very reluctant to grant it in the first place. Since 1990 journalists of the private press and their newspapers have, as we will soon see in detail, suffered as victims of the selective application of a repressive press law, yet they have been unable to organise themselves into a strong union capable of defending and promoting their interests. Teachers, tutors and university lecturers are similarly disorganised, preferring to go in for sinecures rather than fight for professional interests (Jua and Nyamnjoh 2002). In general, attempts to empower civil society in the country have yielded little fruit. And this is true no matter what aspect of society is considered.

If the opposition has stayed divided, unable to agree on a common strategy or a consensual candidate, the ethnic and regional factor of mutual distrust and suspicion is largely to blame. Since July 1991, when four parties headed by leaders from the same Beti ethnic group as President Biya dissociated themselves from *la coordination des partis de l'opposition* because of the Yaounde Plan of Action, the rift between opposition parties has only grown wider. Instead of seeking a common platform, parties have fallen easy prey to the entrapment of primordial bonds, and so have their militants, who have tended to vote along regional and ethnic lines. The ruling CPDM party has not only capitalised upon such differences in the opposition, it has further encouraged the proliferation of ghost parties, whose militants put together 'cannot fill up a telephone booth' (Tchop Tchop 1997), with the sole aim of thwarting the efforts of real opposition in Cameroon. To weaken the opposition even further, government has, since the reintroduction of multipartyism, encouraged the creation of regional and ethnic associations 'to compete for "party" status and access to state resources' (Nyamnjoh and Rowlands 1998: 321). In January 1996, it went even a step further when it modified the constitution to provide for state protection for minorities and state preservation of the rights of indigenous populations. The rise in and importance of ethnicised elite associations are an obvious consequence, and so is the increase in violent polemics about 'ethnic cleansing' and the removal of 'strangers', who in many cases are second- or third-generation descendants of migrants (Nyamnjoh and Rowlands 1998; Geschiere and Nyamnjoh 2000; Monga 2000; Socpa 2002).

From what precedes, it is clear that the democratic process in Cameroon has been stalled. Surveys and undoctored election results repeatedly indicate that the bulk of Cameroonians want a change for the better. They want an active say in matters of public interest and freedom from the misery to which they are being held victim. When you converse with them as individuals, listen to popular music and satirical comedians in bars and public places, or monitor the popular *radio trottoir*, that is unmistakably the impression one gets (Essono 1996; Nyamnjoh and Fokwang 2003).

It is quite common to hear ordinary Cameroonians say, 'On ne se tape même plus le corps ici. On attend' ('We've given up. Let's wait and see'). Thus the bulk of Cameroonians, despite the re-introduction of multipartyism, continue to be compelled to abide by decisions taken without their consent or participation. They continue to have little impact even on their most pressing problems and interests, as the political, economic and social changes that they yearn for are being planned, executed or thwarted according to the one-best-way logic of the one-party era. Those who do not share a political platform with 'us' cannot be right; they must be dishonest, traitorous, unpatriotic. How can they afford not to see things the way we do? It is a case of recycled monolithism, of pseudo-democracy given out in gift parcels, of democracy by remote control; a situation in which the genuinely thirsty have little real chance of quenching their thirst for freedom and participation.

Democracy of any kind is yet to become a way of life – a culture – in Cameroon. So far it has served mainly as face powder, an empty concept or slogan devoid of concrete meaning used to justify reactionary propaganda by the CPDM and its acolytes on the one hand, and revolutionary propaganda by the opposition and some pressure groups on the other.

With political parties being rather slow and increasingly incapable of delivering democracy, attention should normally turn to the other branches of civil society. But then, which of the pro-democracy NGOs, associations, trade unions and other civil organisations created or revived in Cameroon as alternative voices, are indeed free of the contradictions that plague opposition parties? How many of them can justify their existence beyond a mere ploy to target foreign donors for the personal enrichment of their founders? One finds that the emerging civil society is being infiltrated by organisations that are quite undemocratic in orientation. Some of them are known to have been sponsored by the ruling party to protect the government by countering the activities of other associations fighting for greater empowerment and meaningful liberal or popular democracy.

In the absence of a vigorous civil society and creative initiative, Cameroonians in their numbers continue to perceive the state as the sole source of personal enrichment and reward, and of massive frustration and neglect. Thus are stifled the ambition and enthusiasm of those keen to contribute towards the empowerment and edification of the dispossessed. As has been observed repeatedly in poverty studies and by casual contact with ordinary people, Cameroonians have since the 1990s been a lot poorer than they were at independence in 1960. Yet there is talk of the country having maintained an impressive 4.5 per cent economic growth in the year 2000. Corruption is thriving, and the elite few are swimming in opulence from embezzlement and kickbacks (Tumi 2000).[12] And the government does not want to be held accountable for this or to be criticised for not making things better. Nevertheless, its high-handedness, arrogance and absolute power imply that the government can afford to distance itself and ignore the desperate cries of the disenchanted and disenfranchised masses. Liberal democracy, even by African standards, is yet to take off in Cameroon.

How have the media situated themselves in all this? What role have they played in enhancing or frustrating popular aspirations for democracy of any kind in Cameroon? The next five chapters address these questions and more, beginning with the role played by the official media (state broadcasting institutions, the state print media and publishing corporation), in Chapter 4.

Notes

1. See *Jeune Afrique Economie*, October 1991, for Bishop Ndongmo's personal account of his tribulations.
2. *Cameroon Tribune*, 30 May 1990.
3. *Cameroon Tribune*, 4 July 1990.
4. See *Cameroon Tribune*, 4 July 1990; emphasis added.
5. See SOPECAM 1991 for a complete collection.
6. See *Cameroon Tribune*, 20 February 1992.
7. See *Cameroon Post*, 6 January 1992; *Le Messager* (English), 21 February 1992.
8. *Le Messager*, 3 August 1991.
9. See *L'Expression*, 30 October 1992.
10. See the Catholic Bishops' Pastoral letter of 17 May 1990, criticising the president's silence on important issues.
11. According to *The Herald* (no. 279, 1996) a disillusioned illiterate 'Takumbeng' woman who had seen leaders come and go, voted in and out, had this to say of the 1996 local elections: 'Candidates who stand for elections are like birds without feathers. We the voters give a candidate his feathers – each vote being another feather. When he has enough feathers off he flies and we never see him again.'
12. See also Pastoral Letter of the Bishops of Cameroon on Corruption, no. 22–23, 2000.

4

The Official Media, Belonging

and Democratisation

This chapter examines the part the official broadcast and print media – Cameroon Radio Television (CRTV) and *Cameroon Tribune*, respectively – have played in the ongoing democratic process in Cameroon. It seeks to answer the question whether these state-owned institutions have adequately informed the public on democratic values. It asks if they have adopted democratic instruments themselves in their practice of journalism. This question is all the more legitimate granted the often repeated claim by these institutions during the 1990s that they were in the service of democracy, as public institutions funded by the taxpayers. The Cameroonian public, regardless of whether or not they own a television and/or a radio set, have regularly paid an imposed 'CRTV tax' over the years.

In Cameroon, broadcasting was a state monopoly until April 2000, depending entirely on the authorities for its very existence. Whether under the colonial administration between 1940 and 1960, the Ahidjo regime from January 1960 to November 1982, or the present Biya government, the relationship between the state and the broadcast media has basically remained the same. Throughout the 64-year history of broadcasting in Cameroon, those in power have sought total ownership and control of the broadcast media. The laws and regulations in force have, until April 2000, always excluded every other form of ownership and control. In contrast to some African countries, Cameroon remained one of many where the legislation never allowed alternative forms of ownership an opportunity, if only to prove themselves economically, politically or culturally incapable in the 'demanding task of nation-building'. This was the case in spite of the fact that the constitution guaranteed various freedoms, including those of expression, the press and enterprise.

This chapter starts with a brief examination of the role of broadcasting as defined by the state prior to the 1990s, as a background to the place of broadcasting in the current democratic struggles. It deals with how the colonial and postcolonial governments justified the state monopoly, and examines some of the strategies, overt or covert, used by the various regimes to control the broadcast media.

The Colonial State and Broadcasting

Since television did not make its debut in Cameroon until 20 March 1985, radio alone existed during the colonial era. Even then, radio was only introduced in the last twenty years of colonialism, when France needed it for war propaganda purposes. Radio transmission for the general public was already a reality in Europe and America by the 1920s (Mytton 1983: 2–3). Between 1940 and 1942, the first radio station was opened in francophone Cameroon in the coastal city of Douala. The French state did not intend it for indigenous Cameroonians but to service the French community during the War (Bebey 1963: 36; Ekaney 1976: 118; Biyiti Bi Essam 1984: 24; Eone 1986: 249–50; Fonye 1988: 13). Just like many other radio stations that were opened in Africa in the 1940s, the aim with Radio Douala was to serve the exclusive interests of the colonists. Thus when the British opened Radio Lusaka in Zambia in 1941, it was 'primarily to keep the local population informed of the progress of the war, to stimulate their war effort and to convey orders in the event of grave emergency arising' (Lightfoot 1965: 27).

At the end of 1944 when the war ended for Cameroon, Radio Douala also ceased to broadcast. In the words of its former director, Radio Douala was a 'child of war' which died when 'war information' ceased to be necessary (Biyiti Bi Essam 1984: 24). When local amateurs decided to reopen it two years later, the French authorities showed little interest in supporting them. They were forced to improvise in order to sustain what was essentially a music station relaying French melodies. But when in 1955 the French felt they needed the radio again, probably to contain the rising spirit of nationalism and clamour for independence in the colonial population, they immediately made available the necessary technical facilities (weak though these were) and brought qualified staff from Paris (Bebey 1963: 36).

The period between 1946 and 1955 was the closest radio came to being privately operated in Cameroon prior to April 2000. With the French state disengaged, the amateurs of Radio Douala, keen on making use of the abandoned transmitter and other facilities, were obliged to turn to advertising. Local businesses were asked to sponsor the station's programmes, with largely metropolitan content. These amateurs, who normally had other jobs and who knew little or nothing about the technicalities of radio, were able to put on 2 hours 30 minutes of broadcasting each day.

In 1955 and 1957–58 two new radio stations opened in the Centre-South and the Northern cities of Yaounde and Garoua respectively, by La Société de Radiodiffusion de la France d'outre-mer (SORAFOM). SORAFOM remained in charge of radio broadcasting in the territory until three years after independence, in accordance with the terms of a convention signed between the new République du Cameroun and France in July 1960. Thus francophone Cameroon had twenty years' experience of radio before independence, but it was an entirely urban elitist medium. For fifteen of those years it was the exclusive privilege of the colonists in Douala and its immediate environs. The network facilities almost always comprised low-powered transmitters with barely 1kW of power catering for urban listeners, and one of 4kW to serve the entire country (Bebey 1963: 154; Ekaney 1976: 118). Colonial radio was a strategic medium to facilitate the task of the French colonists in their wars and against the rising pressure from urban-based Cameroonian nationalists militating for independence.

In British Cameroon, radio was much slower at establishing itself. Having decided to administer it as part of a larger colony, Nigeria, the British had little particular interest in providing a separate radio service for the territory. Not until nationalism was at its peak, and Nigeria was about to obtain political independence, did the British consider the future of British Cameroon. Not surprisingly, therefore, a recording studio, financed by the Nigerian government and forming part of the Nigerian Broadcasting Corporation (NBC), was constructed in 1957 at West Farm Buea in Southern Cameroon. The recording studio, which was equipped with mobile recording facilities and two recording cars, produced local programmes that were then dispatched to Lagos for broadcast (Nkwo 1975: 14–15).

This was a strategy to woo Southern Cameroonians who were used to tuning to Congo Brazzaville or Congo Léopoldville for 'popular Congolese music' (Fonye 1988: 3), which, according to Manu Dibango, 'was the only kind that traveled so easily throughout Africa and Europe' thanks to the impressive investment in powerful radio transmitters in then Léopoldville by Belgian colonialists who thought they were going to live there for a long time (Dibango 1994: 29), yet the strategy failed for technical reasons, mainly weak transmitters (Nkwo 1975: 14). The studio operated in Buea until 1961 when it became part of the national radio at the birth of the Federal Republic of Cameroon. In that year a 1kW transmitter was dispatched from the capital Yaounde to improve reception (Fonye 1988: 3). But Radio Buea was to wait for more than a decade for further upgrading.

When one takes into consideration the short history of radio in francophone and anglophone colonial Cameroon, its low-powered transmitters, the languages of broadcast (mainly French and English) that were alien to most of the people, the low incomes of the majority of the population, the undomesticated contents of the medium, and the circumstances surrounding its creation, it can hardly be said that radio was a mass medium before independence. Communication among the masses remained largely through indigenous channels and by interpersonal forms. The nationalists used such channels and other alternative media like pamphlets, tracks, song, rumour, humour, parody, irony or *radio trottoir* to communicate their dissent and mobilise support for independence.

Broadcasting in the Postcolonial One-Party State

Broadcasting under President Ahidjo (1960–82)

When francophone Cameroon became independent in 1960, radio continued to be operated and managed directly from Paris by

SORAFOM. Only on 1 July 1963 was a new convention signed with France. By this agreement the federal government of Cameroon formally took over ownership and control of radio, its personnel and equipment, on condition that France would continue to provide technical assistance, especially through OCORA, the new name for SORAFOM (Ahidjo 1980: 305). But once in power, Ahidjo was quick to see the importance of the media in general, and of radio in particular, for the consolidation of his power base.

'Nation-building', Ahidjo declared in 1964, is 'our supreme mission', so important a mission that it could not be attained outside the stability of a presidential regime (Ahidjo 1964: 24–5) or the dynamism of Ahidjo's Cameroon National Union party (Ahidjo 1964: 28). Nation-building, entailing socio-economic, political and cultural development, remained a recurrent theme in Ahidjo's writings and declarations until he gave up power in 1982. He never missed the opportunity to stress the importance of radio in attainment of nation-building.

A review of Ahidjo's speeches on the role of information, and the need to use radio and other media for mass mobilization and education of the population, provides a further insight to his understanding of 'Nation-building', 'Development' and 'Participation'. Ahidjo's declarations, as well as subsequent declarations by his successor Biya, could rightly be considered the information policy of the state. In the single-party era one seldom came across any other statements on information, or for that matter other areas of policy, independent of declarations by the head of state and his associates.

The media were expected to play the leading role prescribed by modernisation theorists. The radio in particular, by virtue of the broadness of its appeal, was singled out for the mobilization of the population – both rural and urban – through mass education and information, with the aim of consolidating the national personality and cohesion. As early as 1962 President Ahidjo saw the need to replace or enhance the low-powered colonial transmitters to make radio more accessible to a wider audience. Subsequent stations were opened and more powerful transmitters installed during his presidency, all with the aim of making the radio translate the national life in all its forms, the evolution of the institutions, and ways of life, and to stimulate the population in its adhesion to the communal effort.

Speaking during his inauguration of the new 30 kW transmitter of Radio Yaounde on 29 May 1962, President Ahidjo was unequivocal about the fact that he wanted radio 'to keep the populations of the federation … informed of the efforts deployed by the government to attain the goal which it has assigned itself: the making of the Cameroonian nation' (Ahidjo 1980: 185). To him, radio was particularly well placed to do this, given its potential to be less elitist than other modern media. With radio, he was sure 'to reach the entire population and take the voice of the government to the remotest regions', for the 'absence or insufficiency of information leads to the passivity of the individual', which 'we cannot accept at the time when the task of national edification demands the collaboration of all and sundry' (Ahidjo 1980: 185).

Thanks to quality information disseminated by the radio, President Ahidjo argued, citizens would be able to cultivate their faculties, increase their knowledge, and feed their intellectual curiosity. Citizens, above all, would become aware of Cameroonian realities, aware of themselves as part of a nation, and aware of their duties to the state. Inhabitants of the territory would get to know one another better if information circulated faster and more abundantly. Thanks to such information, Cameroonians would understand their role in the economic and political life of the country (Ahidjo 1980: 185).

While inaugurating another 30 kW transmitter in Garoua on 23 July 1963, President Ahidjo reiterated the special interest his government had in national radio. The fact that radio could be used with flexibility, and that it possessed great possibilities of being adapted to suit different audiences, allowed for the sensitisation of the listeners by appropriate broadcasts and programmes. This aspect was particularly relevant to Cameroon, whose federal character at the time, differences in colonial heritage, and ethnic diversity constituted a real laboratory of unity in diversity. It was with its linguistic, cultural and ethnic diversity in mind that Cameroon had opted for a radio network instead of a single, highly powerful transmitter with multiple programmes and overcharged schedules. Ahidjo also expected radio, the provincial stations in particular, to create programmes well adapted to local needs but in tune with the communal tasks of nation-building (Ahidjo 1980: 303).

On 3 June 1967, Ahidjo went to West Cameroon (formerly, Southern Cameroon) to inaugurate the new transmitter centre of Radio Buea. There, as if paraphrasing Schramm (1964) or Lerner (1964) on the role of the media in the transformation of 'traditional' or 'primitive' societies, he stressed the link between education, information and 'the sacred task of nation-building'. His government had assigned itself the task of giving 'to all the men and women of this country all the chances possible to fulfil themselves, to become informed and efficacious citizens'. The government's mission was to transform mentalities in order to accelerate development, which 'in effect, does not come about without the disruption of structures, habits, traditions and values. Men must be prepared to accept these disruptions to avoid these structures, habits, traditional values becoming ... constraints, obstacles to progress.' Radio was most well placed to ensure that 'these essential tasks' did not fail. It was the place of the radio to mobilize the people for nation-building, prepare them mentally for the changes that accompany development, and reinforce national unity. Information would make it possible for the different regions of Cameroon to determine their collective aspirations under the guidance of the party and the government, and in short 'to become aware of what united them, and to further consolidate national unity and the stability of institutions' (Ahidjo 1980: 768).

On 10 March 1969 in an address to the CNU party congress in Garoua, Ahidjo revisited the theme of the role of the media in nation-building and made a statement that became a cliché among government officials and media practitioners. The role assigned to broadcasting and other media in the statute of the Ministry of Information and Culture following its November 1978 reorganisation was a mere reproduction of all that Ahidjo had said at the congress, which, again, was little different from his previous statements since 1962. The famous maxim was that the media are supposed to 'inform and educate within; expose and persuade without'. To him, the media's task was threefold: Inform, Educate, Entertain. The slogan was to be repeated by broadcast practitioners and administrators whenever they were asked about the country's broadcasting or information policy. Everyone interviewed acknowledged the absence of a blueprint but repeated the above statements, whose very vagueness remained a constant dilemma.

Concerning information, the essential objective was: 'to open bit by bit the minds to a just understanding of the problems of the modern world and to the joy of an authentic national culture; [and] ... to develop in our compatriots an awareness that is as clear as possible of the role which everyone can and must play in nation-building' (Ahidjo 1980: 918). In order to achieve the animation of the masses, and to make them participate more actively and more closely in the management of communal affairs, it was important for government officials and media practitioners to work in harmony. Only through such collaboration could national unity be best consolidated and Cameroon's social democracy best reinforced.

Ahidjo explained what he meant by 'animation'. It did not mean 'to amuse', for Cameroonians were too geared towards their economic and social development to have any time for amusement. To animate the population of Cameroon did not mean 'making them dance' either. Rather, it meant 'to furnish them with programmes, articles and films adapted to the necessities of our development, to explain our actions to them, in order to obtain their active participation in nation-building'. It was to such an exalted task that Ahidjo invited officials and technicians in the media. He promised the media practitioners the total support and confidence of his administration and assured them that thenceforth the Ministry of Information and Culture would be associated with the activities of the different departments, with the aim of properly mobilizing the media institutions in charge of the information and education of the masses. Then he promised them all the resources needed to achieve their mission (Ahidjo 1980: 919–20).

Regarding propaganda abroad, Ahidjo explained that owing to Cameroon's dependence on foreign aid, it was important for the media to convey a positive international image. The duty of the media consisted in publicising the multiple factors of progress in Cameroon; explaining the reasons for the government's policies; and persuading listeners of the well-foundedness of the government's choices. Such information would contribute towards giving Cameroon the right image, capable of attracting foreign investors whose participation was seen to be indispensable to rapid development of the nation (Ahidjo 1980: 918–19).

In a speech at the inauguration of the radio house and production centre of the Bertoua station on 13 December 1978, Ahidjo summarised all he had ever said on the media issue. He stressed more than ever before the idea of 'responsibility' in broadcasting – an idea that was to be taken up with even more fervour by President Biya and his New Deal Ministers of Information or Communication. The Bertoua Radio Station, said President Ahidjo, was going to unite the East Province with the rest of the country, stop the people from tuning to foreign stations in a desperate quest for information, and reinforce and consolidate national unity. This would be in line with the mission of Radio Cameroon as a whole, which remained that of informing the citizens on what went on in Cameroon, as well as elsewhere, with a view to promoting and intensifying the links of solidarity among them on the one hand, and between the people of Cameroon and other peoples of the world on the other. However, this mission to inform had to be carried out 'in a spirit of responsibility' in a way that relates the facts in an objective manner, thus permitting everyone to better appreciate and in full awareness make their contribution to the common task of nation-building.' By 'responsible broadcasting', Ahidjo implied 'the rejection of the sensational and the spreading of unconfirmed news that risks misleading' (Ahidjo 1980: 2130–31).

Broadcasting under President Biya (1982–90)

When President Biya came to power in November 1982, he stated that his immediate concern was to reassure Cameroonians 'that they need not go underground or into exile or desert their families to be able to express their opinions' (CPDM 1985: 35) – an alternative which by implication they had been forced to accept in the past. Describing himself as one without claim to 'any monopoly over speech, reason, feeling or patriotism', he told the Bamenda CNU party congress that his aim was to bring about 'a more open, more free, more responsible society, a society that is more just and hence, a more pleasant society' – a 'New Deal' society (CPDM 1985: 19).

Like Ahidjo, Biya had a special place for the media in his agenda from the outset; and, just like the former, he continued to reiterate its role in his subsequent declarations, speeches and publications. One of his first systematic statements on the role of the media came during an interview with *Cameroon Tribune* on 6 July 1984, in which he defined the place of the media in the era of the New Deal. The role of the Cameroonian media was to 'contribute to the emancipation and the fulfilment of the Cameroonian, to make it possible for him to live his freedom as a true citizen, conscious of his political, civic and social responsibilities'. The media would be seen to succeed only if proving 'capable of stimulating creativity and participation, speeding up the emergence of the national culture rich and proud of its diversities, promoting an economic activity that is source of prosperity and solidarity ... galvanising the feeling of brotherhood within the framework of national values... order... legality... [and] the property and rights of others' (Ndongo 1985: 29).

Biya used the Bamenda CNU party congress of 1985 to remind media institutions and practitioners of their responsibilities towards the state and the people of Cameroon. Convinced that 'a well-informed citizen is necessarily better enlightened about the actual life of his environment', and that such a citizen 'is also more aware of the major stakes in national development, more conversant in his behaviour and better capable of performing his duties to the Nation', he urged the media to animate, orientate and control the national development effort of Cameroon. For information, above everything else, provides the people with the 'additional moral and intellectual arms in the performance of their tasks'. He made clear that the duty to disseminate information aimed at fostering nation-building was not limited to the official media; the private media were just as involved. He hailed 'the new dynamic spirit of the private press whose numerous and varied titles have come, encouraged by liberalization, to supplement the efforts of the official media' (CPDM 1985: 31). His administration was in support of 'any medium of expression that is capable of stimulating creativity and participation and channelling the emergence of a national culture that constantly derives its wealth from its diversity', as well as of any 'medium capable of promoting an economic activity that would serve as a source of prosperity and solidarity' (CPDM 1985: 31–2). Even before 1990, President Biya was convinced that his administration had brought about greater media freedom. In his speeches and interviews, and in the speeches of his various ministers of information and culture (François Sengat Kuo, Professor George Ngango and Ibrahim Mbombo Njoya, in that order), one is given the impression that there was certainly some opening up; and that the winds of freedom and liberalisation had made an impact on the media. Quite a number of media practitioners tended to think in a similar manner. If greater freedom meant that more newspapers or publications were allowed to circulate after Biya took power than under Ahidjo's government (Ndongo 1987), it could well be true. But if it meant the freedom to determine content, to participate in, or to own and control any medium of one's choice and interest, there was little evidence of it before 1990. Any semblance of freedom then was neither institutionalised nor underpinned by law. The repressive press laws of 1959 and 1966 (Bayart 1973; Fonye 1973; Wongo 1977; Ndogo 1980; Mytton 1983; Ndongo 1987) had not been repealed (Tataw 1984; Nji 1985; Lukong 1987; Wongibe 1987), and journalists were still subjected to arbitrary arrest and detention without trial. Biya's idea of freedom, it soon became apparent, was limited to the freedom to criticise former president Ahidjo and Biya's own critics. As soon as the media became critical of him and his government as well, they were punished accordingly. He expected media practitioners and the wider society to 'use the freedom of speech thus regained with an acute sense of responsibility'.

While appreciating the part all media could play in bringing about national integration, Biya saw the coming of television in 1985 as particularly timely, and suited for the task:

This is therefore a particularly good opportunity for us to hail the advent of national television which translates into concrete terms our ambition to become modern. There is no doubt that it will more appreciably consolidate the basis of our ideals of stringency and moral rectitude, liberalization and democratization, further testifying to our efforts to build our country in unity, freedom and social justice. It will also demonstrate our love for peace and our determination to cooperate with all nations in the world in ensuring respect for human rights, our identity and our national sovereignty. (CPDM 1985: 32)

President Biya also expected 'our information and propaganda media' to use the high dissemination techniques now available, to 'help to make the message of unity, fraternity and peace of our great national Party heard, shared and hearkened to both in Cameroon and abroad' (CPDM 1985: 32). In addition to Biya's declarations were statements by his various ministers of information and culture, but most often they were paraphrasing him, and thus said little that was new. It was commonplace for the president to decide what direction to take, and everyone else followed. Policies were often made through his speeches and not necessarily through parliament. Apart from these speeches, very little else was documented or published that could serve as a source of inspiration for aspiring media professionals or researchers.

It is evident from the above that under the one-party state, the broadcast media had the task of implementing government policies. They had to ensure that national unity and integration were consolidated and that Cameroon developed economically, socially and culturally. To succeed in this, uniformity and conformity were expected from the media and cultural organisations of every nature and origin. Despite their statements to the contrary, when pursued to their logical conclusion the arguments levelled by Ahidjo and Biya were the same: government could not afford fundamental differences of opinion and options in a society that was not only underdeveloped, but culturally and linguistically divided. Thus, state ownership and government control of broadcasting prior to 1990, instead of facilitating the creation of genuine social, economic and political institutions, merely served to manipulate the people into compliance with statist notions of unity embedded in 'pseudo-institutions' that hindered 'the process of integration' (Medard 1978: 37–9).

The fact that at Radio Cameroon and Cameroon Television broadcasters talked more of 'the government's airwaves' than 'the state's airwaves' was an indication of how, as far as they were concerned, the distinction between state and government was more in theory than in practice. Shasha Ndimbie, like all the other broadcasters I interviewed in 1988, recognised that, in Cameroon,

The government is the state, and the government can make or break the state; they can choose to represent the people, who are in effect the state, or they can choose not to. So in any case the two are interlocking, one becomes the other, and so on. There is not really any difference; maybe administratively and legislatively there is a difference, but in practice, all is the same.[1]

There is little evidence that the broadcast media in the one-party era had any choice with the government. Whether under Biya or Ahidjo, the government always claimed to know the interests of the state better than the people they were supposed to represent. The message to the media was always that of explaining government's actions and policies to the population; but seldom was it also a question of explaining to the government what the people's real needs and aspirations were, and as articulated by the people themselves. The assumption was that the people were ignorant and needed information, that they needed to be educated on how to transform their 'backward' mentalities, traditions or ways, and to be mobilised and set firmly behind the government's programme of change or modernisation. The assumption was that it sufficed to listen to the media for the government's message, which, if followed without question, would bring about development, unity and integration.

By placing broadcasting directly under the Ministry of Information and Culture, and by making it part of the civil service, the government deprived the broadcasters of the 'professional objectivity' they believed they needed to practise journalism in a plural society. The broadcasters were in a predicament, torn between acting as the mouthpiece of the government and being professional journalists as they understood it. However, their struggle for autonomy was one they experienced more mentally than physically, as the government constantly employed a number of strategies to make them conform willy-nilly. Such strategies ranged from the 'dos and don'ts' of the civil service, to overt suppression of information and sanctions on failure to conform, such as transfers, interrogations by the police, suspensions and detention without trial. Just how much of this has changed with the new clamour for democratisation in the 1990s is the subject of the next section.

Broadcasting in the 1990s

CRTV and the democratic process

CRTV as a government mouthpiece has seldom been popular in the current democratic process. The negative feeling towards CRTV and *Cameroon Tribune* took a turn for the worse following the 'Yondo Black Affair' in March 1990 and the launching of the SDF in Bamenda in May 1990. According to *Le Messager*,[2] on 27 March 1990 lawyer B.W. Muna addressed the Cameroon Bar Association (CBA) in Douala on the eve of the trial of the former CBA president lawyer Yondo Black and nine others, accused of 'holding clandestine meetings in view of producing and disseminating tracts hostile to the regime, insulting to the President of the Republic, and inciting to revolt'.[3] Although the official media were silent on the speech, others saw it as a milestone in the struggle against human rights abuses in Cameroon. The official blackout gave rise to allegations of 'a conscience of guilt', a contention given added credibility when the same official media, silent on the original address, found it newsworthy to air dissenting reactions against lawyer Muna and what his address stood for. CRTV broadcast statements by lawyers Epassy Antoine, Mbian Emmanuel and Ngon A. Bidias, in which the three accused lawyer Muna of using his position as president of the CBA to promote his political ambitions. This tactic was to be typical of CRTV's operations throughout the period of struggle for multiparty democracy in Cameroon.

Following the launching of the SDF, during which six people were shot dead by security forces, the official media attempted to conceal the truth. As Zacharie Ngniman explains, he received a communiqué from 'the hierarchy' asking him to report that the six had been trampled to death. The television used stock pictures in place of what actually transpired, and repeated accusations, to which reference has already been made in the earlier discussion of multipartyism, against John Fru Ndi and anglophone students at Yaounde University.[4] All these allegations, Ngniman was later to confess, were intended by government to disinform and mislead the Cameroonian public (Ngniman 1993: 24–64). Anglophone Cameroonians were termed 'Biafrans', referred to as *l'ennemi dans la maison*, accused of ingratitude and bad faith to President Biya, who had done so much for their region, and asked by then minister of territorial administration, Ibrahim Mbombo Njoya, 'to go elsewhere' if they were dissatisfied with the Cameroon they had (Ngniman 1993: 51).

Taken unawares by the winds of change and by the clamour for freedom and democracy, the official media continued in the same vein. Their struggles to legitimate or justify government action against a background of relentless attacks from the private press and opposition parties only earned them further public disaffection. Instead of adapting in time to accommodate alternative voices, CRTV management opted to stay with the status quo. The official media remained consistent in their pro-government perspective, despite calls for change from the opposition, the private press and members of the public.[5] Some members of the disaffected public corrupted 'CRTV' to mean 'Centre de Re-établissement Total des Voleurs' or 'Confused Radio Television', and journalists of non-Beti origin who failed to take a critical distance from government and the CPDM were given Beti names, while the Beti journalists were simply referred to as *griots* (praise-singers). A unit was created in CRTV to monitor anti-government reports in the private media,[6] and administrative sanctions against critical broadcasters and against 'offensive' investigative journalism by the radio programme *Cameroon Calling*[7] were reinforced.

The reluctance of CRTV to adapt to the changing context provoked an open letter from two of its senior journalists, Zacharie Ngniman and Antoine-Marie Ngono, who complained of their incapacity to perform their journalistic functions freely and of CRTV's lack of credibility. Its failure to feel the pulse and to adapt accordingly was seen by some as a serious disservice to the Cameroonian public (Ngniman 1993: 24–8). The institution made the broadcasters more public relations officials than objective professional journalists. This open letter would also be a source of worry for the two journalists, whom the government could no longer trust as mouthpieces (Ngniman 1993: 48–64). At the CPDM party congress in June 1990, Antoine-Marie Ngono[8] was denied access to the Yaounde congress hall by a military captain, who told him: 'you are no longer to be trusted'. Hence Antoine-Marie Ngono's conviction that 'in Cameroon the state dislikes public service journalists taking the initiative.' This point was reiterated by Boh Herbert, a journalist who resigned from CRTV, when he wrote that journalists with the state-owned media 'tend to report news as the government orders that it be reported, not as it unfolds. Those who try the latter option are soon marginalised or simply thrown out of their jobs' (Boh 1997: 37).

To guarantee that things are done its way, government appoints to positions of responsibility not necessarily those with merit and professional experience, but those who are politically in tune with the authorities. Positions and coverage are assigned along ethnic lines, especially during periods of tension and political controversy (Ntemfac 1993). As Antoine-Marie Ngono observes,

> In CRTV it is the administrative logic that carries the day. The position belongs to the state which can do with a journalist whatever pleases the state. It isn't due to professional merit that one progresses, but rather to political and administrative considerations. That is what makes it possible for young, professionally inexperienced journalists to become editors-in-chief, etc. (Interview, September 1994)

This practice has, according to Bright Nsame,[9] given rise to an 'over-zealous quest for positions of responsibility and other favours' on the part of some CRTV journalists who may 'go to devilish ends and tell blatant intoxicating lies in favour of the regime in place'.[10] There is little communication between management and journalists, except by way of service notes, queries and sanctions (Tabi 1994: 84–102). What the government wants and succeeds in having most of the time are journalists 'confined to the role of praise-singers, churning out shallow press statements that make headline news while corruption, incompetence, economic mismanagement and human rights abuses go unchecked'.[11] The strong tendency, Blaise Tsangue affirms,[12] is for CRTV journalists 'to assume in an absolute manner the role of defence lawyers for the government or regime.'

At times the struggle was not only between journalists, as it was not uncommon to find non-journalists presenting radio and television programmes and even reading news. This is what we learn from Albert Mbida, an insider, in a reply on the FM 94 news programme *Tintamarre*, on 14 February 1993, to Florence Njilie, a typist with CRTV, whom he claimed called him 'colleague' and accused him of taking a bribe from the minister of commerce and industry, Patrice Mandeng Ambassa:

> CRTV is this rare station, about the only one in the world, whose waves and screens are open to people who know nothing about the business. You know as well as I do that not less than three typists present radio and TV programmes, that script writers, producers, speakerines, copyright clerks and translators present radio and television programmes and even read news. And I almost forgot there are even archives and make-up girls and disc-jockeys and guitar boys who present programmes at CRTV.[13]

Despite eventual and increasing claims of having opened up, CRTV remains largely an instrument of selective communication;[14] filtering through mostly what it sees as good and safe for the government. The institution has continued to disseminate the views and values of government and its allies to the detriment of all those who think and see differently. CRTV has consistently worked to exclude alternative voices, while consolidating the position of government and its supporters. It has allowed access largely to those least likely to criticise the prevailing distribution of power, while doing everything to exclude the real opposition. Thus, for instance, following the 1992 presidential elections, when a state of emergency was declared in Bamenda and the SDF leader placed under house arrest, various allegations were made by CRTV against John Fru Ndi, yet he was not given a single chance to defend himself or to express his own views.[15] The minister of information and culture, Augustin Kontchou Kuoumegni, preferred to continue with his monologues on CRTV and *Cameroon Tribune*, rather than take up a challenge by the SDF campaign manager, Bernard Muna:

> to a live debate on the television and radio which you so effectively control and manipulate. You bring all your proof and I shall bring mine. Let us convince the Cameroonian people who the liars, the cheats and the frauds are in this ongoing democratic process. I call the entire Cameroonian people to bear witness, if you refuse this live debate, to the fact that all you have done so far is to lie to them and manipulate the media, to deceive the people and that the government which you claim to represent has never been honest nor fair to the people and that this whole Electoral

Procedure has been an exercise aimed at maintaining yourselves in power to serve interests other than that of the Cameroonian people. Mr Minister, I await your reply with impatience.[16]

In fact, after the controversial presidential elections, the minister of state for communication repeatedly featured on CRTV and in *Cameroon Tribune* 'to set the records straight' or to 'tell the truth', as the government was accused both nationally and internationally of rigging the elections, and criticised for its human rights record. On one such occasion (8 December 1992), he refuted claims made by the Archbishop of Bamenda, Monsignor Paul Verdzekov, in an interview with RFI on 6 December that 400 people were being held in inhumane conditions in Bamenda. The minister contested the figure, described the archbishop's statement as 'unfounded and irresponsible' and condemned the cleric's 'surprising silence on the atrocities committed in Bamenda following the proclamation of the Presidential election results'.

The final report by the American National Democratic Institute (NDI), one of the international observers of the October 1992 presidential elections, contained a section on media access and news coverage of the campaigns. As an outsider view, the NDI report was quite critical of CRTV election coverage of opposition parties. Although each of the six candidates was allocated a daily share of 120 minutes on television and 60 minutes on radio, the NDI noticed irregularities. Apart from the fact that the lion's share of airtime went to President Biya, there were other problems, which included late schedules and outright censorship of opposition broadcasts. The following is an excerpt of the report on the media:[17]

On October 2, CRTV denied airtime for a videotaped segment prepared for *Expression Directe* by the campaign of candidate Jean-Jacques Ekindi. Authorities stated that they rejected the Ekindi segment because it contained 'vociferous attacks' against the CPDM and 'insulting and defamatory words against Paul Biya.' They maintained that their action was consistent with the rules governing party access to state media. After review, though, the National Communication Board overruled the CRTV decision, and Ekindi's tape was shown on October 7. Nevertheless, Ekindi's broadcasts for October 9 and 10 were banned without notice or explanation. The opposition cited the Ekindi incident as evidence that the government was not committed to the principle of equal access to the state-controlled broadcast media.

As part of its evaluation of television news coverage, NDI timed the amount of coverage accorded to candidates from different political parties on October 7. On that day, the government received 142 minutes of news coverage as opposed to 12 minutes for the entire opposition. Similarly, U.S. embassy personnel documented that, for the first week of the campaign, September 26 to October 3, the ruling party received 346 minutes of coverage. During the same period, all opposition parties combined received coverage totalling 124.5 minutes. (IDI 1993: 31–2)

NDI's report was dismissed in its interim version by the minister of communication, who described it at a CRTV press conference as 'an intellectual scandal, illegal, unfounded and not ... objective' and insisted that 'Cameroon has nothing to learn from anybody as far as democracy is concerned' (Ministry of Communication 1993: 256–71). A subsequent study by Boh Herbert and André Parfait Bell, executive board members of the Union of Cameroon Journalists (UCJ), confirmed that despite its editorial policy of impartiality and equity in coverage during elections, CRTV was always biased in favour of the CPDM at the end of the day. Referring in particular to the legislative elections of 17 May 1997, in which forty-six political parties took part, they noted that CPDM, the ruling party, was covered for a total of '2 hours, 1 minute, 51 seconds, being 64.96% of the total air time as against 13 minutes, 52 seconds for the SDF (7.1% of total air time) and 13 minutes, 4 seconds (6.9% of total air time) for the UNDP' (Boh 1997: 92–103).

Luke Ananga, editor-in-chief of television news and CRTV deputy director for information, tried to justify the fact that CRTV was serving and should indeed continue to serve as government mouthpiece, popular disenchantment notwithstanding. He argued that 'CRTV is an instrument of work which is given to an elected government to use to inform the people of this country.' He said that at 'CRTV, the editorial policy which was drawn up in a one-party system hasn't changed, and therefore the vast majority of CRTV journalists, especially those who belong to hierarchy, still work very closely within that old-fashioned editorial policy.... And so that makes the journalist's job ... extremely difficult' (Nyamnjoh 1996b: 37).

To conclude this section on CRTV and the democratic process, it is important to note that CRTV is seen as a government mouthpiece not only by the audience, the opposition parties and the private press, but also by CRTV journalists themselves, some of whom are in key positions of responsibility within the institution. But recognising the fact has not necessarily led to a conscious, concerted effort on the part of CRTV journalists to distance themselves from such subsidiary journalism. As a mouthpiece for government, CRTV has played an essentially public relations role, rather than the role of neutral mediator in the democratic process.

CRTV and anglophone journalism of liberation

If CRTV as an institution has preferred to maintain its traditional role as government's public relations institution, some of its journalists, anglophones mainly, have resisted this tendency. However, in turn, they have been guilty of PR journalism in favour of the opposition or the anglophone cause. For this reason, and also because of the important contribution made by anglophones to the current democratic process (Konings and Nyamnjoh 1997, 2003; Jua 2003; Ngenge 2003), the status of anglophone journalism in CRTV is worthy of investigation.

The anglophone journalists in the official media have, in general, tended to distance themselves from the sort of pro-establishment journalism defined by government and largely taken for granted by their francophone colleagues. The history of turbulence in the official media is principally the history of government's attempt to muzzle the anglophone journalists, most of whom have refused to be co-opted by 'the Francophone mentality of deifying the leader', who is seen as 'always right even in his swimsuit' ('le chef a toujours raison, même en caleçon de bain').[18] The launching of the SDF in May 1990 led to much witch-hunting against the anglophone journalists in CRTV, whom management identified with the new ('illegal') party.

Cameroon Post[19] reports on a meeting the minister of information and culture held in the first week of June 1991 with CRTV journalists, during which the minister implicitly accused English language programmes of being sympathetic to the opposition. Specifically cited were *Luncheon Date* – later on modified drastically by order of the minister, *News Focus*, the 7.30 p.m. news and *Cameroon Calling*, from which Anembom Munjo, Wain Paul Ngam, Asonglefac Nkemleke and Julius Wamey were subsequently suspended.

The minister also attacked television news editor-in-chief Eric Chinje 'for reporting the resignation of CPDM Wouri Section President Jean Jacques Ekindi without announcing the non-resignation of Mifi Section President Joseph K. Tanyi'. The minister implied that this was part of the anglophone journalists' attempts to sabotage the CPDM government. The suspensions were interpreted by the journalists as 'part of a campaign launched by the Information and Culture Minister and CRTV General Manager Mendo Ze to stop the tide of anglophone journalists' objectivity on CRTV'.[20] The minister insisted on the necessity of CRTV journalists respecting the corporation's editorial policy, a euphemism for asking all journalists to see things the government's way.

In a 'confidential' letter to the general manager of CRTV, Prime Minister Sadou Hayatou is said[21] to have called for severe sanctions against anglophone journalists who were using the official media to 'try government'. The prime minister is reported to have accused, among others, *Cameroon Calling* and the *English News* of having 'more and more exhibited reckless abandon ... in their analyses which have of late seemed like an arraignment of government action'. In his letter he complained that 'newscasters on radio and television have tended to express their personal standpoints as if they were those of government.' He concluded by instructing the general manager to 'verify this situation and where necessary address a severe warning to such personnel who should not turn a public service into a private medium with a tendency to teleguide government action'.

While some anglophone journalists in the public media have accepted the role expected of them, others have opted either to leave the system entirely (e.g. Boh Herbert, Charlie Ndichia, Eric Chinje, Victor Epie Ngome, Orlando Bama, Larry Eyong-Echaw, Ben Bongang, Julius Wamey and Ntemfac Ofege), or to distance themselves from official rhetoric whenever they can (e.g. Ebssiy Ngum, Wain Paul Ngam and Asonglefac Nkemleke). According to *The*

Diasporan,[22] of the nearly 50 reporters and announcers who started or joined television in its first three years of existence, 27 (of whom 21 are anglophones) had by April 1994 'departed in bitterness and disillusionment to seek better climes'.

Many anglophone journalists in CRTV who rapidly distanced themselves from their role as government spokespersons or mouthpieces, following the launching of the SDF, rechannelled their energies in the service of the marginalised anglophone community. But using the official media to articulate societal problems and aspirations has met with stiff resistance from the authorities. The turbulent history of critical English language CRTV programmes such as *Cameroon Calling* (formerly *Cameroon Report*), *Minute by Minute* and *Luncheon Date* are sufficient testimony to government discomfort with anglophone critical-mindedness. Popular radio commentaries on politics and society such as *The Rambler* by Victor Epie Ngome, *Letter from the East* by Charly Ndi Chia, *Letter to Joshua* by Ntemfac Ofege, *Letter to Grandpa* by Asonglefac Nkemleke and *Reflections* by Peter Essoka, show how relentless anglophone journalists have been in their quest for alternative avenues as CRTV management blocks or interferes with established programmes.

CRTV management has often silenced or dissipated criticism through the disciplinary transfer of the critical journalists involved. Vociferous and critical newscasters like Julius Wamey have been moved from the newsroom, some like Anembom Munju and Larry Eyong Echaw have been kept away from the microphone, while others like Sam Nuvala Fonkem and Angela Tabe have been re-called to the Ministry for administrative functions. Following the controversial edition of *Cameroon Calling* on multiparty democracy of 6 May 1990, the CRTV authorities ordered the transfer of Ntemfac Ofege and Boh Herbert away from Yaounde, after they had refused to sign an apology letter addressed to the general manager from their colleagues after detention. Instead of going along with this decree, the two preferred to resign from CRTV. As political tensions increased in Bamenda, especially after the launching of the SDF, the governor of the North West province banned the rebroadcast in the local radio of *Cameroon Calling*, claiming that the programme 'incited the population to violence and revolt'.[23]

In June 1992, members of the *Cameroon Calling* production team (Ben Bongang, Zac Angafor and Akwanka Joe Ndifor), among others, were appointed and transferred in various capacities to CRTV provincial stations. It was a move seen by those concerned as a calculated attempt by government to 'kill' a programme that has never ceased to embarrass it. The deputy general manager accused the crew of *Cameroon Calling* of not heeding the numerous warnings from the hierarchy, by continuing to use the programme 'to put the government on trial'. He accused some of the journalists of not hesitating to question the integrity of the highest authorities of the state, but often without any proof to back their allegations. Others, he said, did not hesitate to incite the population to revolt, and by so doing were endangering national unity. He called on them to understand that CRTV is a public utility and a privileged instrument for the propagation of the activities of government.

To 'put an end to this laxity injurious to state action and to the stability of institutions', the Deputy General Manager prescribed, *inter alia*, that *Cameroon Calling* be henceforth taped and no longer presented live, as was the case before then. The taped programme must be submitted for the critical appreciation of either the director of information, his deputy or the editor-in-chief for features. 'The certified approval of one of these authorities is necessary before the programme can be broadcast.' Finally, the above-named gatekeepers were expected to give a weekly report on the effective implementation of this prescription.

On 2 February 1994, the General Manager of CRTV took decision No. 00012 following 'instructions from above', to send Tamfu Hanson Ghandi, Metuge Alfred Sone and Viban Napoleon Bongadzem to the Ministry of Communication. The crime of these journalists was non-respect for CRTV's editorial policy, which Boh describes as having 'an editorial logic that defies all logic' (Boh 1997: 38).

According to Philip Ndi,[24] anglophone interests are marginalised in CRTV because 'there is nobody who actually represents the anglophones at CRTV', and 'decisions are taken arbitrarily and nobody raises an eyebrow'. He argues that 'many decisions are taken not only to frustrate anglophone journalists but to minimise and discredit their efforts.' This marginalisation is true of other spheres of life and activity as well, primarily not because there are no anglophones in positions of decision-making, but rather because those in such positions have failed to use these to empower their anglophone community (Ewumbue-Monono 2000).

As an institution, CRTV has seldom been comfortable reporting the facts about any anglophone movement, initiative or programme of action. An example of CRTV's journalism in this connection is that of the 3 p.m. radio news of Wednesday 27 April 1994 concerning the second All Anglophone Conference (AAC II). An announcement was read to the effect that the AAC II scheduled to be held in Bamenda from 29 April to 1 May had been postponed by the convenors. It was purported to have been signed by Dr Simon Munzu, Dr Carlson Anyangwe and barrister Sam Ekontang Elad – a claim the three refuted. The AAC spokesman, Dr Simon Munzu, prepared a disclaimer for broadcast by CRTV, but this was rejected. CRTV was even unable to provide Dr Munzu with a copy of the announcement alleged to have been signed by him and his colleagues.[25]

Anglophones are of the consistent impression that CRTV is there not so much to respond to their aspirations, but rather to stifle initiative and their sense of identity. The decision to construct the FM transmitter for the South West province in Douala instead of Buea was criticised by anglophone interest groups (e.g. SWELA) and by the media, and taken as another proof of government's bad faith towards anglophones. On a visit to CRTV Buea on Tuesday 16 November 1993, the general manager of CRTV explained that the choice of Douala was purely a technical one made by Japanese technicians, and not political as rumoured. According to the general manager, the Japanese engineers who did the studies during the 'ghost towns' period in 1991 had combed the South West province thoroughly and found its mountainous terrain a disadvantage. However, the anglophone press and opinion leaders still felt that the decision to construct the transmitter in Douala was a political one. They considered that the authorities were so concerned with the oil in Limbe that they feared what might happen if Buea, given the current trend of sentiments among critical anglophone leaders and public, were to be cut off from the rest of Cameroon and made the capital of a seceding West or Southern Cameroon.

Indeed, anglophones are so suspicious of government and its designs that their first instinct is always to disbelieve that the government can act in good faith. In addition, anglophones generally tend to 'see Francophones as fundamentally fraudulent, superficial and given to bending rules: cheating at exams, jumping queues, rigging elections' (Victor Epie Ngome quoted in Atanga 1994: 126). Thus, when Bamenda went without television signals from 19 September 1993 to 24 March 1994, because of a blown tube at the relay centre, there was talk of deliberate victimisation of Bamenda by government. Despite expert reports that the failure had been purely technical, the public was not convinced. They insisted that in other places which had suffered similar blackouts (Sangmelima, Ebolowa and Kousseri) their situation had been corrected within two weeks.

To anglophones, it has seemed clear from the content and language of programmes that television is preponderantly for francophones. French is the dominant language, and French interests seem not only more important than English interests but are even superior to Cameroonian concerns and priorities.[26] Newscasts on CRTV can be, and indeed regularly are, shifted from their normal time slots in order to make way for the transmission of French football encounters. Seldom has any English league match been retransmitted in a similar manner, and it is not often that local matches or Cameroon's own international encounters get televised.

Thus faced with such resistance, critical anglophone journalists in the official media have, thanks to the December 1990 communication law, used the English-language private newspapers, some of them under pen names, to insert anglophone problems, concerns and aspirations onto the national political, cultural and economic agendas. In one such case, Julius Wamey created and ran a column, 'The Postman', in Cameroon Post, and later on published a collection of his pieces in a book titled Where Heroes Go to Die. Sam Nuvala Fonkem is a well-known contributor to anglophone papers and magazines, and his pieces are usually centred around the predicaments of the anglophone community. When The Rambler ceased to exist on CRTV, Victor Epie Ngome created a paper, which he named after it, and continued with the same concerns for as long as it lasted. Ntemfac Ofege has served as editor of Cameroon Post, and created Today since his resignation from CRTV. Together with Boh Herbert and Charlie Ndichia, he created and published *Post Watch*. Boh Herbert, thanks to his mastery of French, became a key contributor to *Challenge Hebdo* and *La Nouvelle Expression*, which for a brief period he translated and published in English under the title *The New Expression*.

Together with their counterparts in the critical English-language press, the liberation journalists of the official media are eager to expose the contradictions and inconsistencies in the policies and actions of the Cameroonian leadership. They argue that until government starts addressing the problems of the anglophone minority, it will remain an obstacle to the country's economic progress and social justice. They criticise the rigid suppression by government of contending social forces, especially those of anglophone origin. They blame most of Cameroon's current socio-political and economic crises on the lack of accountability of successive francophone-dominated governments (Konings and Nyamnjoh 1997, 2003; Jua 2003; Ngenge 2003). They identify with and are proud of the achievements of the Anglo-Saxon culture worldwide. The Anglo-Saxon culture 'has been tested and its validity adequately proved', and all anglophones must take advantage of this identity, 'rather than seeking to be Francophones only to wind up ridiculous cultural mulattoes to be jeered at and patronised'[27] or to be used as gatekeepers or watchdogs to keep off their fellow anglophones while not exactly being part of the action themselves.

The current anglophone journalism of liberation is one of anger and disillusionment. The liberation journalists approach their news gathering with a set of attitudes and opinions which have often biased their news reporting in favour of the anglophone community and the myth of anglophone superiority. The ability of liberation journalists to give all sides of the story, to avoid biased language, comment and opinion in their news stories and reports, has been crippled by the need to present the anglophones as a righteous community in a country turned into a Sodom or a Gomorrah by sensuous, irresponsible squandering and degenerate francophones.

Much as the anglophone community would like its journalists to see things their way, it is in the interest of both the journalists and the community to face up to reality. For social truth is a matter of consensus between competing views, especially in a plural context like Cameroon where perspective is contingent on one's cultural, regional, ethnic and political standpoint. But it also implies that the francophone community and media are ready to make concessions towards coexistence and national integration, which so far has been confined to official rhetoric, while in practice it is fashionable to fan the flames of dichotomies (Chapter 8).

Concluding remarks on CRTV

Although the pro-democracy clamours of the 1990s have weakened state monopoly of radio and television in many an African country, Cameroon is still lagging behind in terms of the liberalisation of broadcasting. In December 1990, competition in broadcasting was legalised in principle, but government vacillated for ten years in setting the criteria for obtaining a franchise,[28] even though the Ministry of Communication had already received, years earlier, no fewer than thirty applications (Boh 1997: 33). As government delayed making known the rules of the game for private broadcasting, it accepted in 1997 a Canadian government offer to create five rural radio stations in Kembong, Oku, Foutouni, Lolodorf and Mouturewa – on condition that they would 'refrain from including any political programming in their broadcasts' (Boh, 1997: 46). A Catholic priest, in apparent defiance of government's delay tactics, set up an FM studio – Radio Lumière – for the broadcast of programmes from Radio Vatican. As did Institut Samba, which set up Radio Reine without authorisation. There was also the proliferation of satellite dishes on rooftops to capture international entertainment television for the elite few who could afford to subscribe to DSTV through Multi-choice South Africa or Canal Horizon from France. A National Communications Council (NCC), provided for in the law, was created and became operational in February 1992. But as a consultative body set up by government, the NCC has so far failed to take any initiatives. In spite of the fact that members are elected, the appointment of the key officials by government has tended to check its desire to be comfortably independent. Anyway, with consultative powers only, it cannot oblige government to implement any of its decisions, and is regularly bypassed by the minister of communication to hassle the few private broadcasters that have managed to operate despite the odds.

Government thus appears to have singled out the broadcasting media to be watched at close range. This is also because it sees radio and television as the most 'mass' of all the media and as capable of hypodermic effects, the assumption being that a government's political fortunes depend very much on how well it has harnessed the broadcast media. And to show just how important the underfunded and overstretched broadcast media are, 'Official ceremonies are very often delayed several hours, if need be, just waiting for the always late television crew to arrive' (Boh 1997: 37). Elections can be won or lost not by the ballot, but by the power to control access to radio and television while keeping the private press in check.

The government not only monopolises broadcasting, it has made broadcasters part of the civil service. This has meant that civil servants or politicians with little or no knowledge about the media are often charged with overseeing the way radio and television are operated. Professional broadcasters become subservient to these bureaucrats, who determine appointments, salary scales and promotions, and who are expected to approve every initiative beforehand, no matter how technical or urgent. This is unduly harmful to creativity and frustrating to talented broadcasters, who are likely to give up entirely, or to become absorbed by the bureaucratic machinery. There is a chronic lack of job satisfaction that has pushed some journalists either to quit or to 'seek job satisfaction by stringing for other less prestigious but professionally more satisfying jobs in local private newspapers or foreign radio and television stations' (Boh 1997: 38).

Any claims that media avenues have opened up remain suspicious. The situation, however, is certainly less blatantly manipulative at present than before 1997 when the SDF had no parliamentary representation. Frozen attitudes are thawing, and the state media are as likely to report John Fru Ndi and the SDF today as they are to grant interviews and issue press releases to the state media. That notwithstanding, the fact that the government continues, even in 2004, to intimidate and censor private broadcasters further drives critical political voices into clandestinity and forces upon them a sterile menu of mostly imported entertainment and sport.[29] As recently as July 2000, one could hear Professor Gervais Mendo Ze, who has been general manager of CRTV for over fourteen years and has masterminded most of the manipulation that has kept President Biya recycling mediocrity and perfecting the insensitivities of illegitimate power, boasting that his CRTV journalists were *Les Lions Indomptables de l'audio-visuel*. At the 1992 presidential elections, Paul Biya had presented himself as *l'homme Lion*, imbued with the power, courage and intention of protecting Cameroon from 'les marchands d'illusions', of whom John Fru Ndi and his SDF were presented as champions by the CRTV. In taxis, market places, bars, chicken parlours and elsewhere, Biya's message was seen by ordinary people as a corruption of reality. He was a lion no doubt, but his mission was not to save. Rather, he was asking for five more years to accomplish his devastation of Cameroon and Cameroonians. Such alternative interpretations never made their way onto CRTV, not even through the other presidential candidates whose campaign broadcasts were heavily monitored and censored. Jean-Jacque Ekindi, for example, as foremost *chasseur du Lion*, would have his trenchant campaign counter-offensives banned by CRTV management. Cameroon, in short, had space only for three indomitable lions: President Biya, the CRTV and the national football team, whose victories and fame the president and CRTV caricatured through manipulation and corruption.

This guarantees that the indomitable lion of politics shall appropriate the victories and fame of the indomitable lions of football thanks to facilitation and manipulation by the indomitable lion of broadcasting. It makes it possible for government to feed the people not with the facts but with the options only, so that they cannot and never should think for themselves. Truth, the indomitable lion of politics (Biya) has never tired of affirming, comes from above and rumour from below (*la vérité vient d'en haut, la rumeur vient d'en bas*).

By regularly feeding the public with falsehood and denying the opposition forces the opportunity to demonstrate otherwise, the CPDM government has attempted for over a decade to persuade the public that it should take its world of appearances as the true reality. There is neither corruption nor embezzlement – repeated reports by Transparency International and also by nationals notwithstanding. State television portrays only a selfless effort at nation-building by a benevolent President Biya, his ministers, directors and bureaucrats. Tribalism, nepotism and inequalities do not exist, only national unity, balanced regional development and the equitable distribution of the 'national cake'. Documented evidence to the contrary is simply brushed aside as coming from 'people of bad faith' who are blind to the merits and achievements of 'the indomitable Lion' of politics who has made Cameroon the pride of Africa.

As the CPDM government vacillates with face-powder democracy, ordinary people are gradually drained of interest and hope, and change for the better becomes like endlessly waiting for a birth. The sentiment was captured perfectly by Les Maxtones du Littoral in their celebrated tune 'Doleibe (10f) la suite de l'affaire', in which a woman pregnant from a casual fling after a grossly underpaid night out with a deceitful client finds herself waiting for over twenty-four months to have her baby. The doctor, whose responsibility it is to reassure, is impatient with the woman's impatience: 'il faut attendre. Tu es pressée pour aller où?' Hence the cry of desperation: 'on attend l'enfant l'enfant ne viens pas'. Taken advantage of by President Biya and his callous indifference to cries of betterment from ordinary folks, Cameroon has become like a woman waiting indefinitely to give birth to democracy. And like in 'Doleibe', the child might well be bald and infested with jiggers by the time it is born (Nyamnjoh and Fokwang 2003: 191–200).

If CRTV and its journalists are to make an active and positive contribution to democratisation, their focus must be on the common denominators and not on what puts Cameroonians asunder. Unless they can detach themselves from their own values and beliefs by seeking to report facts with utmost fairness and balance, they will continue to misrepresent and distort the very democracy they purport to promote.

Cameroon Tribune, SOPECAM and the Democratic Process

The reaction of *Cameroon Tribune*, the official newspaper, to increasing demands for pluralism and democratisation has been similar to that of CRTV. Reference has already been made to the false allegations the paper published against John Fru Ndi upon the launching of the SDF, pushing the latter to sue for libel. However, public dissatisfaction with the paper's uncritical support of government and the CPDM was evidenced by a significant drop in sales, following the new communication law and the subsequent proliferation of private newspapers critical of government. Writing in May 1991, Philippe Gaillard of *Jeune Afrique Plus*[30] noted that sales of the French-language edition of *Cameroon Tribune*, which prior to the reintroduction of multi-party politics in 1990 used to be more than 60,000 copies a day, had fallen to less than 20,000. As for the English-language edition, readership dropped to less than 2,000. Among certain sections of the public, *Cameroon Tribune* was nicknamed 'Pravda', owing not only to its role as the government's voice but also for the fact that 'a medallion featuring the head of state accompanied by a "thought for the day"' was published daily on the top right- or left-hand corner of its front page 'in an effort to illustrate the omnipresence of the *commandement* in the furthest corners of daily life' (Mbembe 1992: 18–19, 2001: 121). The CPDM and the presidency have pushed to the fore two academics, Augustin Kontchou Kuoumegni (a professor of law) and Jacques Fame Ndongo (a practitioner of semiotics and director of the state school of journalism, ESSTIC), who played a key role in the CPDM–government communication strategy. The former became minister of state for communications following the 1992 elections, a post he held until 1998 when he was made minister of state for foreign affairs. For his part, Jacques Fame Ndongo served as communication adviser and strategist for the CPDM party and government. Much of the government's communication theory and practice was largely credited to this man (Takougang and Krieger 1998: 118–19), who in 1999 was finally rewarded with the Ministry of Communication after a brief period as rector of University of Yaounde I.

As a printing and publishing house, the government-controlled SOPECAM (publisher of the official paper) chose to stay out of business and risk closure as a result of financial difficulties, rather than allow for free competition between the opposition and the pro-government press. Under the instigation of the Minister of

Information and Culture, SOPECAM in 1991 set up a unit to scrutinise the critical private newspapers before deciding whether to print them. Questioned on this by journalists of the private press, the minister declared: 'You are not at all compelled to bring your newspapers for printing at SOPECAM. You bring them there if it serves your interest.'[31] At this time SOPECAM was virtually a monopoly, as others were yet to enter the market.

Another mechanism of control used by SOPECAM was to delay printing of, or not print at all, the private papers for an alleged want of materials. During the Yaounde plan of action in July 1991, many opposition papers were not printed. The reason given by SOPECAM was that the blockade imposed on Douala seaport by the 'ghost towns' had made it difficult for them to import the material necessary for printing. But the pro-government *Cameroon Tribune* and *Le Patriote*, for example, continued to be printed.

According to *La Messagère*,[32] SOPECAM, using paper shortage as the excuse, proposed that the French edition of *Le Messager* 'cut down its print run from 80,000 copies to 10,000 … while the English Edition which was beginning to rise towards a 30,000 print run was ordered down to 5,000'. *Le Messager* retorted by offering to buy its newsprint from abroad.

However, following devaluation in January 1994 and given the worsening economic crisis, the job of SOPECAM and the other censors in MINAT was made easier as the price of newsprint skyrocketed, forcing Rotoprint, in February 1995, to increase the cost of printing, thereby forcing most newspapers out of circulation.

All that SOPECAM did the papers in question perceived as censorship. They decided to look elsewhere to print their papers, and only those without a choice stayed on. In reaction, Benjamin Zebaze, publisher of *Challenge Hebdo*, set up a private printing house, Rotoprint, at Bonaberi in Douala. In the quest for alternatives, other papers (e.g. *Cameroon Post*, *Post Watch*, *The Herald*, *Cameroon Life* and *Times and Life*) went across to Nigeria, and when they ran into difficulties printing in Nigeria most of them reverted to Rotoprint. The government, which must have felt defeated, sent troops in May 1992 to besiege Rotoprint, making printing difficult. This siege clearly reached such an intensity during the time preceding and shortly after the October

1992 presidential elections that even the owner of Rotoprint, Zebaze of *Challenge Hebdo*, was forced to start printing in Nigeria as well. The witch-hunt by SOPECAM against the critical private press put SOPECAM in dire financial straits. From 1991 to 1994, SOPECAM workers had to go on strike repeatedly before their salaries were paid. The 'serious financial crisis and other difficulties' of SOPECAM were admitted by its general manager during its 4th extraordinary Board of Governors' meeting on 26 August 1992.[33] During the meeting, the board chairman recommended cuts in the workforce and further reductions in order 'to rescue the company from collapse'.[34] The massive lay-offs that followed were a further sign of the company's weakened financial position. *International News Hebdo* had been taken to court and sanctioned in 1991 for predicting this financial crisis.[35]

Cameroon Tribune and SOPECAM behaved no differently towards independent-minded journalists than has CRTV. To supplement the efforts of CRTV and *Cameroon Tribune* in their fight against the SDF and other opposition forces, the CPDM government has often co-opted local papers and wooed the foreign press for favourable coverage. When the foreign media run 'favourable' stories, usually paid for from public coffers, these are amplified locally by the official media. According to Professor Titus Edzoa, a very close collaborator of Biya who resigned on 20 April 1997 after fifteen years in government and who is currently in prison for daring to do so, President Biya paid *Jeune Afrique Economie* FCFA 1.5 billion, 'pour défendre les intérêts du Cameroun dans un dossier de liquidation de banque à l'extérieur' (to protect the interests of Cameroon abroad in a Bank liquidation file).[36] The Paris-based Cameroonian publisher of *Jeune Afrique Economie*, Blaise Pascal Tallah, who in the early 1990s identified strongly with pro-democracy forces in Cameroon and the continent, has been severely criticised for his about-face on the need to criticise repression in favour of the reactionary CPDM party and government, and accused by some of the local papers of practising mercenary journalism in the service of dictatorship. *Jeune Afrique Economie*'s shoddy journalism, implicating the SDF and the SCNC with the attempted revolt in the North West province, caused further public indignation and earned it rejection among critical anglophones and SDF supporters (Konings and Nyamnjoh 2003: 104).

Their pro-establishment zeal notwithstanding, *Cameroon Tribune*'s and SOPECAM's serious financial problems have compounded the difficulties of news gathering and news production and made the paper even less credible in its current bilingual edition. The lack of job security for *Cameroon Tribune* journalists has negatively affected professionalism as they seek to make ends meet through unprofessional practices, usually referred to in a derogatory manner as *le journalisme de Gombo* (Tueno Tagne 1996). It is a phenomenon so common, and perceived by journalists to be so normal, that they tend to speak of their source increasingly as *mon gombo personnel* and of their field recording equipment as *gombophone*. Thanks to brown envelopes, individual journalists are able to get by while the already heavily indebted public media, as institutions, are plunged further into the red (Boh 1997: 147–8).

The above account leaves little doubt that the government has been firmly in control of the state-owned broadcast and print media, and that it has used these institutions mainly for its public relations, while doing all it could to filter critique and stifle opposition. The prospect that this opposition could turn to the private print media for a voice had made the government reluctant to liberalise the laws regulating the practice of journalism. Chapter 5 discusses government's cosmetic attempts at reforming media law, as well as the consequences of its selective application of administrative censorship on the critical private press.

Notes

1. Interview with Shasha E. Ndimbie, 25 February 1988.
2. English edition, 10 July 1990.
3. For more on the trial, see Paddy Mbawa's 'blow-by-blow account' in *Cameroon Post*, 7 May 1990.
4. John Fru Ndi, dissatisfied with the way *Cameroon Tribune*, in particular, had reported and commented on the events, was later to file a libel suit against the paper, SOPECAM and three others, and to claim FCFA 400 million.
5. See *Cameroon Post*, 27 February 1991. An opinion poll dubbed 'Concours de Griots', which was aimed at establishing the degree of unpopularity of official media journalists, was conducted by *Galaxie* among its readers (12 March 1991).

6. See *Le Messager*, 5 February 1991, for details.

7. See 'CRTV and anglophone journalism of liberation' below.

8. Interview, 30 September 1994, Douala.

9. *Cameroon Post*, 20 October 1993.

10. The most zealous supporters of the regime, it has been observed, are journalists of the same Beti origin as president Biya and the general manager of CRTV, Professor Gervais Mendo Ze (see *Cameroon Post*, 9 March 1994, for the case of Alain Belibi and Jean-Marie Nka'a).

11. *Le Messager*, Special Edition, 25 April 1991.

12. *Le Messager*, 30 April 1992

13. Albert Mbida, *Cameroon Post*, 23 February 1993.

14. When CRTV does not decide simply to stay mute, its coverage of certain national issues is questionable and consistently in favour of the government (Eone 1994: 12–14). The CRTV has always interpreted events as if the government is always right.

15. Without access to radio and television, John Fru Ndi had to content himself with the private press and foreign media to disseminate his reaction to the Supreme Court decision to declare Paul Biya winner of the elections. His self-proclamation as president-elect in Bamenda on 21 October 1992 (see *L'Expression*, 22 October 1992) would certainly have had a greater effect had it been carried on CRTV, which the government used to dismiss the self-proclamation as 'anti-democratic, grave, anti-national, disgraceful, irresponsible', and to warn that the government 'will take all the necessary steps this situation calls for' (see also *Cameroon Tribune*, 22 October 1992).

16. Bernard Muna, communiqué of 20 October 1992.

17. See *Cameroon Post*, 3 May 1993, for more excerpts.

18. See Asonglefac Nkemleke, SCNCForum@egroups.com, 27 April 2000, on 'Anglophone Appointees and the Anglophone Problem'.

19. *Cameroon Post*, 6 June 1991.

20. Ibid.

21. See *Cameroon Post*, 30 July 1991.

22. 14 April 1995.

23. See *The Herald*, 3 January 1994.

24. *The Herald*, 13 January 1993.

25. For more, see *Cameroon Post*, 29 April 1994.

26. Eric Chinje recalls (see *The Diasporan*, 14 April 1995) that during his years as editor-in-chief for television news, there was a strong 'Francophone Lobby', the membership of which ranged from a team of police investigators 'demanding to know why there was so much English on television', to the French ambassador who claimed that Eric Chinje was not a friend of France ('vous n'êtes pas un ami de la France') because anglophones on television 'were outperforming the francophones'.

27. *Cameroon Post*, 27 May 1991.

28. See Prime Minister's Decree No. 2000/158, 3 April 2000.

29. For the censor of 'Magic FM', 'Freedom FM' and 'Veritas' in 2003, see www.cpj.org/cases03/africa_cases03/cameroon.html; for more, see www.rsf.org/article.php3?id_article=8926.
30. May–June 1991.
31. See *Cameroon Tribune*, 13 February 1991, for full text of the minister's reaction to accusations of censorship at SOPECAM.
32. 2 September 1991.
33. See *Cameroon Tribune*, 28 August 1992.
34. For more on SOPECAM, its problems and its role as censor, see *La Vision*, 28 November 1991; *La Messagère*, 17 March 1993; and *Cameroon Tribune*, 28 August 1992.
35. See *Cameroon Tribune*, 28 May 1991, for a report of the court case between SOPECAM and *International News Hebdo*.
36. Interview granted *L'Expression*, 5 May 1997.

5

The Legal Framework
and the Private Press

One of the greatest threats to media freedom in Africa has been the reluctance on the part of most governments to liberalise press laws. Even where there was such liberalisation in principle, government tended to introduce, by underhand or roundabout ways, measures and practices that effectively curtailed press freedom. Chapter 1 provided a general overview of press laws and media control in Africa. The current chapter takes the Cameroon experience as one case study that illustrates the general theme. It examines the legal framework within which the private press operates. It takes a critical look at the law and how government has employed it in a selective manner in order to stifle a private press it perceives as threatening. Once again we note how reactionary states and governments have chosen to pay lip service to liberal democracy, while doing the opposite in practice.

Press Control under the Colonial and One-Party State

Although Cameroon was one of a limited number of West African countries to have developed a press before independence, little subsequent support for it ensued. Instead, increased censorship and political repression, together with financial problems, made it extremely difficult for the press to operate (Bayart 1973). Starting during colonialism and continuing under Ahidjo, severe press censorship remained a daily reality in Cameroon despite the positive rhetoric of the postcolonial leadership. Under President Biya before 1990, despite the political change of 1982, and the discourses proclaiming greater openness, few reforms took place. Prominent among the obstacles to press freedom were the press laws of 1959 and 1966. This section takes a brief look at the development and regulation of the press prior to 1990.

The history of Cameroon's press begins with the German occupation of the territory. Among the very first papers to be created was *Elolombe ya kamerun* ('The Cameroon Sun'), a mission paper. The early papers were published both in German and in a few of the local languages (Mytton 1983: 42). Under France, heavy censorship and repression proved stifling, and it might appear contradictory to refer to the period between 1955 and 1958 as 'the golden age' of the press in Cameroon. But it should be recalled that this was the period when increased pressure for independence forced France to issue the *Loi Cadre* and to tolerate a certain amount of freedom of expression despite itself.

Brief though it was, this period was actually the closest Cameroon came to having press freedom and plurality of views before 1990. In French Cameroon, during the years of nationalism and struggles for independence, a number of privately owned papers arose to serve as the mouthpieces of the nationalists. More out of sheer pressure than the desire to open up, the colonial authorities briefly allowed the publication of a plethora of papers between 1955 and 1958. By 1959 there were seventy-one publications in French Cameroon alone, because almost every militant group wanted a propaganda machine of some sort. The publications were usually very political, edited mostly by politicians, and in a majority of the cases the articles were written by an individual with specific political interests to defend. But they were very short-lived, partly because of financial difficulties and partly as a result of the colonial censorship. Thus while the pro-establishment *Presse du Cameroun* survived, the radical *La Voix du Peuple du Cameroun*, *L'Etoile*, *Lumière* and *La Vérité* of the UPC (Le Vine 1964: 148) were seriously affected. In July 1959 alone, six pro-UPC newspapers were suppressed, namely *L'Opinion au Cameroun*, *Kamerun mon Pays*, *Ma Patrie le Cameroun*, *La Nation Kamerunaise*, *le Travailleur Kamerunais* and *Le Paysan* (Le Vine 1964: 181–291).

In the English Southern Cameroon, on the other hand, the press was much slower in establishing itself. Throughout the colonial period the territory was devoid of indigenous newspapers. Books, periodicals, films and other vehicles of news and information were scarce. For most of the time, oral communication was the norm within or between different ethnic groups. But as an administrative part of the Nigerian Federation, Southern Cameroon did benefit from British and Nigerian newspapers. Prominent among these were the *Daily Express* and *The Times* of Britain, and the *Daily Times*, *Daily Express*, *Eastern Outlook* and *West African Pilot* of Nigeria. As it had no paper of its own, it was no surprise that coverage of Southern Cameroon throughout colonialism remained peripheral, 'haphazard and halfhearted' (Fonye 1973: 15–16).

The first newspapers in the region, *Cameroon Times* and *Cameroon Champion*, were both started in 1960 as an attempt by Southern Cameroonians to fill the information gap left by marginal coverage in the British and Nigerian press (Fonye 1973: 23–4; Tataw 1984: 26–30). To Fonye (1973) and Tataw (1984), *Cameroon Times* could not have been created at a more appropriate time, for it played a major role in the unification effort, especially as the Nigerian and British media waged a propaganda war against reunification with francophone Cameroon. Although Southern Cameroon did not have a press of its own during colonialism, it 'inherited a free press tradition' through its association with the Nigerian and British press (Fonye 1973; Tataw 1984; Nji 1985; Lukong 1987; Wongibe 1987).

Most of those who eventually started papers of their own in the region had either worked as vendors for British and Nigerian papers or studied abroad where they imbibed Anglo-Saxon press practices (Tataw 1984: 21–5). The consequence was that anglophone Cameroonian papers such as *Cameroon Times*, *Cameroon Champion*, *Cameroon Observer*, *Mirror*, *Cameroon Post*, *Iroko*, *New Standard*, *Newspot* and *Cameroon Telegraph* had more in common with the Nigerian Press (whose 1917 press law remained basically liberal in character despite a series of repeals in 1941, 1954 and 1957) than with the 'heavily censored' francophone Cameroon alternative (Tataw 1984: 70–85; Nji 1985: 35–6). On unification, anglophone Cameroon inherited the problems of francophone Cameroon, where censorship was perennial as Cameroon's first president attempted to crush the opposition within the francophone areas. The curfews that were imposed in guerrilla strongholds, together with progressive control of the press, encroached into the 'democratic state of West Cameroon and put an end to the growth of a free press and freedom of expression' (Nji 1985: 36). Tataw refers to the repression as 'the last nail in the coffin of press freedom' in anglophone Cameroon (1984: 14–15).

An independent francophone Cameroon had a rich colonial past to draw inspiration for its repressive stance towards a free press. For example, a highly repressive version of the October 1923 decree regulating the press in France was applied in Cameroon (Bayart 1973: 50–51). On 1 October 1936 the colonial administration issued a ministerial order 'prohibiting the circulation of magical pamphlets, soothsaying or occultism in traditional languages', all as defined by the French, and on 24 June 1939 a decree suppressing 'the distribution and circulation of tracts of foreign origin' was passed (Nji 1985: 80). Further measures were taken to check against the rising spirit of nationalism. These included intensifying the campaign against publications in the national languages, which the French found difficult to read and therefore hard to monitor effectively.

The main languages of publication remained French and English, even after independence and despite the rhetoric on the need to restore the Cameroonian cultural personality. A few periodicals appeared in Boulou and in a couple of other languages among the plethora of national languages, but that was about all. The early initiative to publish in the local languages would have saved Cameroon from future headaches, had it been encouraged. The consequence is that today the press operates almost entirely in French and English and, therefore, serves mostly the urban-centred minority that can read and write these elitist languages.

In a study commissioned by Unesco, Gahungu (1981) reiterates the linguistic constraints on the development of a press capable of serving the majority of Cameroonians. As a multilingual society with over two hundred national languages, there is the problem of which of these languages to adopt for a national press. The problem is aggravated by religious and cultural differences within the population. But the problem is not so much of a dilemma than the fact that even fewer people can read and write in any of the national languages. It was never in France's cultural interest to encourage the teaching of any other language but French (Fonlon 1964; Mbassi-Manga 1964; Essang 1978).

Ahidjo's tight control of the press started in 1959 when he was Prime Minister of the colonial territory to which France had just granted a measure of autonomy. In that year parliament passed Law No. 59–35 of 27 May 1959, extending the existing controls on press freedom. The law remained the basis of press censorship in Cameroon until its modification in principle by President Biya in 1990.

To indicate the level of Ahidjo's repression, of fifteen news-papers published around the 1960s, only one of them – Cameroon Times – was still being published by 1985 (Nji 1985: 39–40). L'Effort Camerounais, a paper reasonably critical of the government, had a number of its issues confiscated, 'including one in April 1962 which reported the death of twenty-five prisoners in a train on its way to Yaounde, a story the government very much wanted suppressed'. In addition to the seizure, the editor, a Frenchman and priest by the name of Fertin, was deported (Fonye 1973: 102; Bayart 1973: 55). Although the paper survived the early years of censorship, it died in 1974, killed by censorship and a heavy deficit of FCFA 15 million (Wongo 1977: 20–21). The government was equally repressive of social critics and critical intellectuals. Among Cameroonian writers who had their works banned were Abel Eyinga, Mongo Beti and Bernard Nanga.

When Ahidjo became president in 1960, his legitimacy was not universally accepted. Among those who contested him was the Union des Populations Camerounaises (UPC) party, whose leaders felt cheated of victory by the French. Accordingly, France, still believing in its 'Mission Civilisatrice', preferred a moderate who would be easy to manipulate after independence to the radicals who advocated total liberation. Ahidjo was determined to stifle the growing popularity of the UPC. This he achieved with the help of France and through the assassination of Um Nyobe, Dr Moumié and others of its leaders (Mukong 1985: 22–44; Mbembe 1984; Ntumazah 2001).

Opposition to Ahidjo's government and authoritarian style of leadership was to increase after unification with Southern Cameroon in 1961. As an ambitious leader who wanted unquestioning loyalty, Ahidjo sought to create a unified party in a united republic under his unopposed control. With this in mind, a free press was what he needed least. The less the public read or listened to his critics, and the more the government's views were orchestrated and propagated, the better for Ahidjo. With the radio already under exclusive government ownership and control, all he needed was to contain the private press with an iron hand, which he did by introducing or reinforcing the press laws.

For twenty years and more, Ahidjo's control of the press was as tight as was feasible. During his presidency, not only was the press uniform and conformist, but 'freedom of expression' existed only as a statement in the constitution. Cameroonians increasingly tuned to foreign radio stations like the BBC, VOA and RFI, which despite the 'foreignness' of their perspectives were indeed the only 'uncensored' alternatives. They learnt of internal atrocities and abuses from foreign sources because the local media were neither accessible nor had access to information on the state of affairs.

If the number of publications in a country was all that is needed to say whether or not freedom of the press exists, it would be true that Cameroon was freer under President Biya before 1990 than it was under Ahidjo. But to limit oneself to numbers alone is myopic, since the same repressive laws that stifled the press under Ahidjo were maintained under Biya. It is true that in 1982 there were not many publications, and after Biya's accession to power in that year over 55 publications were registered at the Ministry of Territorial Administration. Of this number more than 42 were concentrated in three cities: over 24 were based in Yaounde, the capital city; 16 in Douala, the economic capital; and 3 in Limbe, the oil-producing city. Apart from being more historically associated with the press than most other cities in the country, these three cities had the most prospects for advertising revenue.

Of the 55 publications, only *Cameroon Tribune*, the government-controlled newspaper, was daily (in French). The bi-weekly papers were *Cameroon Tribune* (in English) and *Cameroon Magazine*. All the other papers were weekly, bi-monthly or monthly. Censorship remained a major problem in general and for the private press in particular. A good number of journalists saw the censorship system as serving individual officials and politicians more than it did the 'nation'.

Declarations by President Biya and his various ministers of information and culture tended to confirm the thesis that by freedom of the press they meant nothing more than the freedom to criticise Ahidjo and the critics of Biya's New Deal government. The government set about relativising the concepts of 'freedom' and 'democracy' in order to justify the contradictions between their public statements and their repressive actions.

'Cameroonians enjoy freedom of expression, but they must not misuse it', declared President Biya in a February 1987 interview with the editor-in-chief of Cameroon Television. This statement was most revealing of Biya's attitude to freedom in general and press freedom in particular. He argued that democracy such as existed in countries like Britain, France and the USA was not achieved overnight. It 'is the cumulation of a long process that took centuries, a long process of maturation, of education', he pointed out. When Cameroonians had attained such maturity, they could enjoy full democracy and freedom. For the moment, he preferred a guided type of freedom that ensured national unity, integration and development. Given Cameroon's circumstances, the press could not but be responsible, he rationalised. In his words, even though journalism is a difficult profession,

> We would like the press to manifest an increasing sense of objectivity, of responsibility, not to publish information about which it is not sure, to verify the truth of what it publishes, and to avoid a certain journalistic tendency to chase scandals ... to educate through training and to train through education. We believe that in this fashion, the press in Cameroon, which is already on the right road, can make an increasingly precious contribution to the flourishing of Cameroon.[1]

Taking his cue from President Biya, François Sengat Kuo, the minister of information and culture at the time, warned journalists against taking undue advantage of the period of recovered tolerance and freedom. 'Journalists must work on facts, they must only narrate facts and not manipulate them', he stated. During a national seminar organised on the role of the private press in Cameroon, François Sengat Kuo reiterated the role of the press as follows:

the press in our country must contribute to national unity. In publishing news, therefore, an effort must be made to ensure that a serene national atmosphere is always maintained. This is because our type of democracy is that which seeks to associate all people in the management of their affairs. This preoccupation requires that journalists do not sacrifice the truth for sensation, not to play on the nerves of the public. The press must henceforth also address itself to the rural masses because too much attention has so far been directed at the urban masses – as a contribution to the advent of national integration sought by President Biya.[2]

Despite declarations by President Biya and members of his government, the repressive press laws remained in force. The arbitrary arrest and detention without trial of media practitioners continued. Local and foreign publications were still banned, and the 'catastrophic' technical and economic situation of the private press (Bayart 1973: 52) was far from diminished. The result was the large number of imported and largely politically harmless publications in circulation in Cameroon. Under Ahidjo, Jean-Marc Ela (1974: 15–16) had remarked that Cameroonians were shaped far more by foreign publications than by the local press, and he expressed concern over the fact that these publications reflected a social, economic and cultural reality that was in no way Cameroonian.

On the eve of the democratic struggles of the 1990s, Ela's observations were still valid. So was his call for the promotion of 'a mass counter-culture' that would make Cameroonians more conscious of what was theirs and less attracted to foreign 'images and cultural models'. This could undoubtedly be best achieved with a genuinely free and legally protected local press. Thus, as Bayart concluded in the early 1970s, unless the press in Cameroon was allowed the political, cultural and economic autonomy it lacked, 'its contribution to socialisation and communication within the Cameroonian political system' would remain 'an illusion' (Bayart 1973: 61–2).

Critical Analysis of the 1990 Media Law

In 1990, pressured by both internal and external clamour for liberalisation, the Biya government introduced a series of 'liberty laws'. Among them was a law on 'Freedom of Mass Communication', whose articulation and implementation deserve critical scrutiny. Parliament passed the law (No. 90/052) in 1990. It regulated the press for five years until its slight modification by law No. 6/04 of 4 January 1996. Although on the face of it the law was a marked improvement on previous measures, the new legislation had a catalogue of weaknesses that betrayed a burning desire to police, sanction or control the press. The law devoted 35 of its 90 articles to repressive sanctions against the press. Munzu notes that the law treats journalists 'as people who, all the time, were seeking to jeopardise state interests or to harm other people'. The law's repressive dimensions are compounded by more underhand measures that are not always easy to demonstrate. These include: (i) the permanent or tacit refusal by public authorities to grant journalists access to administrative documents; (ii) the repeated seizure of newspapers, decided upon without notification in writing by the administration; (iii) the repeated violation by the forces of law and order, acting without the authority of a judge, of newspaper offices and printing press premises; (iv) the banning of certain papers shortly before an electoral campaign; (v) the self-arrogation by the minister of communication of the power to censor and suppress the media appearances of rival candidates during a presidential election campaign (N'Thepe 1993).

On the issue of responsibility for libel, Ewumbue-Monono notes that the law is silent on who is liable in cases of reproduction of libellous material in the case of the print media and of defamatory broadcasts in that of the electronic media. The law is equally silent on plagiarism, obscene publication and seditious libel, and vague in its concept of 'conflict with principles of public policy' expressed in Sections 14, 17 and 51 (Ewumbue-Monono 1992: 28–9).

The law's other weaknesses include the fact that it did not recognise Cameroonian proprietorship of any news publication originating from outside the territory. The condition that two copies of such foreign publications must be deposited at the ministries of foreign affairs, territorial administration, communication, and justice twenty-four hours prior to circulation betrayed 'the resolve of the Cameroonian legislator to police information from abroad'. Like the press law in other francophone countries inspired by the French Law of 29 July 1881, the Cameroonian law authorises MINAT to ban the distribution, circulation and sale in Cameroon of foreign news publications.

In practice, a MINAT civil servant 'is given the absolute right to determine public order and propriety' (FES 1993b: 12). At MINAT, the practice was to take newspapers intended for censorship to the assistant director for political affairs, who was also sub-director for public freedoms. Mbida (1995) criticised such concentration of censorship in the hands of one person and wondered just how possible it was for a single civil servant to read effectively, in time, all the newspapers produced or sold in Cameroon.

The publisher could choose to deposit for scrutiny either dummies or copies of the printed paper, 'in real terms, created a confusing situation', especially as some administrative authorities 'demanded the exclusive deposit of dummies which would enable them to carry out partial, less spectacular, though more coarse censorships' (FES 1993b: 12). The law was subject to divergent interpretations on the issue of censorship and allowed for the censor to act in an arbitrary and whimsical manner. It was also 'at the root of a serious conflict between the administration and the private press – a conflict that took its toll on press freedom' (FES 1993b: 12–13). Although provisions were made for a publisher dissatisfied with the way censorship was conducted to take their case to court, the law did not make this very practicable.

The Law as Interpreted by Government

Government paraded the new law as an 'anthem on the freedom of expression', and claimed it could be counted among the most liberal in Africa.[3] Addressing African experts at the first regional meeting of the International Programme for Communication Development in Africa (IPCD), in Yaounde on 17 March 1993, the minister dwelled on the 'numerous innovations' brought about by the law: 'the setting up of a newspaper has passed from a system of authorization to one of declaration: it guarantees journalists free access to all sources of information – sources which are protected.' He stressed that, 'Except in case of judicial inquiry and at the request of the state counsel, or on the authorization of the judge, the law forbids the searching of the premises used for the design, manufacture, production, printing and conservation of mass communication organs.' It opens broadcasting up to competition, thus bringing to an end the state monopoly by allowing for the setting up of private radio and television stations. With a law like that, the minister affirmed, quoting President Paul Biya, no one needed any longer, in order 'to express himself, go underground, live in exile or abandon his family'. The fact that a multiplicity of titles were started in the private press soon after the law was passed was interpreted by the minister as testimony to the liberal nature of the said law and of the New Deal government. All this was sufficient reason for the minister to claim that so far as the promotion of press freedom was concerned, 'Cameroon and UNESCO are on the same wave length'. He added, 'Like UNESCO, Cameroon is convinced of the determining role of the press in spreading the freedoms of which our societies have a great need in order to pursue democratic and socio-cultural transformations.'[4]

So why the administrative censorship and general hostility and brutality towards the press? Why the contradiction of President Biya's very own prescription that: 'local newspapers should provide our population with more diversified information reported on various viewpoints and should lead to a free discussion of ideas which is one of the essential options of our policy of openness, democratization and liberalisation'?[5]

The minister had the following explanation: in order to ensure public order and good morals, the Cameroonian state 'exercises a sort of legal control on the press, thanks to some legal measures providing for a censorship that is extremely light and symbolic'. For, 'poorly managed, poorly used, freedom of expression can prove harmful to the consolidation of social balance and especially to national integration and peace.' Some papers, the minister stressed, did not respect the law, the professional code[6] of conduct and the principle of objectivity, impartiality and the search for truth dear to journalism. Censorship was thus necessary against those who would want to use freedom of expression as 'a pretext to install intellectual terrorism and total anarchy or a sort of return to the state of savagery'.[7]

According to the minister's perspective, every administrative measure taken against certain newspapers or journalists of the private press critical of government could be explained by a lack of respect for the law or for the professional code of conduct. However, Cameroonian journalists were yet to agree on a professional code as such. And it is precisely this explanation that was advanced each time the government had to seize or suspend a paper.

Suspensions

On 1 September 1991, the minister of information and culture issued a press release confirming the suspension in August by MINAT of seven newspapers, namely *Le Messager, Challenge Hebdo, La Nouvelle Expression, Galaxie, International News Bi-Hebdo, La Vision* and *La Messagère*. It was stated that they had not complied with the provision that obliged publishers to submit four copies of their papers to the senior divisional officer, no less than four hours prior to distribution.[8] The suspension, it said, would be lifted as soon as the papers were ready to respect the law. The press release was carried on CRTV radio, but not the reactions of the editors or publishers. Of the seven, five applied for a pardon while promising to respect the law, and were thus back in circulation before 10 October 1991. Only Pius Njawe of *Le Messager* and *La Messagère* insisted that he had always respected the law in question.[9] He waited until January 1992 to resume circulation, following a period that saw enormous national and international pressure put on the government.

This re-authorization was followed by a period of relative calm when the private press functioned with a minimum of administrative hostility. After April 1992, however, censorship intensified. The editorial team of *Galaxie* was brought to court and sanctioned for publishing an article that accused Minister Andze Tsoungui of MINAT of having given the contract for ballot papers to his own firm and, when he was minister of defence, for having used military planes to transport pharmaceutical products for his son.[10] On 6 July 1992, *Galaxie* was suspended for non-respect of the law.[11] On 20 August, there was court action against *Le Messager, Galaxie, L'Opinion* and *Dikalo* for 'failure to submit copies to the legal authorities'. Between 4 and 11 September, on the eve of the 11 October 1992 presidential elections, the government again suspended *Le Messager, La Nouvelle Expression* and *Challenge Hebdo*.[12] But this time, three papers reacted by changing their titles: *Galaxie, La Nouvelle Expression* and *Challenge Hebdo* became respectively *L'Ami du Peuple, L'Expression* (and later *Expression Nouvelle*) and *Challenge Nouveau*, and they continued to publish and circulate in a clandestine manner. Aware of this tactic, the prefect of Mfoundi in Yaounde in 1997 denied authorisation to *Mutant*, a new creation by the publishers of 'the French language weekly *Mutations* which, at the time, was banned by an administrative order and had won a court decision in favour of its reopening but was facing trouble with seizures' (Boh 1997: 33).

Arrests, detention, trial and imprisonment

From December 1990 to July 1998, at least twenty-one major cases of arrest, detention, and in some cases trial, of journalists and newspaper proprietors can be documented. The most frequent allegation was that the journalist in question had brought into disrepute the president, a member of government or parliament, or another official or institution of state. Other cases have involved well-connected individuals who thought themselves victims of libel. Among the most prominent cases are a series involving Pius Njawe of *Le Messager*, whose problems with government are the most familiar internationally. Already, in December 1990, just after the new law was passed, Njawe and Célestin Monga were tried and given suspended sentences of six months each for publishing an article deemed offensive to the president and parliament. In 1993, Pius Njawe was detained after he reprinted an article from *La Lettre du Continent* captioned: 'While the Economy Dies... 6 Billion for the Mvomeka'a Golf'.[13] The official reason for his arrest and detention, as given by the acting state counsel Foe Jean-Claude Robert, was to find out how Njawe had come by a confidential document whose contents appeared in an article of *La Messagère*[14] captioned: 'Moutomé Wants to Incriminate Fru Ndi'.[15] Eventually, on 17 August 1993, Pius Njawe of *Le Messager* and Benjamin Zebaze and Martin Waffo of *Challenge Hebdo* were given suspended sentences of six and five months, respectively,[16] for publishing confidential material from the Ministry of Justice and Keeper of the Seals.[17] In

February 1996, Pius Njawe and Eyoum Ngangue were found guilty and fined FCFA 2.5 million for an article in the satirical *Le Messager Popoli*[18] which was judged contemptuous of the head of state and parliamentarians, for having referred to them as 'salauds' and 'cons'. On 24 December 1997, Pius Njawe was arrested and detained for ten days after publishing, under a pen name, Franck Essomba, an article alleging that President Paul Biya had suffered a heart attack.[19] For refusing to disclose his source, he was subsequently tried, fined FCFA 500,000 and sentenced to two years' imprisonment, only to be released in October 1998, following presidential clemency, which he insisted he did not seek.

On 10 August 1995, Paddy Mbawa of *Cameroon Post* was imprisoned at New-Bell Douala and fined FCFA 15 million following a six-month sentence for libel against businessman John Epee Mandengue. The sentence was subsequently increased following further libel charges by the same businessman, and again following a charge by the government for 'spreading falsehood'. Released on 16 August 1996, Paddy Mbawa had to flee the country in order to avoid a mountain of other charges by Mandengue and the government.

In November 1997, Evariste Menounga of *Nouvel Indépendent* was arrested and detained at the gendarmerie in Yaounde, where he was interrogated in connection with an article allegedly libellous of minister of public works Jean Baptiste Bokam in the newly created *Le Front Independent*. In July 1998, Patrick Tchoua of *Jeune Détective* was arrested and detained at the Kondengui prison for linking the minister of state for finance and a parliamentarian, Emmanuel Mbiam, to 'a mafia network that plunders state coffers'.[20] He was subsequently charged together with Nana Essaie, who, he confessed, had dictated and corrected the story, then paid him FCFA 100,000 to publish it.

These cases of arrest, detention, trial and imprisonment, of which there are many more examples, do not seem to have decreased following modification of the law in January 1996. If anything, empowerment of the courts by the January 1996 law seemed to have exacerbated the precarious relationship of critical journalists with government, as well-documented accounts of harassment, arrests, detention, trials and imprisonment have shown since 1996.[21]

Seizures

The most common form of sanction against the press is seizure. There are numerous examples. Amougou reports from his study of official documents at MINAT that between 1991 and 1993 a total of 144 issues of different newspapers were seized for reasons of 'public order'. Of this number, 27 issues of 13 different newspapers were seized in 1991; 68 issues of 27 newspapers, including *Jeune Afrique Economie*,[22] were seized in 1992; and 49 issues of 15 different national newspapers and 1 foreign publication, the French daily *Libération*,[23] were seized in 1993. According to Amougou, the 'inflated' number of seizures in 1992 is sufficient demonstration 'that the private press was a target or privileged field for application of public order when government announced its strategy to restore state authority'. It was also an indication of government's preoccupation with public order before, during and after the presidential elections of 11 October 1992 (Amougou 1994: 164–7).

The Law as Interpreted by the Press

The newspapers, for their part, do not share the government's interpretation of the 1990 law. They claim that they have always respected legal requirements. Between 1990 and 1996 the press law gave them two distinct options regarding the state censorship provisions. According to section 14 of Law no. 019/052 of 19 December 1990, each publisher shall submit to the Senior Divisional Officer, Governor or MINAT:

> no less than four hours prior to distribution, two copies or two brush-proofs signed by him.
> The four-hour time-limit shall be reduced to two hours for daily newspapers....
> The Newspaper issues thus submitted may be censored in whole or in part where there is a conflict with the principles of public policy.
> The censorship decision may be appealed against before a competent magistrate who must make a ruling within one month following the date he is seized of the matter. (SOPECAM 1991: 34)

The publishers' first option was to print only after administrative approval by MINAT. Their second option was to proceed with printing, submit copies for censorship and wait for four or two hours; if there was no reaction from MINAT, they could make their papers available for circulation. The papers suspended or simply seized were those which chose the second alternative. It would seem that the government, from its own point of view, made a serious error of judgement when it adopted the 1990 Act. The measure created a loophole. This is perhaps explained by the fact that the law 'was hurriedly drawn up' to meet a political agenda in the face of 'the tempers which rose with the clamour for democratic reforms' (Ewumbue-Monono 1992: 29).

Having adopted a law that it found burdensome, the government embarked on a selective application of it 'without any shame' (Ponus, *Challenge Hebdo*, 19 May 1992: 2). Ponus argued that if the government were to apply the law strictly, the private press could not have been accused of not respecting it. He explained himself thus:

> Section 14 ... does not make clear (out of forgetfulness?) if the four hours in question are working hours or not. It does not even make clear if once the dummies or the copies have been submitted, the newspaper publisher is bound to come back for them in order to have an idea on what has been decided. Which implies that it is, without doubt, up to the administration to do everything to bring its decision to the knowledge of the publisher and this notification has to be given within four hours following submission.
>
> Hence, a publisher who makes his compulsory submission of two copies at 8 am, can place his paper in the market at 12:01 pm if by then he still has not received any notification from the censor. And in this case, all seizures would be illegal.
>
> In the same way, when the administrative submission is made at 5:45 pm, the paper can, following the same conditions, be placed in the market at 9:46 pm, without any evil intention to disrespect the law.
> It is this second option (post-impression censorship) that the majority of private newspapers habitually use and which some 'authorities' consider, wrongly, as acting illegally.

By choosing the second option, the press did of course make life difficult for the censor, who was left very little time to do the work effectively. This was especially the case in Douala, where the majority of private newspapers were based. With very limited reaction time, the censor might resort to arbitrary decisions, which could work against the papers in question. As Erik Essoussie (a censor with over eight years' experience and deputy director in charge of political affairs at MINAT) confessed, before 1991 he even used to correct grammatical and spelling mistakes in the papers brought to him for censorship. But the multiplication of titles and the lack of time soon made it impossible for him to continue in such a fashion.[24]

The problem was that the censor's right to edit, extending even to newspaper stories already mounted on dummies, and to prescribe the words to be used in the process, made him an 'editor' more powerful than the publisher of the paper. Lack of training in journalism was no obstacle to the work of censorship. Contradictions were bound to arise and attract criticism. One censor turned down a story in Douala that was accepted for publication in Yaounde; in another incident the same censor approved an edition, then later reversed his decision and ordered the newspaper to be confiscated.

The private press and a critical public hardly understood what criteria the censor used to decide what was fit for the reader's mind. They would have liked the editors to be able to censor their publications themselves, as was the case in most countries, and be charged in a free and fair court if they offended anyone in the exercise of their duty. This point was echoed by journalism lecturer Antoine Wongo Ahanda, who in April 1998 lamented the stifling of peer control with excessive laws: 'in Cameroon, they want to bring everything back to the law, so much so that even ethical problems are taken to court' (Ahanda 1998).

In the face of such official hazards, and with increasing economic hardship, any editor was bound to think twice before printing an edition before the censor had seen it. As François Aby Donfack remarked during an interview, 'it is true that one can print the paper and take copies to the censor. But there is the risk that after printing 20,000 copies for about FCFA 1.5 million, you are told by the censor to delete a phrase, and all the 20,000 copies have to be destroyed and reprinted without the phrase in question.'[25] Although this is an extreme example, it nevertheless highlights the enormous risk for the editor of full use being made of the law.

Such economic risks, as described by François Aby Donfack, were compounded by the devaluation in January 1994 of the franc (FCFA) and by a 40 per cent rise in the cost of newsprint in January 1995. The papers reacted by raising their prices by 50 per cent – some from FCFA 150 to FCFA 250, others from FCFA 200 to FCFA 300. This meant that even fewer Cameroonians would be able to afford newspapers. In mid-1997, Boh remarked that of the 600 or so legally permitted newspapers, barely 100 had 'been published more than half a dozen times whilst only 50 of them or so continue to be published on a more or less regular basis', with only some 20 qualified to be classified as 'serious'. The government's bilingual paper, *Cameroon Tribune*, remains the country's sole daily (Boh 1997: 34). Thus the devaluation compounded the predicament imposed on the press by the MINAT censor and SOPECAM.

By 1995, the private press could account for no more than ten titles, down from over twenty in its heyday. By August 1997, the leading papers in French were *La Nouvelle Expression, Cameroon Tribune, Le Messager, Challenge Nouveau, Le Quotidien, Generation, Perspectives* and *Le Patriote*; and in English, *The Herald, Cameroon Post (The Post)* and *The Witness* (Boh, 1997: 38–9). Keye Ndogo has argued that public apathy by pro-government readers in the face of a highly politicised and tribalised press was responsible for the decline. Between 1990 and 1992, the press had contented itself with 'revelations of political and financial scandals on which the public seemed to feast'. However, other factors must be taken into consideration, such as the fall in the purchasing power of Cameroonian workers, most of whom 'lost between 65 and 70% of their salaries in January and November 1993', and the 1994 devaluation which led to 'the rise in the cost of newsprint on the international market' and forced 'Cameroonian publishers to raise the cost of their newspapers'.[26]

It must be noted that pro-government private papers such as *Le Patriote, Le Témoin, La Caravane, Lettre du Cameroun, Nouvelle du Cameroun* and *Cent Rires* experienced no censorship, seizures or suspensions for five years. This fact was widely taken to indicate that 'public order and good morals' could only be violated or endangered by a press critical of government. Yet a cursory overview of the contents of the pro-government papers shows that they were far from being without polemical content or a willingness to cover scandal (Guiffo 1993; Ndongo 1993; Land 1997); neither did they respect the professional code of conduct. As an example, Le Patriote[27] published an interview it had supposedly conducted with Mongo Beti, in which he 'Demolishes Mrs Frances Cook [the US ambassador] and denounces his "friends" of the LAAKAM' (a Bamileke elite association; see Nyamnjoh and Rowlands, 1998); yet it was an interview that Mongo Beti did not recognise, judging from his declarations shortly after publication.[28] Earlier Le Patriote[29] had published a letter purportedly written by the elite of Metta in the North West province to John Fru Ndi, in which they declared 'We must lord it over all tribes in Cameroon'; and a supposed 'diabolical plan' by the SDF 'To do everything to bring about the collective resignation of all cabinet ministers.... To lead in this way President Biya to resign or to convene a sovereign national conference....To chase all Bamileke out of the North West ... [and] To abolish all traditional chiefdoms.'

In a series of articles in 1993 headed: 'Dossier Independent Press: Serious attacks on press freedom under a fascist regime', La Messagère[30] accused the Biya government of wanting to suppress the independent press in the aftermath of multipartyism. In one, Eyoum Ngangue described the critical private press as victims of denigrating language by government, the official media, and the pro-government private press. Terms such as 'opposition press', 'rag', 'a certain press' and 'gutter press', were used. The official press, for its part, missed no opportunity to accuse them of 'lack of professionalism, of intoxication, of supporting opposition parties, of criticising government action for the sake of criticism'.

It should be added, however, that although the private press has been denied formal access to official information, it has nevertheless been used constantly by government officials to settle scores, or, by those sympathetic to the opposition, to embarrass the government. This accounts for the many political and financial scandals revealed in the private press since 1990, often with copies of confidential documents in support.

Most journalists believe that the critical private press's only crime has been its consistent refusal to succumb to state violence, or to concede that Biya and the CPDM had won successive elections in

Cameroon fairly; that is, to quote Hilary Kebila Fokum, one of their number, their refusal to see anything 'wrong in hauling verbal grenades at an inefficient regime, where corruption has seeped into every orifice and ventricle'.[31]

Not only journalists and publishers suffered under this press regime. Also targeted by censorship were newspaper vendors. As attacks on the critical press intensified during crises (for example, the 'ghost town' period of 1991 and early 1992), so too did actions against vendors. Vendors were made to understand that they were not free to sell what they wanted or what the public liked. Despite the law which gave them the freedom to sell all publications without exception,[32] they often found themselves forbidden to sell certain papers critical of government. Between 1990 and 1996, when administrative censorship was underwritten by the law, the censor virtually obliged vendors to sell *Cameroon Tribune*, *Le Patriote*, *Le Témoin* and all publications favourable to government. In 1991 and 1992, when various critical papers continued to be published despite their suspension, vendors sometimes sold these papers by inserting them inside *Cameroon Tribune* or other pro-government publications. As Nicolas Tejouemessie[33] observed at the time, 'vendors are persecuted night and day because they contribute ... to the fight for freedom of expression.'

A study by Amougou (1994) documents the way the state in recent years has attempted to justify its censorship and suppression of the press. Working with articles 14, 17, 23 and 24 of the 1990 law on Freedom of Mass Communication, the censor and other administrative organs have clamped down on newspapers deemed to have divulged 'sensitive and secret information'. Underlying this exercise of state power is the notion that the internal and external security of the state, and serenity in affairs of a diplomatic and judicial character, are more important than the citizen's desire or right to know.

Amougou's study reveals the grounds on which the censor has sought to justify the exercise of this power. The following are the main reasons furnished for state action against offending publications:

- the need to protect public authorities against falsehood;
- untruths or falsehoods that are seen to threaten national unity or cohesion;

- treating the president with contempt;
- incitement to revolt against government and public institutions;
- treating the constituted institutions and functionaries with contempt;
- national secrets and diplomatic secrets;
- judicial secrets;
- possession of copies of confidential administrative documents.

This battery of state rationales for control of the press has led to such a scale of censorship, official seizures, suspensions, bans, intimidation, invasion or sequestration by the police or military, that it would be difficult to claim that the December 1990 law on communication changed much in practice (Nyamnjoh 1996b, 1996c).

Modification of the 1990 Media Law

A National Forum on Communication was organised by the Ministry of Communication in Yaounde on 29 August–1 September 1994, to address critical issues pertaining to all aspects of communication in Cameroon. Despite its rich and comprehensive recommendations, the amendment of the communication law some fifteen months later addressed only narrowly the issue of administrative censorship and other minor issues. Media practitioners were quite dissatisfied. On 4 January 1996, law No. 96/04 was promulgated, amending certain provisions of the 1990 law. Under the new law, newspaper publishers are no longer expected to submit their dummies or papers for administrative censorship by civil servants. However, other administrative sanctions like seizures, bans and suspension have been maintained, with possible severe financial consequences for the press. The process of starting a newspaper has been made more difficult by requiring a lot more paperwork. A declaration by the would-be publisher, as provided for in the 1990 law, is no longer sufficient. The new law empowers the administrative authority either to grant or reject an application. In this way, the law has reinstated the principle of prior authorization, which was abolished in 1990.

Furthermore, the 1996 law allows individuals who believe that their honour, dignity, esteem, reputation or private life have been injured to obtain an edict providing for the seizure of a newspaper by the administrative authority. The latter thus enjoys a power similar to and in conflict with the judiciary, and can take unilateral action against newspapers on the basis of an individual's request. Also, the new law allows for a search of the premises of a press organ by the police without warrant and without any judicial action, if the administrative authority considers that public order is endangered. The 1990 law authorised such a search only in cases of judicial inquiry.

There is thus little reason for optimism about the abolition of blatant administrative censorship. What the press has supposedly gained in the new measure has been taken away in the same law by more severe provisions than obtained previously. Giving the judiciary a greater say is commendable in principle, but it presupposes an independence from the executive that has not been evidenced by recent cases against journalists. One such case is that concerning Pius Njawe of *Le Messager*, who was imprisoned for two years for reporting in his paper that President Paul Biya had suffered a heart attack. In addition to being at the beck and call of the executive and administration, some judges know little about media law beyond what is provided for in the penal code. Here the president, ministers, parliamentarians and all state institutions are considered to require protection from the public's right to know.[34]

This turbulent relationship between government and private press, even after the new media law, only highlights further the administration's impatience with dissident views and its distaste for critical publications. President Biya is yet to grant an interview to any of the private papers in Cameroon. The private press has no formal access to coverage of the president's daily activities, which is reserved for CRTV and *Cameroon Tribune*.

The president's indifference to the private press has been so frustrating that one of the papers, *Challenge Hebdo*,[35] published an imaginary interview ('frank and face to face') with President Biya at his home village of Mvomeka'a. According to Ombe Ndzana, a regular contributor at the time, this paper was seized in Yaounde. He pointed out that the reason *Challenge Hebdo* had resorted to an April Fool's Day spoof instead of a real interview was because of the marginalisation of the private press by those in power. How can the president expect a friendly private press when his attitude to it has always been less than friendly? As Boh Herbert put it, 'Who do you blame when it is easier for the press to get SDF leader Mr. John Fru Ndi to speak than it is to get a member of government or the Speaker of the Assembly?'[36] Almost eight years later, upon the imprisonment of Pius Njawe in January 1998, little had changed for the better. The president of the Union of Cameroon Journalists (UCJ), Amadou Vamoulke, even though a member of the central committee of the ruling CPDM party, recognised the tension between government and the press and urged them to work to resolve their differences: 'there is urgent need for dialogue between government and the press, so as to break the ice of suspicion, prejudice, contempt and what have you, separating them'.[37]

If the law and its selective application have made it very difficult for the critical press and its journalists to function freely and to fulfil their democratic pretensions, public sympathy for this press has waned largely because of unprofessional and unethical practices on their part. These practices and their effects are the subject of Chapter 6.

Notes

1. *AfricaAsia* 41, 1987: 28, 35.
2. See *Cameroon Tribune*, 25 July 1984.
3. See *Cameroon Tribune*, 18 March 1993; *La Messagère*, 23 March 1993.
4. See *Cameroon Tribune*, 18 March 1993.
5. Quoted by Emmanuel Tataw, *Cameroon Tribune*, 14 December 1990.
6. Although Cameroonian journalists were yet to agree on a code, by 'respect de la déontologie professionnelle', Kontchou meant that every journalist should be guided by the need 'for total restitution of facts, respect for the public, honesty, verification and cross-checking of sources' (*Cameroon Tribune*, 16 January 1991).
7. See *Cameroon Tribune*, 18 March 1993.
8. See *La Messagère*, 2 September 1991, for details.
9. See ibid. for his argument.
10. See *Challenge Hebdo*, 8 April 1992; US Department of State 1993: 35; *Galaxie*, 17 March 1992.
11. See *La Nouvelle Expression* (*Spécial Solidarité Galaxie*) 3 August 1992; *Challenge Hebdo*, 15 July 1992.

12. See *La Messagère*, 17 March 1993; *Le Messager*, 13 August, 2 September and 16 September 1992.
13. See *La Messagère*, 11 May 1993.
14. 26 April 1993.
15. See *La Messagère*, 18 May 1993.
16. See *Challenge Bi-Hebdo*, 20 August 1993.
17. See *Challenge Nouveau*, 22 April 1993 and *La Messagère*, 16 April 1993.
18. See 'Un rejet de la loi constitutionnelle', *Le Messager Popoli* 129, 1 December 1995.
19. See *Le Messager*, 22 December 1997 for the article.
20. See *Jeune Détective*, 25 June 1998.
21. See for example *Le Messager*, 12 May 1997; and reports by the Paris-based Reporters Sans Frontières for 1996, 1997 and 1998.
22. *Jeune Afrique Economie* 155, May 1992.
23. *Libération* 3764.
24. Interviewed by Gallagher, 13 May 1991.
25. For more of the same argument, see *Challenge Hebdo*, 19 June 1991.
26. See Njawe's reply to Keye Ndogo in *Jeune Afrique*, 13 April 1995.
27. 10 December 1992.
28. See *Fraternité*, December 1992; *Expression Nouvelle* 4, December 1992.
29. 28 June 1991; 20 August 1992.
30. 17 March 1993.
31. *La Messagère*, 2 September 1991.
32. See section 30 of Law no. 090/052, 19 December 1990.
33. *Challenge Nouveau*, 25 February 1993.
34. This is a point recognised by the Union of Cameroon Journalists (UCJ), who, in February 1998 drew the prime minister's attention to this in a memorandum, in which they argued that the press law was not well known, especially by magistrates who preferred to apply 'the penal code … in its severest form in courts' (*L'Expression*, 18 February 1998).
35. 1 April 1992.
36. *Cameroon Post*, 19 November 1990.
37. See his article 'Démocratisation apaisée et liberté de la presse', *L'Expression*, 19 January 1998.

6

Professionalism and Ethics in the

Private Press in Cameroon

This chapter provides further empirical substantiation for the professional and ethical concerns raised and discussed in Chapter 2, drawing on the particular experiences of journalism in Cameroon. Given the liberal democratic mission of the press, the basic assumption in this chapter is that the private press can best serve multiparty democracy by adhering to democratic norms itself. Being professional by mediating in an honest, balanced, fair or neutral manner is the best way for the media to unite society around a liberal democratic culture. If the law on Freedom of Communication has made it difficult for the private press to operate freely and to contribute to the democratisation of society, the private press has on its part compounded that difficulty with its unprofessional journalism. Ignoring or downplaying the latter, as some over-sympathetic analysts and media scholars have tended to do, is either dishonest, paternalistic or both. It does not help the democratic aspirations of ordinary Africans, as it tends to play into the hands of opportunistic or mercenary journalism. Again, these shortcomings on the part of journalists and the media point to shortcomings in liberal democratic assumptions about Africa.

The Private Press and the Journalism of Excesses

The private press has seen democracy in purely political terms and has defined the democratic process as the struggle between those who have Cameroon's best interests at heart and those who are out merely to satisfy selfish interests and greed for power. Depending on what side of the political spectrum a paper finds itself on, truth derives either from the opposition or from the government. There is little respect for evidence, honesty, fairness, balance or neutrality, as 'excessive enthusiasm ... and downright cynicism ... seem to dominate the press scene' (Menang 1996: 327). Journalism has become an exercise in turning a blind eye to the shortcomings of political allies, while exaggerating the weaknesses of the paper's political opponents.

Such partisan journalism is little informed by the professional canons of honesty, accuracy and fairness.[1] The ability of politicised or partisan journalism to give all sides of a story, to avoid biased language, comment and opinion in news stories and reports, to dwell on the issues and avoid *ad hominem* remarks, has been crippled by the tendency to break Cameroonians down into the 'righteous' and the 'wicked' depending on whether they are in opposition or in government, or simply depending on their ethnic group and region of origin. Even the general secretary of the Union of Cameroon Journalists (UCJ), Boh Herbert, agrees when he writes: 'Whatever their approach to news treatment, Cameroonian newspapers ... tend to be poorly concealed spokespersons of political parties and movements, the public relations instruments of certain personalities, financial power houses, tribal and/or ethnic pressure groups.' These papers 'often have a constantly changing editorial policy depending on which interest groups are funding the edition', given how used to 'accepting brown envelopes' journalists in Cameroon are (Boh 1997: 40). One gets the impression that being good or bad is much less a question of what one is or what one does than a question of where one stands politically. Such partisanship blinds journalists to their professional beliefs and ethics, to the fact that 'their mission is ... to enlighten and not to indoctrinate the public' (Owona 1995: 135).

In the current democratic process, Cameroonian journalists (both official and private) have been accused of professional impropriety, not only by government and other prominent political actors, but by the general public and even by fellow professionals. The press

has been accused of 'journalistic hooliganism', of 'observing a conniving silence' over certain happenings while being 'irresponsible
and reckless' in reporting others, thus bringing Cameroon 'to the
brink of civil war'. The private press has been accused of using 'ef-
fortlessness and frivolity' to mask 'its numerous shortcomings'.[2] As
Grégoire Owona, deputy secretary-general of the CPDM, remarked
of the press shortly after the October 1992 presidential elections,[3]
'the current trend in Cameroon is to resort to invective, denuncia-
tion, calumny and even insult.... And all those who slander and
denounce would like the public to see them as heroes, threatened
and persecuted.'

Boh and Bell, in their study of press coverage of the 17 May 1997
legislative elections by CRTV and fifty-five newspapers, concluded
that, apart from the Catholic bilingual bi-monthly *L'Effort Camerounais*,
which was balanced, impartial and fair, the tendency was for news
editors to 'keep out information which contradicted their own
political convictions or that did not serve those convictions' and to
defend blindly the side they backed. While the CRTV and *Cameroon
Tribune* championed the cause of the CPDM, its journalists often
bending over backwards to make themselves politically acceptable
by doctoring the flow of information, the private press, through
editorials, opinion and comment, tried to persuade voters in favour
of this or that political party or candidate. Thus, for example, of a
total of 44 pages published on the election campaigns by *L'Expression*,
32 were devoted to pro-opposition stories, 12 to neutral articles
on voter education, and none had anything positive to say about
government or the ruling CPDM. Generally, 'news stories published
with the unique intention of informing voters were hard to find',
with some papers dismissing as 'out-of-fashion' the UCJ's call on all
journalists to be 'reporters, not supporters' (Boh 1997: 91–114).

To illustrate these practices of news filtering, blind support and
failure to cross-check by journalists, Boh and Bell cited several cases.
One was the pre-election violence in which five people were killed
and tens of others injured in the kingdom of Rey Bouba in Mayo Rey
Division. CRTV and *Cameroon Tribune*, the state-owned media, made no
mention of this information in any of their bulletins, editorial pages
or broadcasts. In the same way, they dramatised carpet-crossing from

the opposition to the ruling CPDM, while playing down or staying mute on resignations from the CDPM to join the opposition. The news filters of the pro-opposition press, on the other hand, proved so receptive of the Rey Bouba violence 'that the overall angle of all reports arraigned, judged and sentenced the one person these news organisations held responsible for the violence: the Lamido of Rey Bouba', CPDM baron and hardcore supporter of the status quo. The pro-opposition press did not raise any critical questions on the possible involvement of other local forces in what had happened. 'For the dozen of them that reported on these incidents, none of them from on-the-spot or eyewitness accounts, the Lamido was guilty as charged even before being heard.'

A second case described by Boh and Bell concerned two constituencies in the Far North and South West provinces where voting did not take place on 17 May. Neither CRTV Maroua nor CRTV Buea reported the facts of the situation. Instead, CRTV Maroua reported that voting was going well in the Far North province, only to turn around at the close of the polls to announce 'that voting would take place there the next day'.

A third case involved the photocopy of a letter supposedly written by the government delegate to the Douala Urban Council, Thomas Tobbo Eyoum. 'In the letter, Mr Tobbo Eyoum was reportedly informing President Biya of the fact that he had created ghost polling stations to favour the ruling CPDM.' The pro-opposition press 'comforted themselves that the photocopy was that of an authentic letter and went to the press with it lashing out on Mr Tobbo Eyoum for cheating'. The pro-government press, for their part, 'came to the rescue of the Government Delegate forcefully asserting that the letter was a fake and "cleansing" the CPDM official of any wrong-doing'. 'None of the 15 pro-opposition and 12 pro-government newspapers that published the story, many of them in two successive editions, bothered even once to cross-check with the person concerned and to include his point of view in their story' (Boh 1997: 102–12).

This practice of news filtering is commonplace in daily journalism, as papers generally tend to 'focus on scandals and gossip when these involve political "opponents", while at the same time withholding facts that might harm political "favourites"' (Menang 1996: 327).

Focusing on the critical private press, Albert Mbida[4] accuses it of selecting for insults, defamation and scandals only public authorities or individuals sympathetic to the government. Ahanda, in the same paper, makes the same point in his letter to the journalists of the anti-government private press. His implication is that this press, essentially Bamileke-owned and -controlled, observes a conniving silence over the financial misdeeds of the opposition politicians and Bamileke businessmen 'who import champagne and declare mineral water at the customs, those who have not paid their taxes for decades'.

The private press is seen as leaning 'too overtly towards commentary and opinion', (Boh 1997). It has also been blamed for outright sensationalism. As Zachee Nzoh-Ngandembou, an experienced journalist, observes, 'every newspaper you read frightens you. It predicts doom and prescribes hellfire.' He accuses the critical private press of 'uncivilised behaviour' by seeking to confront an indecent government with indecent language, and wonders whether the press 'couldn't ... use more decent words and still convey the same message'.[5] This concern is shared by Nga Ndongo, a journalist and university lecturer, who concludes, based on a content analysis, that 'courtesy and propriety do not seem to be among the most commonly shared commodities of the Cameroonian private press', and that it seems as if the papers were competing for 'the best insult' or the insult that is 'the most coarse, the most indecent and the most harmful' (Ndongo 1993: 153). The main target of such insults has been Paul Biya, his ministers and other CPDM barons. Nothing in the profession justifies the use of indecent language, especially if journalists are to respect the fact that 'the urgency of the message should not give rise to shoddiness of form' nor to rage (Agbor Tabi 1995: 8).

The private press has equally been libellous. Evidence is the volume of court cases and letters to editors complaining about defamation and falsehood (Ngah 1998). Indeed, this area is so rich in data that it requires a separate study.[6] For now, it suffices to note that the most recurrent criticism of the private press in this regard is the tendency to rush to publication without thorough investigation. Little is done to verify or to cross-check information, and it is not uncommon to find journalists writing under false or pen names, or publishing interviews without the authorisation of those concerned. Newspapers are known to be sponsored by some individuals or interest groups in order to blackmail others. In certain cases, government has succeeded in infiltrating the opposition and the press by using journalists and newspaper proprietors apparently committed to democratisation and change.[7] In almost every letter to the editor I examined during my study, the complainant questioned the professionalism of the journalist or paper concerned (see Chapter 5; Nyamnjoh 1996b: 109–16; for examples).

Albert Mbida[8] is one of those who believe the private press would be less libellous and defamatory were the sanctions by the law more severe. Using the case of *International News Hebdo*, he argues that the private press does not worry about being taken to court because sentences are usually very light, and are often suspended. Since the private press repeatedly attacks state authorities and selectively publishes only scandals that concern members of government or their supporters, Mbida thinks that suspended sentences should be abolished 'in order, on the one hand, to offer public authorities effective protection, and to cancel out the moral and material benefits that accrue from committing the offence, on the other.' But before making the law more severe, it should be ensured that it is applied in a fair manner.

According to the Friedrich Ebert Stiftung (FES) study (1993a) on public attitudes to the media, the CRTV *vox pop* for its radio programme *Cameroon Calling* of 21 February 1993, and critical readership reaction in the press, Cameroonian journalists are seen as mouthpieces for competing political pressure groups by the public (see also Tanjong and Ngwa 2002). Journalists are under enormous pressure to please the financial and political pipers for whom they work. Although quite critical of being criticised themselves, the private press journalists do not hesitate to judge, instruct, moralise and condemn others. Nga Ndongo sums up such double standards thus:

> The paper, it's true, is always right. Even when it is wrong or mistaken, it remains stubborn in a thousand and one ways – procedures, twists and turns, quibbling and frozen views, in the manner of a lawyer, just

to prove that it is right, while its critics are wrong or too dumb to understand. (Ndongo 1993: 145)

Not only is the public aware that the journalists are partisan and self-interested; it is also concerned by the fact that it is difficult if not impossible to find journalists who go for the truth and who treat it with the respect and distance that a news story deserves. But the private press suffers from the delusion that those who appreciate and encourage its partisan and tendentious journalism are representative of public opinion in the country. Thus there is a tendency in the critical press to see censorship always in terms of government's desire to keep Cameroonians in ignorance and seldom in terms of the desire to protect Cameroonians from mass-mediated falsehood.

Some journalists do not deny the press has been 'spurious', 'crudely sensational' and 'lavishly libellous', but they, like Ngoh Nkwain,[9] argue that the profession and the courts should be allowed a free hand to deal with these excesses. Others, like Hilary Kebila Fokum,[10] argue that while the private press may be 'excessively sensational', it cannot be claimed that such sensationalism has been pointless. Citing as an example the contest between President Paul Biya and the Muslim community over a piece of land in Tsinga-Yaounde, Fokum argues that had it not been for the private and 'aggressive' press, President Biya would not have yielded control of the land to the Muslims. It is therefore thanks to 'the searchlight of the private press' that today people are able to 'see through that darkness' imposed by government on issues of vital importance to them. Thus his conclusion: 'Now that politicians have started vomiting in broad daylight the hectares of land they swallowed in the heart of the night, the private press should not relent.' It should encourage others to follow the example of the Muslim community by marching until the national conference is granted and 'missing billions from the treasury' are recovered.[11]

This attitude, as we have seen in our overview of media and democratisation in Africa, can be found in many other countries, where journalists have come to realise that, were they to publish only verified facts, corruption and poor governance would virtually destroy their societies. Sometimes, the scarcity of credible news sources, coupled with financial difficulties and inadequate training, leaves journalists at the mercy of rumour and uninformed allegations (see Chapter 7). This and other explanations notwithstanding, journalism that has little or no respect for evidence, fairness and accuracy cannot, in a liberal democratic context, be termed professional, no matter how popular with the disaffected or with distant observers in the West. This lack of professionalism exacerbates the fragmentation of civil society and often serves to heighten ethnic tensions.

Lack of Professionalism and Adequate Organisation before 1996

In 1992 Michel Epee observed that journalism was one of the rare professions in Cameroon 'whose members were still not organised under a structure capable of checking against adventurers and opportunists seeking to join its ranks' and of working 'to defend its own interests'. His observation is still largely true of Cameroonian journalism today despite the creation in 1996 of the Union of Cameroon Journalists (UCJ). What accounts for the lack of adequate organisation and unity around a common set of values and interests? The reasons are many.

Most journalists in the private press, and some in the official media, have blamed the government for not facilitating the creation of a professional association for all journalists. They argue that the government instead has done much to discourage professional solidarity. Journalists of the official media were not, until 1996, allowed to join or form professional organisations of any kind, even though fellow civil servants in the medical and legal professions had such organisations. The view of those in the private press is that the authorities have never been in favour of a serious professional association working without state interference. According to certain critics, government has always wanted journalists confined to the role of praise-singers, churning out official statements that made headline news while corruption, incompetence, economic mismanagement and human rights abuses went unchecked.

As Chief Bisong Etahoben argued as editor of *Cameroon Post*,[12] 'afraid that unity within any professional or cultural body could work against its tall walls of oppression and repression, the Ahidjo/Biya governments made it impossible for professionals to come together as one body that could iron out the little controversies among professional colleagues'. The government, in order better to divide, encouraged the 'tendency to distinguish between members of the official and private press to the extent that even socials involving a member of the one side and that of the other can easily be interpreted as an attempt at buying the one to the other's side'. The fact that government was most concerned with the 'excesses' of the critical private press further strained relations between the official and private media, as most journalists of the official media were afraid 'to be seen even entering the offices of private newspapers lest they be thought to be selling official secrets', or suspected of writing against the government under pen names.

Unlike their counterparts in the official media, very few journalists in the private press can boast professional training of any kind in or outside a formal school of journalism. As a result, journalists in the official media tend to consider themselves professionally superior to their 'marginal' or 'illiterate' 'colleagues' of the private press, even though the vast majority of these have at least a GCE Advanced Level Certificate (Boh 1997: 143). The official journalists' air of superiority has alienated their private press counterparts, and there is little transfer of 'professional know-how'. As Chief Etahoben further remarked, the best way to show how much they knew was for the official journalists to teach their counterparts what they knew, and not simply to laugh at their ignorance.[13] The consequence, Eone notes, has been that relations between the official media and the private press have been 'mediocre and replete with suspicion and mutual scorn' (Eone 1993: 3), bringing about what Dominik Fopoussi termed 'a schism amongst people of the same profession'.[14]

Prior to the creation of the UCJ in 1996, some journalists argued that it was inexcusable for journalists who were so keen and ready to lecture, ridicule, moralise and criticise others not to muster the time and courage needed to unite themselves in a single, autonomous, active, professional association. According to one such journalist, the absence of a professional grouping before 1996 was less due to government bottlenecks than to infighting among journalists. While journalists of the state media were 'at each other's throats undercutting one another for armchair positions, those of the private press are glued to a battle for survival of the fittest'. The tendency to discredit certain units of the profession and to undercut one another has led to undue rivalry among journalists. Without press centres and clubs, 'not even common professional jokes can be shared!'[15]

As long as the press continued to postpone defining its own duties and protecting its rights by self-discipline and self-regulation, it was always vulnerable to external forces that desired a controlled press. In 1992, Prime Minister Simon Achidi Achu issued a code of ethics for journalists.[16] But the latter rejected it due to a lack of consultation and because the code did not reflect their concerns (Boh 1997: 41; Ngah 1998). To Hilary Kebila Fokum, it was only by discarding 'the cloak of division' and forming 'a strong and viable union' that journalists can cease to be 'the punching bags of influential personalities'.[17]

Asunkwan[18] of the Ministry of Communication laments the fact that in Cameroon journalism remains a profession wherein 'there are no elders' and where the young are not prepared to learn from the old hands. This has added to the chronic lethargy in the profession. He indeed had a point when he claimed, in 1993, that the lethargy had been too long, for if under the single-party regime journalists could explain their lack of organisation and solidarity by government interference and laws limiting the freedom of association, such an explanation was hardly valid for the period between 1990 and 1996 when the legal barriers against association and organisation had been lifted. Keen as they were to blame others for their disunity and disorganisation, the journalists did not succeed, even once, in coming together to examine critically the state of their profession. Even when organisations interested in having journalists better organised had taken the initiative in inviting them to workshops, attendance was either poor or the discussions dwelled more on polemics and external factors than on internal problems.

Whether one blames the government, the quest for stardom, individualism, or the superiority complex of some and the inferiority complex of others for the lack of unity among Cameroonian journalists during the first five years of the current democratic transition, divisions within the ranks of the profession had brought about a catalogue of problems: 'Today we are witnessing all sorts of excesses and revelations that bring disgrace and discredit to the entire profession.'[19] The absence of an association to regulate admission into the profession had resulted in:

> indiscriminate recruitment by the owners of some newspapers, of journalists devoid of any training and for whom the word 'ethics' did not mean much. Overnight, propelled into obscure newsrooms, pen in hand, they let loose their emotions and their imagination to the detriment of evidence and information.[20]

The Union of Cameroon Journalists (UCJ)

Before Cameroon became a one-party state in 1966, associations of journalists existed in both francophone and anglophone regions. The first ever was the West Cameroon Association of Journalists (WCAJ), created on 27 July 1965, with headquarters in Limbe (then Victoria) and with Patrick Tataw Obenson of *Cameroon Outlook* as its president. A short time later, the Association Nationale des Journalistes Professionnels du Cameroun (ANJPC), headed by Auguste Moutongo Black, was created in the francophone region. Their tasks included working in favour of press freedom, promoting better professional standards, and seeking recognition of journalism as a profession. With the unified party came le Syndicat National des Journalistes Professionnels du Cameroun (SNJPC), created on 28 January 1969, with a membership of 115 journalists. In 1972, the association became an arm of the Union Nationale des Travailleurs Camerounais (UNTC), which was itself an organ of the sole party, the Union Nationale Camerounaise (UNC). Other, short-lived, attempts made at creating associations included the founding, in September 1972, of the Syndicat National des Employés de Presse et la Formation Privée (SYNDEPP) and Le Syndicat National de la Presse Privée et Mass Média (SNPPMM), whose president, Dominique Fouda Sima, was appointed president of UNTC within the UNC. Not only were the two positions incompatible, but since Dominique Fouda Sima was remunerated as president of UNTC and held a prominent position in the central committee of the ruling party, it was difficult for him to be impartial. In a desperate quest for a meaningful nationwide association, the Cameroon Association of Journalists (CAJ) was created in June 1979 to replace WCAJ, following reunification of the two Cameroons in 1972. But the Ministry of Territorial Administration was reluctant to grant authorisation to any association created outside the framework of the single party. Hence, not only was the CAJ illegal, it had enormous difficulties meeting, given that its members were dispersed throughout the country and were often too poor to muster the funds needed for such meetings.

Following the December 1990 liberalisation laws, some attempts were made to form professional associations, but these were either specialised (e.g. the National Association of Professional Media Women (NAPMEW), the Association des Journalistes Economiques du Cameroun (AJEC)) or were founded along regional or linguistic lines (e.g the Cameroon Association of English-Speaking Journalists (CAMASEJ) and the Federation of Cameroon Media Professionals (FCMP) of the North West province). As for the Organisation Camerounaise pour la Liberté de Presse (OCALIP), this is not, strictly speaking, an association of journalists. Even if most of its members are journalists, OCALIP is open to all with an interest in promoting press freedom, democracy and human rights in Cameroon. Others, such as the Cameroon Anglophone Journalists Association (CAJA), created in May 1992, hardly survived their first meetings.

The first clear indication that government was willing to consider some degree of freedom of association among journalists, both private and official, came at the National Forum on Communication held in Yaounde in 1994. Among the recommendations made was that a code of ethics be drawn up and adopted by journalists, not politicians or government, and that this be designed along professional and universally recognised standards but adapted to the Cameroonian context. It was also recommended that a National Order of Journalists be created, and that journalists of the public media be encouraged to create their own association, syndicate or federation.

After the forum, and given the ever-mounting cases of unethical and unprofessional journalism, it dawned on journalists that prolonged failure on their part to organise themselves and agree upon a code of ethics could serve as a pretext for government to impose its own code, as it had done in the past. Sources at the Ministry of Communication indeed indicated that the ministry was preparing a project for the creation of an association of journalists, as well as drawing up a code of ethics. The creation of the Union of Cameroon Journalists (UCJ) was not easy. From the beginning, the Friedrich Ebert Stiftung (FES), which funded the initiative and provided material and moral support, was careful to prevent the divisions that had neutralised similar initiatives in the past. It made sure that journalists of both the official and private media were involved from the outset and that emphasis was placed on purely professional issues. At the first meeting, common professional problems were identified and the need for solidarity and credibility was highlighted. Soon afterwards, FES promptly assumed an observer status when a steering committee was elected. The meetings were numerous, delicate and demanding, but eventually bore fruit and the UCJ was born on 18 January 1996, shortly after the law abolishing administrative censorship was promulgated and the courts were given the powers to sanction libel and defamation.

The UCJ was the first major association to be created in the current democratic transition with membership from both the private and official media; thus its members have great hopes for it. Since its creation, the UCJ has put in place a code of ethics, defined conditions for the issue and withdrawal of press cards, and created subcommittees in charge of enforcing various aspects of professionalism (e.g. ethics and discipline). Its aims include: promoting solidarity among journalists; protecting their rights and freedoms; defending their moral, material and professional interests; encouraging and promoting the development and respect of a professional ethic by journalists; fostering better working conditions and standards of living for journalists; promoting freedom of expression and of the press; and working for the training and betterment of skills for journalists.

Among the UCJ's existing sectorial or specialised associations are the following, some of which existed before its creation: the National Association of Professional Media Women (NAPMEW), headed by Carol Ijang Akutu of CRTV; the Association des Journalistes Juristes (AJJ), headed by Guy Roger Ebah of CRTV; the Association des Journalistes Sportifs (AJS), headed by Abed Négo Messang of CRTV; the Association des Journalistes Animateurs (AJA), headed by Lazare Amougou of CRTV; the Association des Journalistes Economistes Camerounais (AJEC), headed by Emmanuel Noubissie Ngankam, former employee of FES and former proprietor of *Dikalo*. Future sectorial associations will include the Association des Journalistes Politiques (AJP) and the Association des Journalistes Catholiques (AJC). But, as Ngah (1998) remarks, the greatest motivating factor for the creation of these associations is 'the frantic quest for money and personal gain' rather than the promotion of any professional ideals.

The creation of the UCJ and its sectorial associations has not minimised the tensions, squabbles and divisions among journalists; nor has it led to a satisfactory knowledge of the basics and ethics of journalism. Many journalists still ignore the code (Boh 1997: 41–2). The UCJ does not even have a head office, has no knowledge of its exact membership, and receives very little in membership fees from its estimated 478 members. Due to the dispersion of its officials nationwide, and its lack of funds, the UCJ has failed to meet as regularly as was intended at its creation. As Ngah (1998) puts it, 'the lack of funding has a negative impact on attendance at meetings by members, for it is incumbent on the union to pay for travel, board and lodge of members coming from the provinces'. Even the executive finds it hard to meet regularly. Activities are often initiated and conducted by the general secretary alone, and differences have been known to occur between him and the president or treasurer (Ngah 1998). Little wonder, therefore, that many journalists of the private press 'hold that the UCJ is inefficient and a little too quiet on the cases of journalists arrested and detained as well as over the administrative closure of certain newspapers' (Boh 1997: 41).

The UCJ's affiliates tend to compete with rather than reinforce the union. The UCJ goes unrecognised by many journalists (including an impressive number of veterans) and further lost credibility when its president, Amadou Vamoulké, became a member of the ruling Cameroon People's Democratic Movement (CPDM) central committee. Granted government's abilities to manipulate and to divide and rule, some members of the UCJ, notably those of the private press, are still very distrustful of the government. They would rather not have a head office than turn to the government for one. Thus, a suggestion made by Antoine Marie Ngono of CRTV that the Ministry of Town Planning and Housing be approached for accommodation was turned down by journalists of the private press, claiming that it was necessary to steer clear of the government in order to stay independent. Yet funding of certain projects is contingent upon the existence of a head office (Ngah 1998).

These problems notwithstanding, it is only through a well-organised, strong, united and articulate UCJ that journalists are best placed to promote their values, interests and aspirations as a profession. Only such solidarity as guaranteed by a strong, active and participatory union can enable journalists to play a meaningful role in the democratisation of society, and not simply to be pawns in the hands of external (political, economic and cultural) forces that may or may not have the liberal democratic aspirations of society at heart.

Proliferation of Newspapers

When considering the composition of the Cameroonian press, one is struck by the number of registered newspapers. Estimates from MINAT suggest that there are over four hundred titles. What accounts for so many? Explanations range from the simple desire to take advantage of the 1990 Freedom of Mass Communication law that facilitated the process of starting a newspaper, through the need to make fast money from a public freshly out of its reading slumber and keen on national political developments, to the thirst for stardom and for a medium to articulate the views and interests of particular ethnic and regional pressure groups.

Also worthy of note is the unstable nature of editorial teams, whose members have tended to leave and create their own newspapers. The splits have resulted either from disagreements over politics, quarrels stemming from poor treatment of staff by publishers of already well-established newspapers, the desire to become one's own boss and strike it rich if lucky, or pressure from politicians, groups and lobbies in search of journalists to create and run papers at their beck and call. The following cases of splits bring out the different factors that have made Cameroonian newsrooms unstable.

Dikalo was created after its publishers moved out of *Le Messager* in protest against what they saw to be the high-handedness of Pius Njawe, its publisher. Early in 1992, as already mentioned, the government suspended some six newspapers including *Le Messager*. This resulted in a decision by Pius Njawe to suspend the salaries of his staff and to place them on 'technical leave'. But Emmanuel Ngankam Noubissie, Thomas Eyoum à Ntoh and Jean-Baptiste Sipa found this behaviour unacceptable. They regarded Njawe's indifference to the suspension of the paper and to their financial difficulties abhorrent. They openly wondered why, in the face of such vicissitudes, Njawe should go globetrotting and publicity-seeking instead of staying at home to address their predicament.

The *Weekly Post* publisher, Chief Bisong Etahoben of the South-West province, left the *Cameroon Post* in October 1992, owing to what he believed was unfair treatment by his former boss Paddy Mbawa of the North West province. He took with him Ndikum Patrick Tanifom, who also believed he was being underpaid. Like *Dikalo*, Etahoben's *Weekly Post* started with a middle-of-the-road editorial position. It predictably attracted the same scorn from fellow journalists and supporters of the radical opposition. However, before long, the *Weekly Post* had drifted from its editorial line to being an open instrument for hate propaganda against the North West province. Chief Bisong Etahoben, it was alleged, had been sought by some elites of his native South-West province to fight their political battles against the elites of the North West province, believed to be a hindrance to greater political benefits for the South-West elite at the national level (see Chapter 8). Naturally, the paper did not sell well in the North West province, nor among North-Westerners in the diaspora, and all its staff from that province left. Ndikum Patrick, who was editor of the *Weekly Post*, left in mid-July 1993 and returned to the

Cameroon Post with apologies. Francis Wache and Charly Ndichia also broke away from the *Cameroon Post* and created *The Post*, because of differences with Susungi, its new proprietor, an SDF baron.

Ndzana Seme, an Eton (or Beti) and publisher of *Le Nouvel Indépendant*, quit *La Nouvelle Expression* 'on grounds of principles'. He accused Séverin Tchounkeu, publisher of *La Nouvelle Expression*, of having modified the editorial policy of the paper to satisfy the hidden desires of his Bamileke ethnic group. This notwithstanding, Ndzana Seme was himself accused of having a deep hatred for Bulu, whom he believed had not treated his own group, the Eton, fairly. That aside, his vitriolic condemnation of government excesses was not in doubt, and would subsequently earn him detention and imprisonment at the Kondengui prison.

François Aby Donfack[21] regrets the fact that the majority of journalists today came to the profession not because of love of journalism but simply as a means of livelihood – 'un moyen de gagne pain'. Those who are lucky enough to make some money from journalism invest it elsewhere 'instead of ploughing that money back into the profession'.[22] This point is echoed by Mbakop Fouendip Paul, if we are to believe his allegations against Séverin Tchounkeu of *La Nouvelle Expression*, according to which the latter had bought property at Bonapriso for FCFA 50 million and purchased a rice-processing machine for use in Tonga.[23]

These splits and instability, which, quite strikingly, reflect similar splits in political parties and alliances over the past fourteen years of stalling democratisation, have meant that the press has been preoccupied more with internal wrangles of its own than with a concerted effort to promote a free, professional press. A greater sense of unity, solidarity, organisation and purpose would clearly have done more to resolve some of the critical problems that currently plague them and their profession. Interviews with journalists over the past ten years have consistently pointed not only to the fact that they are all aware of these problems and their causes but to what it would take to resolve them. Elsewhere I have discussed at length journalists' views of what their pressing problems and needs are. Over the years these have not varied much from problems they highlighted in 1994 and 1995, when I ran a training programme for journalists funded by the Friedrich Ebert Stiftung. These include: the need for technical know-how or craftsmanship; the ability to define, master and respect the professional ethos; job security; and specialisation (Nyamnjoh 1996b: 148–65).

To conclude this chapter, it suffices to say that such organisation of the profession as discussed above is indeed imperative, if the media and journalists are to play a positive and significant role in the democratic process in Cameroon. If the above discussion has highlighted the professional and ethical inadequacies of the press, it is still to be established how their partisanship, scapegoatism, ethnic biases and other negative practices have impinged upon the adoption and edification of liberal democracy in Cameroon. Chapter 8 discusses multiparty democracy as victim of a press and society that are reluctant to respect a consensual set of values, and that seem united by a common ambition to promote ethnic interests and thereby heighten communal tensions (Nyamnjoh 1999). But first let us examine in the next chapter the widespread use of political rumour and political cartooning as alternative voices in a context stifled and characterised by monolithic politics.

Notes

1. Elsewhere, I have likened it to a literary genre (Nyamnjoh 1996e).
2. See Keye Ndogo, *Jeune Afrique*, 23 February 1995.
3. *Le Messager*, 17 October 1992.
4. *Le Patriote*, 14 June 1991.
5. *Cameroon Post*, 17 July 1992.
6. For an idea of court cases concerning the press between 1990 and 1993, see Datchoua Soupa 1993.
7. See, for example, *Le Front Indépendant* 32, February 1998, for the allegations made by Mbakop Fouendip Paul against Séverin Tchounkeu, proprietor and editor-in-chief of *Nouvelle Expression*, in this connection.
8. *Le Patriote*, 14 June 1991.
9. Ngoh Nkwain, *Cameroon Post*, 30 August 1990.
10. *Le Messager*, 7 January 1992.
11. Ibid.
12. See *Cameroon Post*, 2 April 1992.
13. Ibid.
14. Dominik Fopoussi, *Le Messager*, 30 April 1992.

15. *Cameroon Post*, 17 July 1992.
16. See Decree No. 92/313 PM, 24 September 1992.
17. *Le Messager*, Special Edition, 25 April 1991.
18. See *Cameroon Calling*, 21 February 1993.
19. See Michel Epee, *Le Messager*, 19 March 1992.
20. Ibid.
21. Interviewed, 24 June 1994 in Douala.
22. Interview with François Aby Donfack, 24 June 1994, in Douala.
23. See *Le Front Indépendant*, 23 February 1998.

7

Creative Appropriation of ICTs, Rumour, Press Cartoons and Politics

In a context where ordinary people are peripheral to global trends and subjected to the high-handedness and repression of their own governments, it is easy to slip into metanarratives that celebrate victimhood. But if there is reason to be pessimistic and cynical, there is often, on closer inspection, cause to be hopeful as well. However repressive a government is and however profound the spiral of silence induced by standardised global media menus, few people are ever completely mystified or wholly duped. In other words, there is always room – sometimes through radical or alternative media – for initiative or agency to challenge domination, exploitation and the globalisation of poverty (Downing 2001). Histories of struggle in Africa are full of examples in this connection (Mbembe 1992, 2001; Gecau 1997; Barber 1997), which demonstrate why no understanding of the media is complete without a focus on the radical or alternative media (Downing 2001).

Political control, draconian press laws, selective communication and downright misinformation and disinformation by states in Africa have pushed ordinary people to seek alternative ways of satisfying their information and communication needs. Among these alternatives are what Spitulnik terms 'small media' – 'such as graffiti, flyers, underground cassettes, Internet listservs, slogans, jokes, and rumors', which, despite being rather diffuse and not direct in their dialogues with the state and global structures of repression, nevertheless serve as 'vital and pervasive undercurrents and reservoirs of political commentary, critique, and potential mobilization'. In this way, they deserve their place 'as a crucial part of civil society and the public sphere' (Spitulnik 2002). This chapter examines the ways marginalised Africans have, as individuals, communities and interest groups, creatively appropriated ICTs, rumour and political cartoons, to 'discuss state authority, political accountability, and representation' (Spitulnik 2002: 179).

Creative Appropriation of ICTs

We have already alluded to the networks of various kinds taking advantage of the Internet to push ahead their agenda in situations where the conventional media continue to blunt aspirations for creative diversity (Spitulnik 2002). True, the Internet is not free from the logic of domination and appropriation typical of neoliberalism. But it clearly offers real alternatives, if well harnessed to serve popular social causes. Although connectivity is lower in Africa than in other regions of the world (Jensen 2000; Franda 2002; Leslie 2002), local cultural values of sociality, negotiation, interconnectedness, interdependence and coexistence (Gecau 1997; Nyamnjoh 2002a) make it possible for people to access the Internet without necessarily being directly connected. In many situations, it suffices for a single individual to be connected for whole groups to benefit. The individual in question acts as a relay point or communication node, linking others in myriad ways, bringing hope to those whom otherwise would be dismissed as not belonging (Olorunnisola 2000). Hence, it is much more meaningful to study what Africans *do with* ICTs through enculturation, rather than simply to focus on what ICTs *do to* Africans (van Binsbergen 2004).

In the Cameroonian city of Bamenda, for example, resident telephone lines are grossly inadequate and very defective at best; at the same time Internet connections are difficult to get and expensive. But literate and illiterate alike, eager to stay in touch with relations, friends and opportunities within Cameroon and in the diaspora, daily flood the few Internet points with messages to be typed and emailed for them. Replies to their e-mails are printed out, addressed and pigeonholed for them by the operators who can only afford to check for mails twice a day. What is noteworthy, however, is that the high connection charges do not seem to affect those determined to stay in touch with the outside world. The names of some of the Internet businesses (e.g. '*Allied* Bamenda', '*Sprint* Communications', and '*Mondial* Computers') reflect this commitment. Through such connections, people are able to exchange news on family, projects, events, and developments of a personal and general nature. They are also able to learn about different cultural products and make arrangements to acquire them. It is mainly through this means that Cameroonians abroad do not lose out on local musical releases, publications, satirical humour, artefacts and fashion. Each visitor to the home village is armed with a long list of cultural products to take back. Many bachelors and spinsters in the diaspora would otherwise have given up on marrying from their home village or country, and doing so in accordance with local customs and traditions, were email not there to facilitate contacts and negotiations with parents and potential families-in-law.

Among anglophone Cameroonians, where feelings of marginalisation by the state and exclusion from the mainstream media are high, many people, especially youths, are increasingly turning to the Internet. They use it as a vehicle to air their views on various aspects of their predicament, centring mostly on their territory and community as victim of gross mismanagement by a corrupt and inefficient francophone-dominated state (Konings and Nyamnjoh 2003). Their main channels on the Internet include web pages, discussion and mailing groups.[1] These are created and managed by anglophone youths, usually Grassfielders of the North West province, and mostly based in the American diaspora. Because of their influential nature, these mailing and discussion groups have even attracted the attention of the state, especially after June 2004 when a rumour claiming that President Biya had died in Switzerland was alleged by the government to have been started by an online newspaper, the *African Independent*, and spread the world over by various listservs in conjunction with the cellphone. Following the rumour, the minister of communication issued a press release threatening court action and calling on 'all users of the Internet to be vigilant on the type of information they receive on the Internet, where some editors and producers exploit the new liberty

offered them by the new communication and information technologies, to abuse the credulity of the public and want to give credit to
their erroneous information'.[2] Normally indifferent in the past to this
traffic, government departments and members of the ruling party now
monitor its content on a daily basis, determined to track and close
down websites deemed to be unpalatable. But policing the Internet
is by no means an easy task, especially for an underresourced and
highly unpopular government like President Biya's. Given the flexible
nature of the Internet, real identities of users can be hidden under
ambiguous usernames, making provocative and fearless exchanges more
possible. Those who participate in the discussions mentioned above are
anglophones both in Cameroon and the diaspora, pro-government or
pro-SDF or pro-Southern Cameroons independence. Among them are
the most radical and most conciliatory alike. This clearly highlights
the importance of the Internet in providing the space for anglophone
issues in a state that has stifled such debate and monopolised the
conventional media. Critics of the government no longer feel obliged
to be physically located in Cameroon to be relevant to the ongoing
struggles for democracy, and thus 'challenge the very notion that
processes of civil society always occur within the physical boundaries
of the nation-state' (Spitulnik 2002: 179). Quite strikingly, however,
discussions even at this level tend to reflect the same tensions and
multiple divisions that the politics of belonging and autochthony
have brought to the fore (see Chapter 8). The Internet discussions not
only shape what is discussed in society; they also reflect the inherent
divisions that autochthony brings about.

The same creative appropriation is true of other technologies such
as the videocassette recorder (VCR), photocopier, fax machine and
cellphone. In the 1970s, the proliferation of the VCR coincided with
Ahidjo's domination of radio and apathy for 'la bonne parole officielle'
among the literate urbanites (Djuidjeu 1988). In the late 1980s and early
1990s, photocopiers and fax machines allowed the budding opposition
and civil society organisations to bypass censorship – especially since
the Yondo Black affair and the controversial launching of the Social
Democratic Front (SDF) party. In 1992, when a state of emergency
was decreed in Bamenda and John Fru Ndi of the SDF was placed
under house arrest for contesting the presidential election results, his

party relied heavily on fax machines and photocopiers installed at his residence for staying in touch with the outside world. The government was reportedly embarrassed when its delegation touring Europe was preceded everywhere by faxed documents detailing the massive election fraud. In certain cases, the photocopiers and fax machines were situated in government offices, and were used by civil servants and officials sympathetic to oppositional politics.

The popularity of the fax machine and the photocopier in Cameroon was analogous to the situation in Banda's Malawi where excessive censorship pushed dissidents to adopt both technologies as alternatives. According to Lwanda (1993), the fax machine not only made it possible to bypass the need for official 'clearance' of information before dissemination but also provided for anonymity. Faxing and photocopying also tended to speed up 'the responses of exiles and sympathisers from the outside world' who could communicate 'cheaply, quickly, safely and extremely effectively' with government, NGOs, churches and other institutions in Malawi. 'The Malawi government, though they tried, could not disconnect all business fax machines without hampering the already precarious economic activity of the country' (Lwanda 1993: 270–72).

The latest technology to be domesticated is the cellphone, whose phenomenal ability to spread information, especially when complemented by the Internet and word of mouth, was demonstrated in June 2004 by the rumoured death of President Paul Biya. It took a couple of days only for the rumour to spread the world over, and to put on the defensive a government used mainly to conventional channels of control. Political dissidents or subversives are able to bypass such conventional channels of control, and they are easily tipped off to the possible danger of collaborators in the centre of state power. Dissident action can be coordinated right up to the minute of execution by collaborators who do not have to be physically located in their national territories to be relevant and useful to ongoing struggles. At the social level, diasporic Africans or migrants collectively supply a free phone to someone in a village whom they can call. In the Bamenda Grassfields, for example, marriages, feasts, funerals, crydie, and village development initiatives can no longer pass by any Grassfielder simply because they are in the diaspora. The cellphone has become like the long arm of the village leadership, capable of reaching even the most distant 'sons and daughters of the soil' trapped in urban spaces (Geschiere and Nyamnjoh 1998). The dramatic increase in the sale and theft of cellphones is an indication that this technology has been eagerly grasped by Cameroonians exploring ways of denying exclusion its smile of triumph.

Under the current structural adjustment programme, Cameroon has restructured and privatised some of its telecommunications facilities. In 1998 the Cameroon Telecommunication Company (Camtel) was created by merging Intelcam and the Department of Telecommunications at the Ministry of Post and Telecommunications. Another company created was the Cameroon Telecommunication Mobile Company (Camtel Mobile), an affiliate of Camtel, with the specific duty of installing and exploiting of mobile phones in the country. With this initiative, private investors such as Mobilis (or Orange) and MTN–Cameroon have since extended and improved upon the telecommunications services. From a fixed telephone network of around 87,000 subscribers since independence, Cameroon now boasts more than 200,000 cellphone subscribers for MTN–Cameroon alone. Owning a telephone or being connected by Internet has since 2000 become much less of a luxury for those who can afford it in the major cities. As in South African townships and informal settlements (Thoka 2001), poor and urban dwellers in Cameroon are using the cellphone creatively to stay in touch with rural relatives and through them maintain healthy communications with their roots. Even those who cannot afford a cellphone stand to benefit thanks to the sociality and solidarity of the local cultures of which they are a part. Because the tam-tam remains relevant, even as the Internet and the cellphone are adopted and celebrated (Ngwainmbi 1995; Ras-Work 1998; Spitulnik 2002; van Binsbergen 2004), Africans are able to make the best of all worlds in a context where surviving has long ceased to be a matter of course.

Political Rumour

In Cameroon and most of francophone Africa, political rumour, together with various forms of political derision through word-play dominate what is popularly referred to as radio trottoir (pavement or sidewalk radio) and *rádio boca a boca* in lusophone Africa. This section argues that rumour, defined not as falsehood but as the emergence and circulation of information that is either not yet confirmed publicly or refuted by official sources, is an integral part of the fabric of Cameroonian society. Consumed alike by the rich and the poor, the literate and the illiterate, rumour is arguably the most popular source of information both for the private press and for the information-starved public. The section explains the ubiquity of rumour in Cameroon, not simply by the country's strong oral tradition, but also owing to the rigid control of information and communication by the power elite. In this situation, rumour flourishes as a legitimate source of information for the marginalised majority. Thus rumour, far from being something essentially negative and false – to be rejected as unaccountable and unconfirmed and not to be romanticised (Hyden and Leslie 2002: 24–5), is like the voice of the voiceless seeking to challenge passivity and the oppressive discourses of officialdom (Toulabor 1981; Mbembe 1992, 2001: 142–72; Diamani 1995; Nlandu-Tsasa 1997; Bourgault 1995: 200–205), in the same way that 'alternative small media' function despite their invisibilities (Spitulnik 2002). Rumour, Bourgault observes, 'is underground news, an alternative to the official press, which is tedious, censored, uninformative, and often unintelligible', and as such is a 'free and uncontrolled "medium"', to which 'everyone is a potential contributor' (Bourgault 1995: 202).

Cameroonians are more likely to become informed by rumour than by radio, television or newspaper. This, some may argue, is hardly surprising, given Cameroon's very strong oral tradition: little is put in writing, even by the literate minority. Among the civil servants and administrators, preference for oral communication is motivated by the need for self–protection. Rumour is part and parcel of daily life in Cameroon, and is so popular that various names have been created to denote it: We hear of *radio trottoir*, 'radio one-battery', 'radio kongosa', 'radio 33', 'radio Kaake no-battery', 'FM Malabo', and so on. Implied in these names is the idea that media do not necessarily require technological sophistication to be credible and appreciated.

Can the ubiquity of rumour in Cameroon simply be explained away by illiteracy and the strong oral traditions of the people? Were illiteracy and orality to blame for the love of rumour, would one not expect radio and television to be popular with Cameroonians? Is this the case? Although it is tempting to make the sweeping affirmation that radio and television are indeed popular, a more informed look at CRTV shows that this popularity is more imagined than real. Illiteracy, though a handicap, cannot be an insurmountable obstacle to someone who really believes there is something of value to be got out of a newspaper, especially in a context of sociality, solidarity and coexistence. If illiteracy and orality are not really to blame for the popularity of political rumour with Cameroonians, then what is?

Types of political rumour in Cameroon

To answer the question above, it is important first of all to identify the types of political rumour that are popular with Cameroonians. In journalism we know that news is about important events and great personalities. Similarly rumour targets those in the limelight. A person must be perceived as having a certain standing to be earmarked for comments, rumours and calumny. As Shibutani (Kapferer 1987: 17–18) argues, at the origin of every rumour must be an event that is both important and ambiguous. Again like the conventional media, rumour is involved not only in the dissemination of information about events but also with their interpretation and commentary.

The centralised and overbearing nature of the state in Cameroon makes the president, his activities and collaborators primary targets for rumour. Because the political changes heralded are more claims than reality, rumour has remained very much alive, attending to the information needs of most ordinary people. Taking President Paul Biya and his immediate collaborators as cases in point, almost every important event of their twenty-two years in power has been preceded and followed by rumour. And in all cases, the rumours have been carried both by word of mouth and by the critical private print media. Increasingly, the Internet and the cellphone are vehicles for such rumours, as newspapers go online and electronic discussion networks multiply.[3] A few examples will suffice:

1. When the markets of Foumban (1984), Kumba (1988 and 1990), Bafoussam (1989), Mokolo in Yaounde (1992), and Congo in Douala (1992) caught fire, rumour pointed an accusing finger at the government, saying these were politically motivated 'disasters'. Also, when an attempt was made to burn down Hotel Arcade in Douala on the night of 9 August 1991 by setting fire to rooms 305 and 309, it was rumoured that the government was behind it. Rumour alleged that the authorities wanted to cripple financially the proprietor of the hotel, Joseph Kadji Defosso, whom it identified strongly with the radical opposition at the time.

2. When first lady Jeanne Irene Biya died on 29 July 1992, in the absence of her husband, who was in Dakar at a meeting, it was rumoured that President Biya had arranged for her to be killed and had left the country (for a meeting where his presence was not mandatory) as an alibi. His behaviour, the rumour claimed, was very suspect. Why had he not allowed her body to be laid in state? Why such a rush to bury her? Why had CRTV and Cameroon Tribune, the official media, been so economical with information regarding her 'brief illness', the purported cause of her death? When soon after her death, two European reverend sisters whom she had visited shortly before were found murdered at Djoum, it was alleged that they had been killed because they must have known the truth surrounding the circumstances of her death. Other deaths such as that of Motaze Roger, the president's personal aide, a presidential cook, and Jean Assoumou, were all mysteriously linked by rumour to President Biya.

3. President Biya's marriage to Chantal Vigouroux on 23 April 1994 was preceded by rumours and speculations, some of which claimed that he was to marry President Omar Bongo's daughter. Cameroon Tribune (10 February 1993) and CRTV (bulletins of 9 February 1993) were used to refute a rumour started by a report in International News Bi-Hebdo of 28 January 1993 that the president was to marry Bongo's daughter on 12 February 1993. It was also

rumoured that Chantal Vigouroux had been a prostitute when a bar attendant, and that her twin boys had been conceived with a taxi-driver boyfriend from Bafut in the North West province, who was shot dead by the traffic police after the wedding and the children's birth certificates doctored to preserve presidential prestige. Prior to this, it had been rumoured that Frank Biya, born to Jeanne Irene Biya's sister and only son to President Biya until the marriage to Chantal, had actually been fathered by a late CRTV journalist – Mark Nibo, also of the North West province. The rumour had been intended to present the president as incapable of making a woman pregnant, and to dramatise the role of the North West province (home to John Fru Ndi and birthplace to the radical SDF) as a political and psychological thorn in the president's flesh.

4. Cabinet reshuffles are always preceded by speculation and rumour. Incumbents and aspirants are said to scheme for positions in the cabinet and to employ natural and occult forces to attain this end. Various lodges and fraternities are alleged to play a major part in determining who stays and who becomes what. Among the key players are Rosicrucianism and Freemasonry, both of which are influenced by and imported from France. It was even rumoured at one point that President Biya had financed the construction of one of the Rosicrucian lodges in France (Nouvelle Expression, 15 January and 24 March 1999).

5. After the presidential election of 11 October 1992, it was rumoured that the incumbent CPDM candidate, Paul Biya, had offered the sum of FCFA 200 million to the chairman of the national electoral commission and FCFA 25 million to each of the other members of the commission in order to rig the elections in his favour. Similar allegations were made about the Supreme Court after the legislative elections of 17 May 1997. A salary increase for judges, made shortly before the May 1997 election, was rumoured to have been intended as an inducement by government.

6. During the inauguration of Bill Clinton as US president in January 1993, it was rumoured that he had personally invited John Fru Ndi of the SDF and had failed to tender a similar invitation to

President Paul Biya. This, the rumour held, was a clear indication of American legitimation of John Fru Ndi as the real winner of the 11 October 1992 presidential elections. This rumour provoked the government's spokesman, the minister of state for communication, to organise a series of press conferences to deny that John Fru Ndi had been invited personally by Bill Clinton.

7. Professor Gervais Mendo Ze, general manager of Cameroon Radio Television (CRTV) for over fourteen years, has been at the centre of repeated rumours connecting him with straddling religions. Rumour makes him both a committed Catholic who propounds the virtues of the Virgin Mary on the one hand, and a Rosicrucian whose mystical totem is a boa constrictor that sucks the blood of young virgins whom he entices with money and expensive gifts of necklaces. On 15 February 1999, a girl known simply as 'cousine Elise' phoned the Yaounde FM94 presenter Joly Nnib Ngom, to accuse 'a well placed personality of the republic' with whom she had been going out for six or seven months of having given her an expensive gold necklace in the form of a boa constrictor. Rumour immediately associated Mendo Ze with the girl, and matters worsened when Mendo Ze suspended the presenter of the programme. The rumour was given extended coverage in the private press[4] and widely disseminated in taxis, bars and other public places. Although the presenter was eventually reinstated, the rumour refused to die, and Mendo Ze has since been given the nickname of *serpentologue* to go with *mariologue*.

8. In Yaounde on Christmas Day 1999, four children (one boy and three girls) of the same parents (Ernest and Fidoline Anaba) were reported missing after having been sent to collect change from Maguy Bar Restaurant, where they had earlier bought drinks. News of their disappearance caused pandemonium. Following a search, all the children were found dead with their genitals cut off three days later, in an abandoned Renault 9 car in a garage.[5] Some time after, rumour began to circulate that Professor Mendo Ze had hired someone to carry out the ritual killing since he was known to traffic in human body parts. A few months later, Magistrate Louise Ndzie was savagely murdered in front of his

children at their home in Yaounde. It was alleged that he was the one handling the file on the murdered four children and had vowed to nail Mendo Ze for his occult and diabolic practices. Having failed to persuade the magistrate through his wife (with whom he was said to have had an affair) and with a bribe of several million FCFA, Mendo Ze reportedly asked the wife to hire thugs to eliminate her magistrate husband.

9. In 1999, eight years after the attempted arson attack on Hotel Arcade in Douala, the proprietor, whom it was rumoured the government had wanted to cripple financially for supporting the opposition SDF party, released, at his Union des Brasseries Camerounais (UCB), a new beer named after himself: Kadji Beer. The release was followed by a series of adverts which all started with: 'Il a fallut du temps' (It was worth the wait). These ads were immediately corrupted in certain circles to read: 'Il a fallut du temps, pour que je vous insulte correctement. Les camerounais me boivent, mais ils vous crachent' (It was worth the wait, in order that I could insult you well. Cameroonians drink me, but are revolted by you). Kadji Beer, which instantly became popular with opposition supporters, was interpreted as the proprietor's revenge on President Biya.

10. From 5 to 9 June 2004, it was rumoured among Cameroonians at home and in the diaspora that 71-year-old President Biya, widely believed to be in poor health, had died in Switzerland – only for him to resurface and joke about it: 'The ghost greets you warmly'. He remarked on state radio and television that 'Those who wish me dead have the next twenty years to wait.'[6] The rumour, arguably the most widely disseminated ever in the country's history, benefited from a fascinating combination of the Internet, the cellphone, word of mouth and a popular hunger for democracy to spread far and wide, embarrasing a government unfamiliar with dealing with alternative media. Commentaries in private newspapers and the Internet seemed to suggest a collective, if only symbolic, assassination of President Biya by all those whose aspirations for democracy and the good life have repeatedly been thwarted by the insensitivities of his 22-year regime to basic transparency and the rule of law.

Why political rumour is popular

Such political rumours are innumerable. But what gives them life? What makes them so irresistible, palatable and popular with the public? The reasons are many. It has been observed elsewhere that rumour is most likely to become an alternative source of information during a crisis, when there is a heightened need for information in the public. This is especially likely when the conventional media, for whatever reason, lack credibility.

According to this theory, Cameroon must be in a prolonged state of crisis during which rumour has acquired the status of a legitimate institution of communication for a majority of the population. What accounts for this legitimation of rumour? I see the main reason in government's monopoly over the official channels of mass communication and its clampdown on alternative sources of information.

To tighten its grip on power, the government has actively pursued the withholding and outright manipulation of information. To do this effectively, in addition to laws of repression that muffle private practice in journalism, the government typically employs as journalists those it has taken time to mould into mouthpieces and uncritical proponents of official rhetoric and precepts. Tenacious journalists, if any, are sanctioned or sidelined with overt embargoes on sensitive news items or institutions, capricious censorship, suspension without pay, demotional transfer, administrative appointments away from the microphone or the virulence of their pens, interrogations by the police, arrest and detention for months without trial (see Nyamnjoh 1989: 174–94; see also Chapter 4).

Treated thus, the bulk of the public has had little choice but wholeheartedly to embrace rumour as the only uncensored source of information on national events and prominent personalities. The scarcity of information critical of government (the president in particular) in the official media has left Cameroonians vulnerable to everything alternative. The rigid control of information by government has made Cameroonians generally suspicious and incredulous towards the official media and almost too uncritical vis-à-vis anything anti-government or foreign. The fact that the government often reacts with hysterical denunciations of critical reports by foreign media, and against the

Internet, cellphones and an individual journalist in the case of the rumoured death of President Biya, has only hardened public attitudes against its 'noble' truth.

Rumour, far from being falsehood because not confirmed or accounted for, is the undoctored counter-truth of citizens questioning life at the margins of state power and skewed indicators of newsworthiness. Given that there is no absolute social truth, truth becomes what the public believes it to be. And since the government has confined the official channels of communication to its own truth, the people's truth is expressed by way of rumour: rumour defined not as falsehood but as the emergence and circulation of information that is either not yet confirmed publicly or refuted by official sources; rumour as a sort of 'black market for information', seeking to provide understanding of important events on which the official sources are silent (Kapferer 1987: 25). As Kapferer (1987: 22–5) points out, to the public the dividing line between information and rumour is not an objective one; it is subjective, the result of people's convictions. When someone is convinced by a message brought by a relative, friend or acquaintance, he or she will consider it true. But if he or she doubts it, the same message is qualified as rumour. Once qualified as rumour it ceases to spread. Kapferer sees rumour as the public's attempt to dialogue with the authorities, for, by revealing secrets and suggesting hypotheses, rumour forces the authorities to speak. It challenges the status of government or the conventional media as the only authorised voice or channel of communication. Rumour, he argues, is like spontaneously taking the floor to speak without being invited to do so, and often in opposition. Official disclaimers do not convince, just as official and credible no longer go together. As parallel and sometimes counter-information to official information, rumour is a counter-power.

The concern shown by the Cameroonian authorities over the spread of political rumour shows that rumour makes them ill at ease. Thus the question: if rumour is invariably false information, as the government claims, then why worry about it? After all, the truth will always triumph. As Kapferer (1987: 16) observes, rumour worries not because it is false, but because it is information that the powerful cannot control.

Wherever it has been studied, *radio trottoir* (epitomised by rumour and political derision) has proved itself the perfect medium of communicating dissent and discussing the powerful in unflattering terms. In Togo (Toulabor 1981; Ellis 1993), Zaire (Diamani 1995; Nlandu-Tsasa 1997), São Tomé e Príncipe (Seibert 1999: 389–403), Cameroon (Mbembe 1992, 2001: 142–72) and elsewhere in Africa (Ellis 1989; Bourgault 1995: 200–205), *radio trottoir* has proved effective not only as a vehicle for popular and informal discussion of power and current affairs by urbanites in particular (Ellis 1989) but also as a counter-power: the 'poor person's bomb' (Mbembe 2001: 158) or the 'weapons of the powerless' (Toulabor 1981: 69) in the face of government arbitrariness, water cannon, tear gas and guns. Usually in the form of 'anecdotal gossip', *radio trottoir* serves the poor as 'a phenomenon of revenge and a rebuttal of censorship' (Yoka cited in Devisch 1995: 623) against 'the totalitarian discourse of the Party–State', often through the display of 'an extraordinary verbal creativity' rich in humour, parody and irony (Devisch 1995: 623–4).

In his study of the postcolony, Mbembe argues that political derision or humour directed at the autocrat is an attempt by ordinary people to present the powerful as ordinary mortals with the same appetites and nature as any other person. 'Hence the image of, say, the President's anus is not of something out of this world – though to people's great amusement the official line may treat it as such; instead, people consider it as it really is, capable of defecating like any commoner's.' Through ridicule, Mbembe argues, ordinary people can tame state power and render it powerless. The autocrat thus stripped of his aura or magic becomes domesticated – a mere idol, a familiar friend or a member of the family as much for the ruled as for the rulers (Mbembe 1992: 8–9, 2001: 109–12). By this logic, President Biya's rumoured death was intended not so much as a fact, but rather as a wish or as a reminder to him and those who assist him in making an illusion of democracy that he is a candidate for death like everyone else.

Ellis argues that 'Africa's new press' shares many characteristics with *radio trottoir*, including identification with certain values, beliefs and outlooks commonly held by the population, some of which may appear bizarre and highly implausible to Western reporters and readers

(Ellis 2000: 225–6). In this regard, it is noteworthy that most of the rumours in Cameroon discussed above were also reported in the private press as news stories, a trend common throughout francophone Africa (Bourgault 1995: 204). That the press often readily sacrifices its canons of rigorous investigation, objectivity and proof (à l'occidentale) is also indicative, I would argue, of a journalism under constant pressure to be grounded in the popular epistemologies of African societies, where reality is not simply a question of appearances and truth is not always what is legitimated by 'official' or 'confirmed' sources (Mbembe 2001: 142–72; Nyamnjoh 2001b).

Cartooning and Democracy in Africa

As the most distinctive feature of radio trottoir, rumour, as noted above, defines itself in opposition to official discourse that it challenges and seeks to replace. The same is true of political cartooning in general, which could be described as a sketched or caricatured version of rumour about the high and mighty in society. Such forms are an unequivocal confirmation of the fact that withholding relevant information from the public results in desperate attempts by the public to invent that information, and that such inventions are seldom a flattering mirror of the status quo. While there is obviously no consensual interpretation of political cartooning, I am critical of any suggestion that such cartooning has little impact simply because it has failed to bring about a change in the status quo. These forms of communication induce gradual and cumulative effects.

One of the instruments of the current democratic process in Africa has been political cartooning. Cartoonists have mushroomed everywhere in the continent since 1990, most of them focusing daringly and narrowly on politics, and few surviving the rough and tumble of politics or journalism to be of sustained service to democratisation. In the words of Tanzanian Godfrey Mwampembwa (Gado), a staff cartoonist with Nation Newspapers in Kenya, cartooning 'emerged as a growing profession' in most African countries with the introduction or reintroduction of multiparty politics in the 1990s. Political changes, he argues, 'brought greater freedom of expression as well as of the press', which 'injected new life into newspapers, magazines and the publishing industry generally'. Until then, censorship, both self-imposed and administrative, had made it extremely difficult for artists to be creative and critical towards the ruling elite. Even so, some cartoonists managed to work during this period, 'despite the dangerous times'. Before the current waves of liberalisation, the fear of reprisals by cartoonists severely 'limited creativity'. Some were deported from their countries while others were forced underground. Thus, prior to the 1990s in many African countries, 'it was unimaginable' that key political figures would feature in cartoons, 'even in so-called independent newspapers' (Mwampembwa 1997: 17). In the 1970s and 1980s more muted forms of criticism were the norm. Excessive control of conventional channels of communication largely accounted for the popularity and importance of *radio trottoir*.

Today not only has *radio trottoir* become more open and more daring, but cartooning has joined the bandwagon of political commentary and satire. The situation of cartoonists has changed remarkably. Caricatures of presidents and their ministers are no longer uncommon in the press. In Nigerian newspapers – the *Guardian* and the *Times* for example – cartoons depict political leaders and the military, their partners in power, in very stereotypical fashion. Associated with the Nigerian politician in cartoons are such words as: 'rigger, thug, area boy, hidden agenda', terms that imply 'a cheating, deceitful, crooked, and corrupt individuality, and emphasize the politician's lack of morals and ignorance and contempt for justice and fairplay'. Through such cartooning, the politicians are stereotyped as 'completely selfish, self-centred, and self-indulgent, lacking in any altruistic thought, action, or motive', and being completely at variance with those they purport to serve. The military, in general, are depicted as forceful, disdainful of propriety, indifferent to established rules and regulations, and as having 'a tendency towards absolutism and totalitarian control' (Medubi 2000: 200–205).

In rare instances cartoonists have earned the respect of distinguished leaders in a country. South Africa is a case in point, where within a few years of the end of apartheid cartooning has blossomed and political cartoonists are highly regarded. Jonathan Shapiro (Zapiro) is a leading South African cartoonist based in Cape Town. He is arguably the best known but is also the most well liked and the most disliked of South African cartoonists. His strength is clearly in the fact that his work leaves few indifferent. Most people in South Africa, from the great to the ordinary, have had something to laugh or cry about in Zapiro cartoons. So have the lowly and the mighty in other countries, including neighbouring Zimbabwe, whose President Mugabe is a favourite target. In 1996 Nelson Mandela acknowledged Zapiro as 'exciting and quite accurate', and in a foreword to Zapiro's 1997 collection Archbishop Tutu praised his passionate desire for South Africans to be good to one another and to the world, by 'showing up our weaknesses and shortcomings' as a nation of diversity and as a young democracy (Zapiro 1997). To the Mail and Guardian, he is simply 'South Africa's best political cartoonist', a talent he is quite willing to share, as was made clear to me in an interview (Nyamnjoh 2000b) and also at a workshop I organised in Gaborone on 'Political Cartooning and Democratisation in Southern Africa' (Mason 2001).

At the workshop in question, which was held in Gaborone, 8–10 November 2000, cartoonists from South Africa, Botswana, Swaziland, Zimbabwe, Malawi, Zambia and Tanzania discussed common issues, shared the secrets of their profession and talked about the possibility of setting up an association of African cartoonists. Censorship is still a very real problem for many, although it often takes the shape of more subtle forms of self-censorship by newspaper managers and owners. Swazi cartoonist Thulani Mthethwa reported that it is considered 'in poor taste' and 'anti-Swazi' to portray King Mswati III in cartoons, and is simply not allowed. Innocent Mpofu, cartoonist on the Herald of Zimbabwe, felt it would be imprudent for him to attend sessions where Zapiro was presenting, because of the latter's unflattering portrayals of Mugabe. Mpofu is not allowed to employ caricature in his work and restricts himself to broad social themes.

Malawian cartoonist Deguzman Kaminjolo described the flowering of political cartooning in his country during the heady days of 1993 and 1994, when Hastings Banda was forced by a withdrawal of foreign aid to submit to a national referendum and election, both of which he lost. Opportunities for emerging cartoonists were created by a new spirit of openness and critique, reflected in a rapid proliferation of independent newspapers. According to Kaminjolo, some twenty Malawian cartoonists emerged to celebrate previously unknown levels of freedom of expression, and it was not uncommon for political cartoons to appear on the front pages of the independent papers. Today, Malawian freedom has waned, and cartoonists who enjoyed momentary prominence have faded back into obscurity. In Botswana, where the private press has been relatively free since the early 1980s, government and cartoonists have learnt to tolerate one another and to provide for a common responsibility to democracy and social harmony, according to the self-taught cartoonist Billy Dikeme Chiepe (1996: 31–2). Interestingly as well, both Zambia and Tanzania enjoy vigorous cartooning cultures. Cartoonist Trevor Ford (Yuss) is a Welshman from Cardiff who has lived and worked in Zambia since the late 1960s. As cartoonist for the *Post* of Zambia, Trevor Ford has enjoyed a limited degree of freedom to record the country's travails, despite its steadily failing currency, declining standard of living, and government desire to control.

According to Tanzanian cartoonist David Chikoko, Tanzania's first multiparty elections were held in 1995, and the democratically elected Benjamin Mkapa, an ex-journalist himself, has always held cartoonists in high esteem. The president has been caricatured so often that he is reported to have quipped: 'I can't even remember my own face!' Most of the eleven Tanzanian dailies use strips and political cartoons, and the country has about a dozen humorous periodicals. There are twenty or more active cartoonists working in Dar es Salaam alone, mostly on Swahili papers. One paper, *Sanifu*, a recreational tabloid, is more than half-filled with cartoon strips, rendered in a variety of styles, all in Swahili. Most of the cartoonists work in the vernacular; few of the English-language papers carry cartoons.

In other parts of Africa, the attitudes of the powerful are still as hostile as in Malawi, Zimbabwe and Swaziland. Thus proliferation of cartooning notwithstanding, cartoonists in general continue to have 'a raw deal from government monopolies and the publishing industry', with few of them able to 'get jobs or even to freelance' (Mwampembwa 1997: 17). This is partly because cartooning is either ignored or inadequately promoted by schools and other institutions of training. Hence the tendency for cartooning to be seen as a part-time occupation by people who normally earn their living from doing other things (Mwampembwa 1997: 17; Monga 1997: 148–9).

Indeed, in most parts of the Third World, comic art has not until recently been given much attention. 'As a field, it was banished to the lower echelons of the art and journalism professions, its practitioners ignored and overworked' (Lent 1997: 4). Yet comics have a tremendous potential to foster developmental projects and democratisation, and in certain cases have succeeded impressively (Lent 1997: 5–6, 2001). It is a potential that is all the more promising for Africa where 'the public follows cartoons (editorial, strip and comics) much more than before and people comment on them and react to them' (Mwampembwa 1997: 18). During an interview with Zapiro, I was overwhelmed by the sheer volume of personal correspondences and newspaper articles from South Africans of all walks of life, reacting to his cartoons (Nyamnjoh 2000b).

Political cartooning in Cameroon

Cartooning existed in Cameroon before 1990, but political cartooning was rare, given the repressive laws in place. Censorship, according to Celestin Monga, was what pushed some Douala-based journalists of the private press (Le Combattant, Challenge Hebdo, Le Messager) to begin political cartooning. At first, cartoon pages were not considered to be 'threats to public order'. The censor initially 'did not pay much attention to political caricature, estimating that its impact was negligible'. 'Easy to understand and unusually funny', cartoons 'attracted readers in both rural and urban areas, increasing the readership of the private press, even among illiterate groups of the population. Their success was so fast that the number of newspaper buyers in 1991 was almost four times as great as in 1990' (Monga 1997: 147–8). When cartooning started, it was rather harmless, but after 1991, when it became more political and critical, exposing to public ridicule even what President Biya did between the sheets in his most private moments, the attention of the censors was also drawn to them. Subsequently, cartoons were censored, and cartoonists detained, for being too daring in their 'misrepresentations' of the president and his appetites.

Much of Cameroon's political reality has, on a weekly basis for the past fourteen years of democratisation, been summed up and vividly captured in cartoons. 'Pomposity, venality, corruption and self-importance particularly in public figures' (Thomas and Lee 1997: 2) have invited a critical response from cartoonists working in many newspapers, 'usually in the form of a barb aimed at deflating inflated egos' (Thomas and Lee 1997: 2). While almost every newspaper publishes cartoons, only some (e.g. *Le Messager Popoli, L'Expression de Mamy Wata, Herald Observer*) have specialised in cartoon journalism. These run news stories mainly in cartoons, limiting conventional writing to the barest minimum. Among the leading cartoonists are Nyemb Popoli (*Le Messager Popoli* and *Le Messager*), Jean-Pierre Kenne (*Challenge Hebdo*), Tex Kana (*L'Expression de Mamy Wata* and *La Nouvelle Expression*), Go'away (*Cameroon Tribune*), Gaby (*Mutations* and *Herald Observer*), and Abou (*Galaxie*). Cartoon journalism has sprung up to meet the challenge of political derision (Monga 1997; Mbembe 2001: 142–72), and like most of the critical private press in general, it has singled President Paul Biya out for its most venomous bite. As Mono Ndjana puts it,

> exaggerating every detail of the President's anatomy, sometimes with an immoral twist, has become the stock-in-trade of cartoonists who take special delight in cataloguing every single one of his presumed faults and shortcomings. Going to these sources alone, a foreign reader would immediately think the country is ruled by a gruesome monster. (Mono Ndjana 1997a: 76–7)

Not all cartoonists are critical of the establishment, however. This is how Celestin Monga sums up the political messages of Cameroonian cartoonists:

> Being affiliated with a governmental media, Go'away is usually full of praise for President Biya's government; he only targets the opposition leaders and always tries to depict them along the lines of the official discourse, whereas Popoli, Kenne, Tex Kana, who do not formally belong to any political party, strongly oppose Biya's regime and devote most of their loops to criticizing his policies. (Monga 1997: 149–150)

These neat dichotomies between cartoonists according to political affiliation, true of the early 1990s, have evolved with more and more cartoonists showing increasing disillusionment with both government and opposition, and sometimes, as in the case of Nyemb Popoli, appearing to take over as the Messiah – the only one really capable of defending the interests of the people – or avoiding the temptations of 'the politics of the belly' (Bayart 1993). Increasingly, they see everyone seeking power as either corrupt or corruptible. Cartoonists use the giving and acceptance of bribes as symbol of this corruption, with President Biya repeatedly depicted as a cunning fisherman, fishing with bales or wads of banknotes, targeting opposition leaders and other critical voices in civil society, inviting them to shut up and join the club of those with a mission to bleed the poor to death with pillage. In line with this perspective, the ruling elite are caricatured, lampooned and stigmatised, and their acronyms or slogans creatively corrupted to negate what they claim to stand for. This is a cynical view shared by journalists and the wider public, where it is common to talk of politicians as self-seeking. People are not judged by their ideas but by their bellies, which are seen as either hungry or overfed, threatening or threatened.

Staging natural and supernatural fights for access to the national manger (la mangeoire) for a piece of the national cake is a regular theme in the caricaturing of politicians, opportunistic elites and pseudo-intellectuals. And so is sex. Opposition politicians who yield to the tempting offers of government are depicted as cheap prostitutes, and, generally, a debasing form of sex is portrayed as a weakness which not even the most powerful man in the land can resist. The general manager of Cameroon Radio Television (CRTV) is represented as a boa constrictor who relies on drinking the menstrual blood of adolescent virgins for political survival. Indeed, politicians, the military and others in power at different levels of society are represented as men consumed by phallocratic passions, and they are ridiculed and debased by the girls and women they often imagine themselves to be debasing (Mbembe 2001: 142–72). The young and poor are thus imbued with a fascinating sense of agency in their acts of deceptive submission and strategic resistance; they are presented as accepting the 'gifts' of the government during election campaigns in exchange for promises to vote for the ruling party. In their treatment of these themes, the cartoonists employ new forms of everyday wit and new languages 'that people invent in their daily struggle for survival as a collective response to oppression' (Monga 1997: 151–2). These cartoonists draw extensively from pidgin English, which they blend with French and some of the popular national languages to give a new language rich in innuendo, irony and sarcasm, and which expresses the predicament of the common man in ways unmatched by the English and French of the power elite. Very often, the 'cartoons are filled with popular jokes derived from the painful decay of the social fabric' (Monga 1997: 151–2), jokes which they share with satirical comedians (Jean-Michel Kankan, Dave K. Mocktoi, Tchop Tchop, Antonio, Kouokam Nar6, Mechekan L'Africain, Tchop Die), popular musicians (Eboua Lottin, Lapiro de Mbanga, Prince Ndedi Eyango, Petit Pays, Soustain Parole, Donny Elwood, Longue Longue, etc.), and columnists (Rotcod Gobata, Daniel Rim, etc.) (Nyamnjoh and Fokwang 2003). Celestin Monga sees in their cartoons a translation into laughter of the 'strong sense of collective anger' among Cameroonians. Employing a wide range of coarse and subtle humour, the cartoonists create a constant clash between personal thoughts and official discourse, common sense and official logic, private interests and public responsibilities (Monga 1997: 151–2).

An increasing number of Cameroonians of all walks of life follow cartoons much more than before, and people comment on them in buses, taxis, bars and other public places. Some also react to them through letters, telephone calls or by word of mouth to the cartoonists or the newspaper for which they work. Little wonder therefore that cartoonists are increasingly frowned upon by politicians.

How effective is political cartooning?

The cartoons, sketches, illustrations, drawings or models produced in Cameroonian newspapers are subject to multiple interpretations. Like every communication, they are likely to mean different things to different people depending on their social positions or the relationships they entertain with the power elite. At the level of analysis, Mbembe suggests that the text and the drawings of the cartoonists could actually be analysed separately, especially as 'The expensive richness and extraordinary density of the graphic sign contrast, very often, with the poverty and banality of the comment that accompanies it or attempts to voice it' (Mbembe 2001: 159).

Mbembe argues that the first effect of the loss of total control by the president (whom he calls 'the autocrat') would have been to put him out of sight by so arranging things that he ceases to be 'in front of' people as 'something to see'. 'But the paradox is that in seizing the power of public imagination, the artist amplifies the autocrat's pervasive presence.' Although there is the obvious aim, in these cartoons, of 'weakening' the autocrat and his signs, Mbembe argues, 'The fact, however, is that there is no way of weakening the thing that does not, at the same time, account for its shadow and its doubles.' The cartoonist,

> far from signing the 'thing' in death, rather intensifies its presence by enclosing the subject in a mixture of fascination and dread, a sort of consciousness whose peculiar feature is to be hallucinated ... to the extent that it is the autocrat who offers speech, commands what is listened to and what is written and fills space to the point where he is still being talked of even as the act of creation is claiming to debase him. (Mbembe 2001: 160–65)

Hence his conclusion that 'the hallucinated subject' is still very much 'the beast of burden' or 'the jester' of the autocrat: 'The autocrat sits on his subject's back, harnesses him, and rides him. And makes him shit. Which they do willy-nilly. As a sign of vengeance, if necessary.... Is the subject aware of being taken over by the demoniac thing? How to escape? By breaking the demon? By coating it with excrement? The cartoons that we have been looking at do not yet tell us' (Mbembe 2001: 167–8).

I would argue slightly differently. The fact that President Paul Biya, or the autocrat, to quote Mbembe, dominates discussions of public affairs, current or otherwise, shows how influential he is in public life. But do such discussions in the press, cartoons and *radio trottoir* make him more or less powerful? Mbembe seems to imply that his power would diminish if the public were less preoccupied with him in this way. But I think that it is also important that we pay critical attention to the light in which he is presented. Paul Biya is generally portrayed in very negative terms, which obviously has a greater effect than if the press were simply to ignore him as if he did not exist. Fewer channels refer to the autocrat in the illustrious terms of the past. Even among the Beti, who share the ethnic origins of the president, critical Bikutsi songs have emerged to challenge support for someone who has repeatedly failed to deliver on his promises (Essono 1996; Nyamnjoh and Fokwang 2003). Thus it is crucial to consider the way such discussions or public representations of the autocrat are conducted, since they may either threaten his myths and powers or reinforce them. The very existence of censorship is an implicit recognition of the destructive potential of political cartooning to the 'good image' of the autocrat. Judging from widespread administrative censorship, therefore, and from government's preoccupation with controlling alternative voices, one could say that political cartooning provides a vehicle for dialogue between the governing and the governed – a very useful function in a society where there is little consensus and where neither government nor the opposition seem to be in a hurry to arrive at it. In this way, political cartooning has a similar function to that served by *radio trottoir* and satirical comedians over the years, even under the one party state.

All but one of the cartoonists I have studied are very critical of the president and blame him for almost all of the predicaments ordinary Cameroonians have endured. He is portrayed as an uncaring, unavailable, unaccountable person, who delights in taking holidays in Europe or in his home village and enjoys 'Le Chien Noir' in the company of his youthful mulatto wife and a few cronies. He loathes dialogue, and allows corruption, mismanagement and social decay to run unchecked for a price: total and unconditional loyalty. The president's presence in these critical media is therefore different in that he is not the traditionally orchestrated father of the nation, a visionary, a genius of virtue, a god. He is demystified, rendered ordinary and mortal, demythologised and indeed replaced, eventually, by the cartoonist who, in the face of repeated failures by the power elite, increasingly sees himself as the substitute – the Messiah, the source of hope and salvation.

The effects that cartoons have upon the lives of Cameroonians are far from simple and direct, tempting though it may be to think of the media as powerful tools capable of directly stimulating their audiences. Even a quick look at how actively the disaffected resist government manipulation through state-owned media enables one to understand that media effects are not direct, simple and immediate, and the masses not so passive and helpless as is often suggested. People react to different messages with creativity and agency. They 'may welcome, accept or collude in some cases, but in others they may ignore, select, reshape, redirect, adapt and, on occasions, even completely reject. Even when the same material is available to all and widely consumed, the eventual outcome may vary considerably' (Halloran 1993: 3). To what extent one is influenced by cartoons depends also on one's social situation. Anti-establishment cartooning does not alone suffice to bring about change in Cameroon. The fact is that political cartoons have to act in association with other factors to effect political change, and in that way serve to weaken the forces of repression.

The effect of political cartoons should thus not be measured in terms of their ability to provoke intense resistance. Media effects are far from being direct; rather, they are gradual and cumulative, and usually depend on other factors. Cartoons in Cameroon may not have succeeded in inciting Cameroonians to rebellion, and may indeed 'be thought to have the opposite effect by giving harmless vent to anger and hatred' (Barber 1997: 5), as Mbembe (2001: 142–72) is inclined to argue. Nevertheless, they do show the importance cartoonists and the public (judging from widespread consumption) attach both to keeping a record and providing repression with an unflattering mirror of its excesses and deafness to popular demands for change.

Such creative responses make clear that it is far from the end of the story simply to acknowledge disempowerment and marginalisation. Ordinary Africans are refusing to celebrate victimhood. It is therefore important always to explore how people at the margins of power, wealth and the mainstream media strive to survive. People always find creative ways of making ends meet and of keeping hope alive in hopeless situations. The contention, then, is that Cameroonians and Africans have found myriad ways of participating as active agents in national life and global socio-economic processes, their victimhood notwithstanding.

Notes

1. Examples include www.southerncameroons.org; scncforum@egroups. com; Camnet; Camernetwork@egroups.com; and SDF Forum.
2. See www.africanindependent.com/Cameroon_biya_mort.html for the rumour supposedly started by Ndzana Seme, a Cameroonian journalist now based in the USA, and *Cameroon Tribune*, 8 June 2004, for government disclaimer.
3. See Ambazonia.indymedia.org/en/2004/01/652.shtml for Ebale Angounou's 'Blood: Biya's Power Lotion', and www.africanindependent. com/Cameroon_biya_mort.html for Biya's rumoured death.
4. See *La Nouvelle Expression*, 24 March 1999; *Le Messager*, 7 April 1999; *L'Anecdote*, 6 April 1999; *Mutations*, 1 April 1999; *Dikalo*, 30 March 1999; *Perspectives Hebdo*, 26 March 1999.
5. See *The Herald*, 29 December 1999.
6. See www.africanindependent.com/Cameroon_biya_mort.html; www. wagne.net/messager/messager/2004/06/1670/messager.html; and 'Cameroun: L'Affaire Biya', *Jeune Afrique l'Intelligent*, 13–19 June 2004: 16–20.

8

Liberal Democracy:

Victim of a Partisan and Ethnic Press

One of the main findings of this study is that the media have assumed a partisan, highly politicised, militant role in Africa. They have done so by dividing citizens into the righteous and the wicked, depending on their party-political leanings, ideologies, and regional, cultural or ethnic belonging. By considering the Cameroonian experience, we seek to understand how scapegoatism, partisanship, and regional and ethnic tendencies in the media have affected their liberal democratic responsibility to act as honest, fair and neutral mediators – accessible to all. We do this by looking at polarisation in the press and at how the media have shaped and been shaped by the politics of belonging since the early 1990s.

Almost everywhere in Cameroon, citizens expect the urban elite – including journalists and media proprietors –, to make inroads into the modern centres of accumulation. Since the state is a major source of patronage and resources, it, together with other economic institutions, must be manipulated to divert the flow of finance, jobs and so forth to the home regions from which the heterogeneous urban population originally derive. Thus these elites are under pressure to act as facilitators and manipulators with respect to the state. Through elite development associations, they lobby foreign agencies and NGOs to provide their home villages or regions with new sources of wealth and livelihood (Fisiy and Goheen 1998; Nyamnjoh and Rowlands 1998; Geschiere and Nyamnjoh 1998,

2000). In return for so doing, they may be rewarded with neo-traditional titles in their home villages. These honours confer on them symbolic capital that is not expressed in material wealth but sustained by 'the conspicuous display of decorum and accompanied by public respect' (Fisiy and Goheen 1998: 388), which in turn can always be exploited for political ends at regional and national levels. In certain cases, investing in the village is a way of consolidating success in the city, especially in the politics of ethno-regionalism (Nyamnjoh 1999; Monga 2000; Socpa 2002). According to Goheen (1992), the 'modern big men' or new elite, for whom the ethnic area of Nso in the Cameroonian Grassfields is the home village, are able to redistribute their personal wealth to those back home in exchange for neo-traditional titles 'without giving up their ability to accumulate'. In this way, they continue to take an active role in the traditional government of their home areas. At the same time their rural ties lead them to consider customary law and local opinion when making national decisions. They thus become 'mediators between the local and national arenas, the interpreters as well as the architects of the intersections between customary and national law'. This is a project for which the elite concerned recruit journalists and the media for purposes of information, communication and public relations within and between communities, and also with the state and the outside world. The Cameroonian cases point to the interconnectedness and interpenetration that one might expect between citizenship and subjection, the cosmopolitan and the local, the individual and the collective, which make popular understandings of democracy in Africa far more complex than simplistic notions of liberal democracy would otherwise suggest.

While the following discussion clearly highlights the shortcomings of ethnicised and politicised media in liberal democratic terms, it also points to the limitations of liberal democracy in a context where people are obliged or ready and willing to be both citizens and subjects. They identify with their ethnic group or cultural community on the one hand (ethnic or cultural citizenship), and the nation-state on the other (civic citizenship). The argument for democracy as both an individual and a community or cultural right (see Chapter 1) cannot simply be dismissed when there are individuals who, for one reason or another, straddle both the realm of individual rights (liberal democracy) and the realm of group rights (Nyamnjoh 2001a, 2002a; Werbner 2002; Mazonde 2002; Nyati-Ramahobo 2002; Rowlands 2004; Englund and Nyamnjoh 2004).

A major characteristic of Africa's second liberation struggles since the 1980s has been a growing obsession with belonging and the questioning of traditional assumptions about nationality and citizenship almost everywhere. Identity politics are central to the political process. Exclusionary conceptions of nationality and citizenship have increased. Group claims for greater cultural recognition are countered by efforts to maintain the status quo of an inherited colonial hierarchy of ethnic groupings. As ethnic groups – local majorities or minorities – clamour for status, they are countered by an often aggressive reaffirmation of age-old exclusions informed by colonial registers of inequalities among the subjected. This development is paralleled by an increased distinction between 'locals' and 'foreigners' and between 'indigenes' and 'settlers' within and between countries, with the emphasis on opportunities and economic entitlements.

Even in South Africa and Botswana, where the economies are relatively better off than elsewhere in sub-Saharan Africa, xenophobia is rife against migrants from other African countries in economic downturn. Referred to derogatorily as *Makwerekwere* (meaning those incapable of articulating local languages that epitomise economic success and power), some of these migrants come from countries that were very instrumental in the struggle against apartheid (Comaroff and Comaroff 2000; Nyamnjoh 2002b; Morris and Bouillon 2001; Crush and McDonald 2001). Such tensions and boundaries between 'undeserving outsiders' and 'entitled nationals' are eloquently captured by Phaswane Mpe in *Welcome to Our Hillbrow*, a novel about a part of Johannesburg where 'citizens' fear to tread because criminal and violent *Makwerekwere* have made themselves at home in and imposed a reign of terror on Hillbrow (Mpe 2001). Even South African nationals from the ghettoes, townships and bantustans of the former apartheid dispensation, who are yet to graduate from subjection into citizenship in real terms, have been co-opted by the rhetoric of abundance and success under threat from unregulated immigration. Polarisations and tensions are exacerbated by the racialised lexicon, categorisation and registers of the apartheid era that have fed into the new South Africa, where even progressive academics are in no hurry to deconstruct and reconstruct. A consequence, by no means the only one, is that recently South Africans of Indian descent have come under scathing attack in a pop song by Mbongeni Ngema, a popular Zulu musician. Titled 'Ama-Ndiya', the controversial song claims to 'begin a constructive discussion that would lead to a true reconciliation between Indians and Africans', and accuses South African Indians of opportunism and of enriching themselves to the detriment of blacks, who are presented as the more indigenous but most exploited nationals. If the Indians are to be taken seriously as belonging to South Africa, they must display greater patriotism and stop straddling continents. In this way, elite capitalism becomes less the problem, as black nationals for whom socio-economic citizenship remains an illusion scapegoat *Makwerekwere* and increasingly Asians. This raises questions about the meaning of the juridico-political citizenship guaranteed by the constitution of the new South Africa (often touted as the most liberal in the world), where the socio-economic and cultural cleavages of the apartheid era are yet to be undone in a way that is beneficial to the majority of the victims of apartheid.

Everywhere in Africa, traditional policies of inclusion and emphasis on wealth-in-people over wealth-in-things are under pressure from the politics of entitlements in an era of accelerated flows of capital and migrants (Geschiere and Nyamnjoh 2000), and a context where governments of weak states feel obliged to be repressive while keeping up appearances of democracy. In discussions of democracy and rights, this heightened sense of cultural identity cannot simply be dismissed as 'tribalism' and consigned to the past (Taylor 1994; Rowlands 2004; Englund and Nyamnjoh 2004). Again, the Cameroonian experience offers interesting empirical material to inform the discussion of how to marry liberal democracy with African cultural, historical, indigenous political and economic realities.

Polarisation in the Press

When the democratisation process intensified after 1990, two main political tendencies in the media stood out. First, there were those who claimed that all the government did was good and in the best interests of Cameroon, and that the radical opposition was void of patriots and motivated only by selfish, regional or ethnic self-interests. This part of the media comprised the publicly owned CRTV and *Cameroon Tribune*, and pro-government 'privately' owned newspapers such as *Le Patriote, La Caravane, Le Courrier, Le Temps, Révélation* and *Le Témoin.*

Second, there were those who argued that all the radical opposition did or stood for was in the best interest of Cameroon, and that the government and its allies were only motivated by the hunger for power and self-aggrandisement. This current comprised the bulk of the privately owned papers, among which were such regular publications as *Le Messager, La Nouvelle Expression, Challenge Hebdo, Galaxie, Cameroon Post* and *The Herald.* The media were, therefore, polarised into two diametrically opposed camps, each claiming to represent the best interests of the Cameroonian people. As Nga Ndongo (1993: 168) remarked in 1993, 'each camp seems to anathematise the other' and tends to consider that 'the God, angels and saints of the other are nothing but Lucifer and demons'. Guiffo, in his study of *Challenge Hebdo* and *Le Patriote*, observed that, while the former held the Biya government 'responsible for all the ills of present-day Cameroon', the latter was thankful for 'Cameroon's luck to have President Biya at its helm' (Guiffo 1993: 183). While Paul Biya was credited by *Le Patriote* for bringing about 'advanced democracy', he was accused by *Challenge Hebdo* of presiding over 'the delinquent state' and by *Le Messager* for 'retarded mediocrity'. And if to *Le Patriote* the opposition was nothing but 'an embittered bunch of vandals thirsty for power', to *Challenge Hebdo* and *Le Messager* 'the opposition are the way to salvation for the people' (Ndongo 1993: 168). Some papers (e.g. *La Gazette* and *Fraternité*) flirted both with the government and with the opposition, seemingly undecided where to belong, without being professional either.[1] Those who strove for the middle ground, like *Dikalo, La Detente* and *L'Effort Camerounais*, were rare, and their reporters tended to be treated with suspicion by fellow journalists.

As ethnic and regional pressures increasingly undermined the nationwide appeal of political parties (Socpa 2002), the press itself also began to reflect ethnic divisions. And soon it was commonplace even for journalists to admit this fact. In 1997, Boh Herbert, general secretary of the UCJ, acknowledged the rise of 'tribal or ethnic papers, buried in a policy of tribal fundamentalism that preaches the truth as known and acceptable to the tribe or ethnic group'. He described the ethnicised press as 'founded on tribal arrogance with an editorial policy ... limited to settling tribal scores (often over land disputes) and to revenge in print the wrongs inflicted on one's flawless tribe by the enemy tribe or ethnic group' (Boh 1997: 44).

Despite constitutional provisions disallowing the creation of parties along ethnic lines, political parties had nevertheless evolved that were clearly based on ethnic divisions in the period of multiparty-ism after 1990. The editor-in-chief of *Cameroon Tribune* argued that the press followed suit. Newspapers committed themselves to defending the interests of parties that relied on ethnic support. He cited *Le Messager* and *Le Patriote* among the very first papers to embark upon the defence of ethnic causes, and these were followed subsequently by *Challenge Hebdo, La Nouvelle Expression, Le Temoin, L'Harmattan, The Herald* and others. Apart from *Cameroon Tribune*, which he saw to be neutral, every other paper, in his view, was to a greater or lesser degree ethnic and partisan. Basically, he argued, 'the camps are Bamileke on the one hand and Beti on the other, coupled with Fulani of the Grand North'. Such newspapers 'rally all intellectuals of the tribe who can participate in the "fight"', often having 'recourse to pen names that shroud the real identity of some fighters in the shadows' (Ndembiyembe 1997: 39–42).

Ethnicity and tribalism have become so important, Chindji-Kouleu notes, that in 1993 a quarterly, *Inpact-Tribu-Une*, started publishing exclusively on the topic, inviting politicians, academics and others to comment on the trend. Chindji-Kouleu's analysis showed that such papers as *Le Patriote, Le Combattant, Le Courrier* and *Elimbi* were fundamentally ethnicising political life in Cameroon, to the detriment of integration and democratisation (Chindji-Kouleu 1997). 'These "Radio Mille Collines"-oriented newspapers' operated without any legal barriers (Boh 1997: 44), a fact which Pierre Paul Tchindji of ESSTIC regretted, questioning why the legal provisions punishing the provocation of tribal or ethnic hatred prior to December 1990 had simply been discarded in the new media law (Tchindji 1996: 58).

This polarisation or ethnicisation of the press is best understood within the framework of the politics of belonging, whose emphasis on 'autochtonie' and 'allogèneité' have subverted liberal democracy and its narrow focus on a homogenous civic citizenship informed by electoral politics where individuals are seen and treated as autonomous and disembedded units (Geschiere and Nyamnjoh 2000; Bayart et al. 2001; Socpa 2002).

The Politics of Belonging

The polarisation in the media reflected a similar division within the Cameroonian public and between communities and regions (cf Socpa 2002). According to Ebssiy Ngum of CRTV, the public preferred partisanship to level-headed analysis.[2] This state of affairs was compounded by the adoption of a new constitution in January 1996 that promised state protection for minorities, the preservation of the rights of indigenous populations, and required that chairpersons of regional councils be indigenes.[3]

Adoption of this constitution coincided with municipal elections, which the opposition SDF party won in some key urban constituencies, including Douala. The result was the creation of the SAWA movement of the coastal peoples, presenting themselves as an 'autochthonous' minority marginalised by newly dominant 'settlers' or 'non-natives' from the Grassfields (Mentan 1996; Sonnè 1997; Monga 2000; Socpa 2002). Supporters of SAWA claimed to be opposing exploitation by 'unscrupulous' and 'ungrateful' Grassfields settlers in the region. SAWA demonstrated against the in-migrating Bamileke in particular, who alone accounted for 70 per cent of the population of the coastal city of Douala. When the SDF won the municipal elections, it selected only one indigenous mayor for the five local councils.[4] This was seen as evidence that Bamileke were ready to use their numbers to exclude minorities in a multiparty context (Sonnè 1997). It was an outcome regarding which Ava Jean, a Beti writing in the pro-government Le Patriote of 11 January 1993, had expressed some misgivings, informed by past conflicts occasioned by a previous law that, in his opinion, had favoured migrants unduly:

The council must be administered by the native populations. In this context, there is much to fear that the Ewondo and the Douala would be eliminated from urban councils since the Anglo-Bami [anglophones and Bamileke] are most likely to win all the seats under the SDF which carries the day with them.... We need a law which guarantees customary property rights. It is in the state's interest to settle populations on their own sacred land which must be protected jealously. (reproduced in *La Nouvelle Expression* 1, 23 May 1996: 12)

The media reflected these ethnic tensions. SAWA and some of the Beti population (Ewondo, Eton, Boulou, Fang), supported by *Cameroon Tribune, Le Patriote* and *L'Anecdote*, hailed the new constitutional provisions as a necessary and timely step to protect minority groups from the asphyxiating grip of expansionist and populous migrants such as Bamileke. But others, articulating their case through the critical anti-government press of mainly Bamileke and anglophone origin, saw it as a recipe for national disintegration. As Zognong argued, instead of facilitating 'national consciousness', the constitution, by encouraging ethnic discrimination, was actually promoting a 'false consciousness' through substituting ethnic citizenship for civic citizenship as provided for in the 1972 constitution. This was all the more glaring as the term 'minority' was deliberately kept ambiguous and thus subject to manipulation (Zognong 1997). Indeed, since 1996 various groups have taken advantage of this ambiguity to fan the flames of divisions in a scramble for resources at national and regional levels (Eyoh 1998a and 1998b; Geschiere and Nyamnjoh 1998, 2000; Monga 2000; Socpa 2002). Critical anglophones, on the other hand, viewed this outcome as a trivialisation of the notion of 'a minority'. They blamed the CPDM government for championing the politics of divide-and-rule to the detriment of nationhood. Some have interpreted the new constitution (and previous ones) as a conspiracy by the state to marginalise the anglophones even further (Mentan 1996: 186–94; Ngenge 2003; Jua 2003; Konings and Nyamnjoh 2003).

Various Bamileke sympathisers have interpreted the new constitution as yet further evidence of 'the Bamileke syndrome' orchestrated against them since colonial times because of their intelligence, their social organisation, dynamism, migratory capacity and populousness

(Lele 1995: 61–96; Shanda-Tonme 1995; Onomo 1997: 114; Zognong 1997: 127–32; Tabapssi 1999; Monga 2000; Socpa 2002). They could argue their case on the basis of observations such as the following, which appeared in a local paper:

> The Bamileke arrive somewhere, hands outstretched and mouth full of insults, begging for land in the name of national unity. Since it is common knowledge that Ewondo men cherish red wine, discussions take place in the bar nearby. Everything is settled. Then starts the shameful exploitation of Ewondo land. Occupation of neighbouring pieces of land is done under cover of darkness. The slightest protest by the legitimate owners is enough to lead the parties in conflict to court where the power of money always has the last word.[5]

In response to such sentiments, Bamileke politicians and intellectuals declared that their ethnic group had been singled out for exclusion since colonial times, and only their dynamism had ensured their survival. Academics at the University of Yaounde are all too familiar with the debate between two philosophers, Mono Ndjana (Beti) and Sindjoun Pokam (Bamileke), on this theme between 1987 and 1991, which was faithfully reported by *Le Messager*. Labelling Bamileke hegemony 'ethnofascism', Mono Ndjana argued that the Bamileke elite manipulated the idea of self-marginalisation as a mobilisation ploy for political power. By glorifying themselves beyond impeachment at the same time as they devalued other ethnic groups, Bamileke were able to convince themselves of their messianic mission. They felt themselves to be the only group capable of bringing into politics the same degree of success that they had already attained, despite all odds, in the domain of economics and commerce, an attitude which this thinker described as a threat to the state (Mono Ndjana 1997a).

The Bamileke elite on the other hand, have always argued that any stigmatisation of their ethnic group was dangerous to national unity and integration. They have never hesitated to make this clear through books, tracts and newspaper articles (Collectif Changer le Cameroun (C3) 1990, 1992, 1994; Monga 2000). In this connection, a group of them came together in March 1990 and addressed a memorandum to President Biya in which they requested that

Bamileke be, without prejudice, fully integrated into the national community (Zognong 1997: 135–6).

They also requested the detribalisation of Cameroon by banning all reference to race and district or province of origin in birth, marriage and other civic certificates. They recommended the abolition of the politics of regional and ethnic balance, arguing that it was against the idea of civic citizenship and placed 'the Bamileke under extinction in the name of promoting minorities' (Zognong 1997: 136–7). This, in the view of most Bamileke critical of the status quo, constituted 'the Bamileke syndrome', and it explained why the January 1996 constitutional reform that made concessions to minority groups could be interpreted by some Bamileke as a conspiracy by the state to marginalise them even further. This view appeared even more plausible as the 1972 constitution had stressed civic citizenship, which the Bamileke had considered in their interest.

Applying the January 1996 constitution, the CPDM government effectively demonstrated that the SAWA and Beti minorities could indeed rely on it for protection against the 'hegemonic' Bamileke or Grassfielders. Soon after the SAWA demonstrations the president signed a decree appointing indigenes as government delegates in ten metropolitan councils where the SDF had won the municipal elections. The installation of these delegates 'in towns considered SAWA (Douala, Limbe, Kumba) was the occasion for all SAWA to meet and "congratulate the head of state" for heeding their call to put a check on the hegemony of non-natives in "their cities"' (Yenshu 1998). In reaction to critics who described the SAWA attitude as shameless political expediency, Jean Jacques Ekindi wondered why SAWA were condemned while Laakam of Bamileke and Essingan of Beti were revered. He vowed, 'this is the time we want to assert and reorganise and nothing can stop us'.[6]

Under the guise of protecting minority interests, the CPDM was able to put its sympathisers at the head of key urban councils where it had lost the elections. This was viewed as a clear message to the SDF and the opposition in general that they stood more to gain by seeking political power within the confines of their home region and village than by pursuing the illusion of power and resources at a national level.

On this point Mono Ndjana, one of the most faithful ideologues of the CPDM, made a most revealing argument during a colloquium in April 1996 on 'Democracy in the Throes of Tribalism'. Defining 'the native' as 'an ethnic citizen of the local ethnic group' and 'the non-native' as 'an ethnic citizen of another ethnic group', he argued that in every African country 'everyone is at the same time native and non-native depending on where they find themselves in the territory'. He then proceeded to explain why democracy in Cameroon should be more of an ethnic right than simply an issue of 'one man one vote':

> We must therefore know that there are small and big tribes, small and big ethnic groups. As a real entity, each of them should be taken into consideration in a well-conceived democracy. When a demographically superior ethnic group is part of the picture, there is a big temptation that in applying the principle of democratic free choice the ethnic multitude would express itself in favour of the ethnic group which, in this way, would stifle those ethnic groups who are demographically weak. It is fair enough to talk of *one man one vote* democracy in principle. But the democratic principle defeats itself when, through this vote, only one ethnic group expresses its hegemony. This in effect amounts to a contradiction in terms, since democracy in this case would be serving the totalitarian interests of those it has enabled.
>
> It is therefore necessary to envisage seriously a democracy that would be that of ethnic groups as long as these groups remain a reality. As I see it, this is the duty of a responsible state, a state that seeks the harmonious coordination of the advantages of sociological majorities with the rights of natural minorities. (Mono Ndjana 1997b: 102–3)

The January 1996 constitution thus endorsed, in principle, the idea of democracy as an ethnic or group right. For every ethnic group was entitled to 'its place under the sun without seeking to push out the others from under the same sun' (Mono Ndjana 1997b: 103). This view effectively denies the idea of a *Cameroonian citizenship*, since even metropolitan areas like Douala and Yaounde, created by colonists and cosmopolitan from the outset, have under the new constitution been claimed by this or that autochthonous group to a degree quite unprecedented. Little wonder therefore, that the appointment of André Wouking, a Bamileke, as Archbishop of Yaounde in July 1999 (to succeed Jean Zoa, a Beti, who died in 1998) should be greeted with indignation by Beti elite, clergy and Christians at the same time that it was hailed by the Bamileke press as a good lesson in national integration.[7]

To those who sought protection as minorities, the price to pay would increasingly be stated in no uncertain terms: 'Vote the CPDM', the only party 'with a solid base or with sufficient appeal' (Mono Ndjana 1997b: 96). This is exactly what the prime minister, Peter Mafany Musonge, himself a SAWA, told SAWA chiefs at a meeting in Kumba on 8 March 1997. In fact, since his appointment in September 1996, Musonge and the pro-CPDM SWELA and SAWA elite have persisted in their invitation to all coastal people to throw their weight behind President Biya and the CPDM. As Musonge put it during a reception in Buea following his appointment, 'President Biya has scratched our back, and we shall certainly scratch the Head of State's back thoroughly when the time comes.' This promise they kept at the 1997 presidential elections, after which Biya rewarded him with reappointment as prime minister (Konings and Nyamnjoh 2003).

The fact that political parties created by SAWA indigenes at the beginning of the 1990s had all failed to take root by 1996 meant that SAWA opposition politicians who had failed to make it at a national level through party politics found in the SAWA movement a singular opportunity to stage a political comeback. In his paper on this movement, Sonnè draws attention to the example of Jean-Jacques Ekindi of the Mouvement Progressiste, who, after four years in the political wilderness, had enthusiastically agreed to coordinate the SAWA movement. In this he was supported by the very CPDM from which he had resigned in 1991 and the leader of which he had challenged resolutely at the October 1992 presidential elections (Sonnè 1997: 187–95). But, as we have argued elsewhere, whether the SAWA movement is a party in the making[8] or can keep its momentum of 1996 without the instigation and support of the CPDM is hard to say, given that the personal animosities which thwarted similar efforts in the past have resurfaced. While the appointment by Biya of Musonge (a Bakweri and South Westerner) as prime minister in September 1996 might have had the effect of weakening the anglophone cause (Konings and Nyamnjoh 1997: 227–8,

2003; Jua 2003), it also brought trouble to the SAWA movement (Monga 2000: 736). At a SAWA movement meeting, Jean-Jacques Ekindi reportedly accused the South West delegation of sidetracking him and wanting to dominate the movement. He lamented that 'Sawa cannot talk of Bamileke domination and later accept South West domination' (Nyamnjoh and Rowlands 1998: 333), his claim to being SAWA too notwithstanding (Y. Monga 2000: 736; Yenshu 2003: 601−5). It thus remains to be seen if it is possible for the SAWA movement (or any similar ethnic or regional movement encouraged by the 1996 constitutional changes) to stay alive and active, should the CPDM and government no longer see the urgency of their alliance. This perspective by no means denies the SAWA movement or any other a cultural content or legitimacy, but it draws attention to how a political elite can seek to manipulate a cultural movement for political ends.

Press and Politics of Belonging from 1996

The increased importance of regional and ethnic politics was indeed marked by a redefinition of editorial policy on the part of some existing papers and the creation of new mouthpieces to take care of ethnic interests. Newspapers such as *The Weekly Post*, *The Star Headlines* and *The Oracle* now extended their interests to include what the SAWA movement stood for in general. New papers such as *Elimbi*, *Muendi*, *The Beacon* and *Fako International* (*Mendi me Fako*) were created to attend more specifically to the political ambitions of the SAWA elite in the Littoral and South West provinces and to oppose Grassfields hegemony as a matter of policy. After 1996, little would escape criticism or comment by this press, including inter-tribal wars in the North West, which it used to deride the warmongering, land-grabbing Grassfielders with their penchant for fighting over trivia. Intra-party squabbles in the SDF would also be highlighted, the aim being to show why John Fru Ndi and his party could not be a viable alternative to the CPDM. During the 1996 and 1997 elections, the press sought, through the rhetoric of 'ethnic cleansing', to encourage a widespread antagonism to 'strangers' as parasites and 'traitors in the house' (Boulaga 1997a, 1997b; Jua 2003). For these papers, it was sufficient for one to be of the Grassfields in order to be accused of harbouring pro-SDF sentiments. Leaning on this press, and armed with CPDM banners, party uniforms and effigies of Biya, opportunistic civil servants, bread-and-butter intellectuals, and tax-evading businessmen and -women were able to manipulate individuals, groups and situations, simply by shouting anti-SDF and/or anti-Grassfields slogans.

As Sonnè notes, the first issue of *Elimbi* on 26 March 1996 co-incided with the launching of the SAWA movement. Initially a bi-monthly, *Elimbi* became a weekly in November 1996, as the politics of belonging heated up. It described itself as 'a regional newspaper' that targeted the people of the coast, paying attention in particular to the activities and news of the coastal elite. But *Elimbi*'s most strik-ing feature was 'the production and dissemination of ideas hostile to the Bamileke'. In this connection, *Elimbi* presented Bamileke as a catalogue of weaknesses ('bearer of all the vices'), among which were stereotypes of Bamileke as 'dirty, thieving, cunning, crafty, deceitful, scattered, sectarian, domineering'.[9]

The Grassfielders also used the private press to fight back. In a similar manner, existing papers redefined their editorial focus, while new ethnic or regional papers sprang up. Bamileke and North West elites used established papers, most of which they owned and/or controlled, to respond to the attack by the SAWA press, interpreting the January 1996 constitutional changes as an impediment to the democratic process. The sheer volume of diatribes, commentaries, opinion and reports related to *autochtonie* and *allogènie* (native/settler) in Grassfields newspapers such as *La Nouvelle Expression*, *Le Messager*, *The Post* and *The Herald*, were an indication of how absorbing the politics of belonging had become since 1996, with equally blatantly ethnic papers like *Ouest Echo* and *Nde Echo* leading the charge. *The Herald* al-though actively pro-anglophone and not outrightly pro-South West province, became narrowly ethnic as it defended a dissident priest, Father Étienne Ntellah Khumbah (of the same Bangwa origin as *The Herald*'s proprietor and editor-in-chief) in a conflict between the priest and the Bishop of the Buea Diocese, Pius Awah (who hails from Bafut in the North West province) (Konings 2003). What the press in general has done is transpose the debate from the streets and neighbourhoods to the public sphere, while staying faithfully ethnic and partisan in their interpretations.

Press and Politics of Belonging Prior to 1996

The reality of an ethnicised press in Cameroon in recent years has only intensified, not initiated, a trend that has deep roots in the country's past. The manipulation of ethnic and regional rivalries is a long-standing strategy in national politics. Popular clamour for democratisation became the victim of ethnic ambition soon after the reintroduction of multiparty politics in 1990. The era of multipartyism from 1990 onwards extended the existing pro-government politicisation of the media to embrace the whole political spectrum. Along with that politicisation came a steady surge of ethnic mobilisation in the struggle for patronage and power (Socpa 2002).

Eonè argues that the 'chronic overpoliticisation' of the press in the aftermath of the 1990 reforms led to a situation where few in the media were able to respect the empirical evidence.[10] The most recurrent themes in the critical private press from 1990 to 1994 attested to this preoccupation with politics. The press dwelled repeatedly on what it saw as the pillage of the commonwealth, economic mismanagement, embezzlement, fraud, lack of accountability, overexploitation of forests, dictatorship of the state and government incompetence. Along with this vociferous criticism came persistent ethnic slurs and undertones. With the Biya government being viewed as Beti-dominated, the opposition press itself was far from innocent in the growth of ethnic divisiveness.

According to Nga Ndongo (1993) and Onomo (1997), both Beti scholars, Beti were presented by this press not only as a demographic and political minority that had all the important posts in government and in the administration, but also as a people whose love for pleasure and red wine, and whose laziness, incompetence, mediocrity, tribalism and propensity to steal from the state, were a danger to the national economy. Bishop Ndongmo, a Bamileke, was quoted in an interview in Le Messager as saying that one of Ahidjo's mistakes was to have handed power over to Beti, a people incapable of handling money (Onomo 1997: 114–15). Beti 'must be chased into the desert or slain even', especially as 'Biya and his people, after having thrown the country into a political and economic crisis, are now preparing themselves to bring about a moral crisis as well' (Ndongo 1993: 131–2). The press in question, Nga Ndongo further argues, indulged in a cruel game of words, aimed at ridiculing Beti: 'the terms *bêtise politique* (political blunder), *bêtise incurable* (incurable foolishness), *bêtisation* (to render silly), which have been the stock in trade of newspapers, are in effect, a cruel game of words on the Beti (Ndongo 1993: 156).

Such simplistic scapegoating by the anti-government private press of Beti as an ethnic group forced Beti, even those dissatisfied with Paul Biya's performance as president, to bury the hatchet and support 'our brother' in power. To Keye Ndogo, if the private press, essentially non-Beti, lost its Beti readership a couple of years into multipartyism, it was because of the ease and frivolity with which this press tended 'to tarnish ... the Beti, under the pretext that President Biya was part of this group'.[11] If their strategy of stereotyping, labelling and insulting Beti succeeded in uniting Bamileke, it had the negative effect of provoking 'the reprobation and opposition' of Beti, especially as it depended on 'the inflation of facts' and 'exaggeration at will' (Onomo 1997: 115).

The results were entirely predictable. A vicious circle of ethnic accusation and counter-accusation ensued. The Beti elite were quick at making political capital out of the reductionist reasoning, simplistic analyses, and sweeping condemnation of Beti by a critical private press dominated mainly by anglophones and Bamileke. They argued, with much conviction and evidence, that it was not by accident that both the radical opposition parties and the most vociferous anti-government private press (*Le Messager, La Nouvelle Expression, Challenge Hebdo, Cameroon Post* and *The Herald*) were anglophone and/or Bamileke in origin and control. In this way, it was easy for them to dissuade their ethnic brethren – Beti masses – from identifying with such 'illusionmongers' who were not fighting for democracy as such but, rather, were simply using democracy as a pretext or short cut to power for the 'anglo-Bami'.[12]

The Beti elite exploited the sense of fear and insecurity of ordinary Beti, dramatising in the press and tracts the 'danger weighing on their land, their property and their survival as a noble people, if Bamileke, who are a vindictive and hypertribalistic people, were to take over power' (Onomo 1997: 115). Bamileke were presented to Beti as an inward-looking, untrustworthy people with whom it was difficult to integrate, and who, on coming to power, would wreak havoc on others, starting with Beti (Onomo 1997: 116).

Little was done in government circles to curb the circulation of anonymous tracts that whipped up sentiments of animosity between Cameroonians of Beti origin and those from other regions and ethnic groups.[13] Instead, they actively encouraged Beti-owned papers such as *Le Patriote*, *La Caravane*, *Le Courrier* and *Le Temps* to counterattack, claiming that Beti had formed a coalition and were determined to chase out of their region 'the invaders of their heritage' (Onomo 1997: 116). Also recruited in the fight was Radio Centre in Yaounde, in which national language programmes such as *Bembelle mbelle ibouc* were infused with ethnic hatred, targeting the 'anglo-Bami' in particular. Angered by this programme, some listeners were reported to have nicknamed the station 'Radio Sept Collines', in reference to the seven hills of Yaounde and reminiscent of the Rwandan 'Radio Mille Collines' (Boh 1997: 47). *Le Temps*, in no uncertain terms, promised war if Bamileke and all those who had benefited during the Ahidjo regime did not stop insulting Beti.[14] Beti spokespersons argued that if it came to war and secession, Beti stood to lose less than others. For one thing, Bamileke were reminded that despite their demographic majority, they occupied less than 10 per cent of the national territory, 'while the Beti are spread over nearly 40 per cent of the territory with rich and abundant natural resources'. Second, Beti elite counted on the support of their Fang 'brothers' in Gabon, made known to them in a declaration to *Le Courrier* by the president of la Renaissance Fang: 'at the moment that we are all discovering the difficulties of co-habitation with peoples whom we have very little in common with, why should we not now envisage working for the unity of the Fang–Béti–Ntoumou?' (Onomo 1997: 117–18).

Anglophones and Bamileke ('anglo-Bami') were presented as the group most covetous of Beti power (Socpa 2002); hence the xenophobic reassurance by Joseph Owona (secretary-general at the presidency) in an interview with Ndzana Seme (an Eton) in Ewondo,[15] at a period when Beti hegemony was most threatened, that a Bamileke will never be president in Cameroon ('A Bamileke at the Etoudi Palace? Never!'). Such otherwise outrageous xenophobic declarations were reinterpreted as heroic attempts by courageous Beti elite to protect and consolidate Beti power in Cameroon. The message in town and village presented Beti elite as watching over Beti interests by making sure that Bamileke hegemony was curbed. For if Bamileke were allowed access to power, Beti would be reduced to nothing: 'you will no longer.have where to dig even a pit latrine. If they come to power, they will chase you out of your houses and occupy them' (Onomo 1997: 119).

This constant harping on ethnic susceptibilities only heightened divisive tendencies at the grassroots (Socpa 2002). When President Biya undertook to make a tour of the provinces in 1991,[16] Émile Awah wrote that 'the country is on the verge of civil war: suspicion reigns, the tribes are pitted against each other, the nation is intoxicated with lies being churned out by a press with a hidden agenda'.[17] As Amougou rightly observed in 1994, front-page headlines like these were a common stock-in-trade: 'The Bami Syndrome', 'Who Wanted to Kill the Wadjos?' (natives of the northern part of Cameroon), 'The Betis or Bêtises', 'Is a Beti State Viable?', 'Are Certain Cameroonian Tribes Preordained to Rule?', 'The Anglo-Bami Alliance, the Challenges: This Time or Never' (Amougou 1994: 44).[18]

In this way even ordinary and rural Beti, who had benefited least from Biya's largesse (Essono 1996), found themselves defending a regime they would normally have joined others to vote out of office. Feeling falsely and repeatedly accused of belonging to 'the tribe of the belly',[19] the ordinary disenchanted Beti, backs against the wall, threw their weight behind 'the chief of the tribe of the belly' and hoped for the best for their bellies. Even when reminded by others that their Beti brothers and sisters in government and the public service had little regard, respect or generosity for their less fortunate kin,[20] the hostility expressed in the anti-Beti press was sufficiently off-putting to make the ordinary Beti take seriously any opposition rhetoric on democratisation.

Given this frozen picture, Onomo argues, ordinary Beti and Bamileke people have, in the current democratisation process, been taken hostage by a minority of politicians and intellectuals 'who speak in the name and direct the actions of these peoples without their mandate'. Another victim has been democracy as the empowerment of the individual. In their quest either to maintain or to extend their traditional advantages, Beti and Bamileke elites have manipulated ethnic belonging to this end, each using liberal democracy as a smokescreen. Beti and Bamileke intellectuals, politicians and journalists have tended to paint a biased picture of Cameroon's problems, each guided by the prejudices and stereotypes they have internalised of the other. The result is a caricature of peoples and politics of the most simplistic kind, much to the detriment of liberal democracy. In broad terms, 'who speaks Beti, speaks Cameroon People's Democratic Movement (CPDM); who speaks Bamileke, speaks opposition parties', and anyone who fails to conform is treated as a traitor or a spy (Onomo 1997: 120–21).

Conclusion

Given the politicisation of the press and in light of its lack of professionalism and respect for evidence, it becomes difficult to argue that it has made a positive contribution to democratisation in Cameroon. The press since 1990 has failed to serve as a platform for the promotion of tolerance and coexistence in a multicultural, multiparty Cameroon. Another consequence was that 'Today, many of our compatriots do not still know that two political rivals can still talk to each other, and even be friends without the one nor the other having betrayed anything or anyone.' Concerning the critical private press in particular, Thomas Eyoum à Ntoh (a journalist with a rich working experience in the major private newspapers) concluded that 'it was itself not a model of tolerance', preferring on the contrary to use insults on 'all those who refused to think the way it wished'.[21] This attitude alienated the people who were attacked by wounding them to the point where they vowed never again to read such discourteous papers, so that press attacks appear sterile self-indulgence.

This chapter has highlighted the limitations of a liberal democratic model that blindly emphasises individual freedoms in a context where actors are also and obviously more committed to group freedoms and solidarity networks. It offers evidence why scholars of Africa should provide the theoretical space for democracy as a marriage of individual, cultural and community interests. Related to our discussion of media, belonging and democratisation in Africa, it is worth noting that the power elite in Cameroon and in most of the continent has failed to domesticate liberal democracy. But it is equally noteworthy that the orthodox version of liberal democracy is fundamentally problematic in its emphasis on the individual, especially in a context like Africa's, where people straddle possibilities in order to maximize opportunities in the face of ever-increasing uncertainties.

An idea of democracy that is more in tune with the historical experiences, the cultural and economic predicaments of African societies and peoples, would certainly have other expectations of the media, as it seeks to empower individuals and communities. Under such an accommodating system of democracy, some of what are currently perceived as failings on the part of the media (e.g. ethnic biases, partisanship, regionalism) could indeed be healthy practices, as it would be quite understandable to have media defending particular group interests openly, rather than in camouflage as is the case under the liberal democratic model. A broader definition of democracy – one that allows for ethnic cultural citizenship as well as civic citizenship and for the straddling of both (where the regime of individual rights and interests is married with the regime of group, cultural or collective rights and interests) – would puncture the illusion in certain journalistic circles that there is such a thing as objective journalism to cater for everyone's interests satisfactorily. It would also debunk the assumption in media circles that facts speak for themselves, or that truth exists independent of how social actors construct and perceive it. A well-mediated democracy would provide for a journalism that is more critical and less pretentious.

Given the limitations of liberal democracy in general, and its failure to provide for an ethnic cultural citizenship that blends well with African notions of civic citizenship, it is hardly surprising that behaviour and attitudes which appear perfectly normal to ordinary Africans have been highlighted and dramatised as impediments to democracy. Like fishermen only able to net fish of a certain size, some observers have concluded that there is little room for democracy in the Heart of Darkness. According to this narrow measure, it is not surprising that various attempts at democratisation in Africa have produced little. As long as one version of liberal democracy continues to be the measure and Africans remain marginal to global processes and opportunities, it is unlikely that the situation will change significantly. As modernity produces malcontents en masse (Comaroff and Comaroff 1993), Africans have become loath to entrust all their eggs (for those who have any) to the liberal democratic basket of holes.

Globalisation and the accelerated flow of capital, goods, electronic information and migration it occasions have only exacerbated insecurities, uncertainties and anxieties in locals and foreigners alike, bringing about an even greater obsession with citizenship, belonging, and the building or restoration of fences. The Cameroonian case stresses that the most fulfilling response to uncertainties and anxieties hardly lies in a narrow and abstract definition of rights and citizenship, nor in a preoccupation with the politics of exclusion and difference within and between groups, local or foreign. The answer to the impermanence of present-day achievements lies in the incorporation of 'strangers' without stifling difference and in the building of new partnerships across those differences. The answer, to draw on Waldon (1995), lies in a cosmopolitan life informed by allegiances to cultural meanings drawn from different sources in the rich repertoire of multiple encounters by individuals and communities alike. Cameroonians have through the years displayed a remarkable ability to open up to one another, incorporating and adapting 'foreign' ideas and institutions, and welcoming 'strangers' from other communities from afar and near. This is indeed a common trait of African communities, where the emphasis has tended to be on inclusion because of a mainstream philosophy of life, agency and responsibility that privileges wealth in people over wealth in things.

Individuals and groups alike must be allowed the creative interdependence to explore various possibilities for maximising their rights and responsibilities within the confines of the economic, cultural and political opportunities at their disposal. Inclusion, not exclusion, is the best insurance policy in the face of the uncertainties to which individuals, communities and states the world over are subjected under global consumer capitalism (Nyamnjoh 2002a). The media can find in this philosophy the inspiration they need for a vision and coverage in tune with the predicaments of their audiences, be these individuals or groups, minority or majority ethnic communities, citizens/nationals or immigrants. The challenge for the media is to capture the spirit of tolerance and coexistence beneath every display of difference and marginalisation, beckoning for recognition as the way forward for an increasingly interconnected world of individuals and groups longing for recognition and representation.

Notes

1. For examples of such flirtation, see *Challenge Hebdo*, 8 July 1992; and also *Le Messager*, 17 July 1992.
2. *Cameroon Calling*, 7 November 1993.
3. 18 January 1996 constitution, preamble and article 57, paragraph 3.
4. The SAWA demonstrators displayed placards with the following messages among others: 'Yes to Democracy, No to Hegemony'; 'No Democracy without Protection for Minorities and Indigenes'; 'A Majority Based on Ethnic Votes is Not a Sign of Democracy but of Expansionism'. They were singing songs in Douala, such as 'This shall not be tolerated in our homeland!'; 'These people lied to us!' 'Where are they going to dump us?' (*Cameroon Tribune*, 14 February 1996; Sonnè 1997).
5. Reproduced in *La Nouvelle Expression*, 23 May 1996.
6. See *Cameroon Tribune*, 18 June 1996; *The Herald*, 19 February 1996.
7. See *Cameroon Tribune*, 19 July 1999; *La Nouvelle Expression*, 21 July 1999; *Cameroon Tribune*, 23 July 1999, for reactions to the appointment.
8. Jean-Jacques Ekindi's call for the SAWA movement to be transformed into 'grand parti Duala' received little support from other SAWA elite, including Samuel Eboua (Sonnè 1997: 188).
9. Some of Elimbi's headlines read as follows: 'The Natives Feel Threatened. Is There a Plot Against Douala?'; 'Natives – Non-Natives. The counter-example from the West Province. Bafoussam: Forbidden City to Non-Natives'; 'The "Hegemonic Plot" is it an Intervention by the Duala?'; 'Why Do the Bamileke Detest Order?'

10. See *Spécial XVème Anniversaire Le Messager*, 28 November 1994.
11. Keye Ndogo, *Jeune Afrique*, 23 February 1995.
12. See Jean-Baptiste Sipa on the 'Bamileke Syndrome', *Challenge Hebdo*, 5 June 1991.
13. See Celestin Monga on 'The Belly Tribe', *Challenge Hebdo*, 15 October 1991.
14. *Le Temps*, 10 April 1991; quoted in Onomo 1997: 117.
15. See *Le Nouvel Indépendant*, 6 January 1994.
16. For a collection of speeches made by the President during these tours, see CPDM 1991.
17. *Le Témoin*, 23 September 1992.
18. For more examples of such headlines, see Boyomo 1995: 25–6.
19. Voices like A. Ebongue de Ngomba's (*Horizons*, 12 June 1991), urging the press and the opposition to understand that 'the struggle isn't against a tribe or an ethnic group' as such, but rather 'directed against a regime made up in the main of Beti for sure, but comprising people from all the other regions', were few and drowned out.
20. See, for example, *Nouvelle Afrique*, 1 April 1997, for Biloa Ayissi's article on 'Le Mal Béti'.
21. *Dikalo*, 8 August 1994.

9

Communications Policies in Africa:
Lessons from the West

In the Introduction we highlighted the importance of the social shaping of information and communications technologies in order to avoid technological determinism. Subsequent chapters have stressed the desirability of democratic practices and media ethics in tune with popular notions of personhood and agency in Africa. These considerations call for communications policies tailored to African realities. Of course, how well the new technologies serve the needs of any community anywhere in the world depends very much on what policies are designed to harness them. This is all the more so in Africa where, in a time of political and social flux, matters of policy vitally affect the relationship between the media and democracy.

Current tensions between liberal democratic rhetoric and the sociology of African societies on the one hand, and between African governments and the media on the other, have been blamed in part on poor communications policies. UNESCO defines communication policies as 'sets of principles and norms established to guide the behaviour of communication systems' in a given country and informed by the political ideologies, social and economic conditions in place (UNESCO 1980: 11). Instead of policies that are carefully considered and comprehensive, however, African governments have tended to content themselves with 'piecemeal legislations that are enacted or decreed in response to perceived misbehavior of the press by government'. These laws are usually employed as drastic measures designed to silence the press in the name of national

security, and in glaring contradiction to 'their pronounced commitment to "democratic reforms"' ('Blake 1997: 258). Many African
governments, Ellis remarks, have yet to find a balance 'which allows
the publication of facts and the airing of views while protecting
individuals against certain forms of vilification' (2000: 222–6). Even
in South Africa, where there have been significant changes since
the end of apartheid (Tomaselli 2002), 'much of the censorship
regulations and other restrictive legislation remain, however, on
the statute books', even if they may not have been invoked since
1994. Indeed, media and communications policy was not a priority
of the Mandela government. Only in 1996 was a Task Group on
Government Communications (ComTask) set up. Its brief, among
other things, was to make recommendations on a new government
communications policy (Van Kessel 1998: 15–16). Rapid advances in
technologies call not only for integrated and comprehensive policies
by governments but entail an unprecedented level of awareness and
monitoring (McQuail and Siune 1998).

Given the importance of communications policies in determining what role the media play in the evolution of any given society
(Linden 1998), this concluding chapter critically reviews Western
trends and debates on media ownership and control. In doing so,
it aims to provide African scholars, NGOs, governments, media
and media rights advocates with examples from which to draw
insights as they seek to make meaningful choices on the future of
communications in Africa. The chapter also presents a policy option
proposed by Cecil Blake, one of Africa's leading scholars in the
field, who recently served as minister of information in post-civil
war Sierra Leone.

Critical Appraisal of Western Ownership
and Control Policies

Most national communications policies attempt to influence, if not
actually dictate, the roles the public and private sectors should play
with regard to communication and media institutions. Explicitly or
implicitly, the assumptions of policymakers about personhood and

agency determine to a large extent specific national policy emphases and priorities regarding a desirable communications sector. While some governments favour private initiatives in the setting up and operation of communications facilities, others prefer to see a larger role for state or public ownership and control. Taking a more conciliatory stance are those uncomfortable with both exclusive state monopolies on the one hand, and purely commercial or private systems on the other.

The whole debate is centred on how best the interests of the public can be served by communication, and is very much informed by competing perspectives on 'the concept of property'. Much, however, depends on whether the public interest is seen as a composite of individual interests, as collective group interests, or as a marriage of individual and group interests (Rowlands 2004). A majority of countries view the communications sector as a most sensitive area, where two contrasting philosophies stand out clearly. Some advocate and practise the 'public-service' view, others the 'business' view. The public-service view is one in which broadcasting, for example, is seen as 'an enriching and limited resource' that should be employed most judiciously to serve the needs and aspirations of 'the entire spectrum of society' (Adkins 1985: 54). It expects broadcasting to function as a public utility 'in the service of the public sphere'. It should guarantee that 'all members of society have access to the information and knowledge they need in order to perform their civic duties', or simply to satisfy their interests and preferences as individual listeners and viewers (Syvertsen 1999: 6). Such broadcasting should be informative and educational, capable of stimulating thought, developing latent tastes for good art of all kinds, and encouraging a proper sense of values, as well as enhancing wisdom (Beadle 1963: 93). The service should provide 'programmes that examine public issues with an incisively critical eye' and that 'provide fora for debate' (Findahl 1999: 18), without being used by individual journalists in a self-serving manner, as was recently demonstrated in the furore in Britain around the condemnation of the BBC by the Hutton Report over claims by BBC defence correspondent Andrew Gilligan that the Blair government had 'sexed up' its intelligence report on Iraq's weapons of mass destruction (The Economist 2004b: 11, 31–3).

The position of the public-service advocates is that collective interests cannot be served if broadcasting is left entirely in the hands of the private sector. The public interest demands at least some, if not total, state regulation (Curran 1988: 292). Although not very popular prior to the late 1980s, one version of this approach in Europe has more recently promoted the use of public-service broadcasting in serving the preferences of individual media consumers rather than culturally interested groups (Syvertsen 1999; Søndergaard 1999). This development blurs the traditional distinction between public-service broadcasting and commercial broadcasting, and makes of 'public service' a 'catch-all for everything good and right in a world where a lot of things are bad and wrong' (Syvertsen 1999: 7–11).

The business view, on the other hand, maintains that only when operated as privately owned business can broadcasting satisfy the whole of society. Free competition among the forces in the market-place inevitably brings the public more services and wider pleasures. Only if government interference and manipulation are avoided will broadcasting be free from undesirable influences and able to serve the public more effectively.

Perhaps one should add immediately that these distinctions are more ideal than real, for there is hardly any country in the world where absolute freedom is guaranteed, or where there is no attempt by the state to regulate communications and the media (Hamelink 1983: 111–12; Downing 1986; Wells 1987: 34; Findahl 1999: 14). Media practitioners and 'journalists everywhere have to work within certain confines, whether of law, custom or economics' (Head 1963: 595). For, as Beadle (1963: 51) rightly notes, 'abstract appeals for liberty', though always exciting, are 'seldom satisfying, because they beg too many questions. Whose liberty? Liberty of what? Liberty for what? How much liberty?'

The ideal of the free press, inherent in Western discourse, has given rise to the mistaken view that Western media systems are indeed totally free of state interference and regulation. Thus Western media have often been presented to the rest of the world as un-restricted systems that operate in an environment where there is 'free flow of information'. Based on this claim, Western countries have often posed as pacesetters for the rest of the world. This position is hotly contested in countries where the free flow of information is considered to be hampered through state regulation of media content (Wells 1987: 24–42).

We can understand how the various ownership and control policies are translated into practice by referring to the research findings of leading communications scholars. I use broadcasting as an example because, although in most societies it is taken for granted that there should be a private press free from rigid government control, there tends to be more controversy around broadcasting, with government interference and regulation more widespread. Recent attempts by the Blair government to harness the BBC are a good case in point.

The well-known cultural theorist Raymond Williams identified two types of ownership and control patterns of broadcast institutions in Europe and North America. One is a broadcasting system dominated by capitalist and commercial interests, but whose proponents, for rhetorical purposes, like to describe it as 'free' and 'independent', as opposed to being a 'monopoly' and under 'state control'. The other is public-service or non-commercial broadcasting. Williams's distinction is between institutions that are privately owned, operated and funded with advertising revenue, and that have as 'their primary aim the realisation and distribution of private profit on invested capital', and other institutions whose concerns are not to make profit, instead devoting revenue 'almost wholly to production and development of the broadcasting service' (Williams 1979: 266).

Public-service television in the USA, in contrast to commercial counterparts, which are funded with advertising revenue, not only has its production funds subject to central control, but is 'member-supported, and survives with great difficulty only by constant local fund-raising' (Williams 1979: 266). Mulcahy and Widoff (1986: 31) find the use of the term 'public' rather misleading in the American context, where, unlike in France and Britain, such broadcasting is independent of the state financially, administratively and in the elaboration of its policies. They note that 'one of the outstanding questions facing public broadcasting is how to administer a national program without a national policy – indeed, where national policy-making has been virtually prohibited' (1986: 32). They argue that 'any discussion of public broadcasting must emphasize the highly circumscribed and decentralized character of the system, especially if compared to the commercial networks' (1986: 31). Furthermore, juxtaposed with commercial television, public broadcasting in the USA, despite its 'significant presence...has a decidedly minority share of viewership'.

Attractive though the idea of public-service broadcasting may be, affirms Williams, it can only function effectively if there is no 'ambiguity about the public interest' and if 'its relation to the state' is clearly defined. Yet it is not always easy to say with required precision what in effect constitutes 'public interest', and what is the relationship between the public institutions charged with promoting such interest and the state. Although Williams was in favour of public-service broadcasting, he did not think that state monopolies were necessarily the best way of promoting the public interest. The reason for his scepticism is that whenever that is the case, 'the state can be correctly identified with a partisan version of the public interest', as our study of Africa has so well evinced. In France, where competitive versions of public interest are active, 'the equation between state and public interest is especially vulnerable, and this leads not only to internal conflicts but ... to complicated international pressures' (Williams 1979: 267).

In France, the constant interference with broadcasting by government along party-political lines proves Williams's point that state monopolisation of broadcasting can lead to all sorts of complications in a multiparty state. It is the case that France has carried out 'a rapid and confused process of deregulation which has led to an explosion in the number of radio and television networks' in the country (Betts 1988: 3). But the tradition in the past has been for every government that comes to power to seek total control of broadcasting by placing its own people at the head of the broadcasting institutions. Accordingly, there have been ten regulatory structures since World War II, each replacing the other to reflect changes in the political arena. Betts describes the nature of the struggles by various governments to control broadcasting in France, and refers to the state of affairs during the Mitterrand and Chirac regimes as examples.

According to Betts (1988: 3), the tradition after every general election in France has been for 'heads to roll' in the broadcasting sector

– 'with the new government appointing its supporters and friends to the key jobs'. Thus, following the 1981 elections, the victorious Socialists not only 'placed their cronies at the head of the public networks', but also reformed the broadcasting authority in order to secure the necessary influence over the regulation of broadcasting. The Socialists were 'anxious to ensure that the right would find it hard to regain control of the broadcasting sector when it came back to power'. To do this, they decided to emulate Britain, whose public-service broadcasting is 'flanked by a private sector'.

The Socialists then proceeded 'to create two new private commercial networks and one private pay television channel to compete against the existing three public television networks'. However, immediately the right came back to power after the 1986 elections,

> Mr Jacques Chirac, the Gaullist Prime Minister, set about dismantling the broadcasting structure set up by the Socialists. The heads of the public networks were replaced and the concessions granted to the new private channel operators were cancelled. The broadcasting authority was replaced by a new Commission Nationale de la Communication et des Libertés (CNCL), a supposedly independent body dominated by Gaullist representatives. (Betts 1988: 3)

Prime Minister Chirac did not stop there, but proceeded to the privatisation of TF-1, France's 'oldest and most influential network', thus scoring a further political victory over the Socialists, who favour nationalisation and more central control.

This struggle speaks for itself. It brings out the demerits of excessive central control and clearly points out how governments might use their position as custodian of the public interest to secure and consolidate power for themselves, their parties and supporters. Williams can thus be said to argue for policies that foster pluralism, though not commercialism, in broadcasting. For him it is possible for the broadcast media to be plural without being commercial, and to be public-service in character without becoming the mere mouthpiece of the government or being reduced to a mere state monopoly. He is apprehensive of any form of political organisation except what Schlesinger (1978) terms 'democratic pluralism', wherein power is shared by 'competitive political parties' in a way that is balanced, and that allows no particular interest to weigh too heavily upon the state. The BBC, which supposedly subscribes to the very same democratic pluralism (Seaton 1988: 263–72), is Williams's prime example of an independent public-service broadcasting institution. It is 'supposed to be … a marketplace for ideas and competing viewpoints, endorsing none, admitting all, a national institution above the fray' (Schlesinger 1978: 166).

To attain a clearer idea of what Williams advocated, let us briefly consider what the BBC is all about. The BBC was created to reflect the plurality of British society in politics and culture. It is public property, governed by an authority whose individual members are publicly appointed by the state for a defined and limited term of office. It is answerable to parliament, to which it is required to make annual reports through the Postmaster General. It operates under terms of reference designed by government and approved by parliament, and it is subject to certain overt government powers of control over the content of its programmes. It has powers to produce its own programmes. Concerning funding, 'the BBC lives on an agreed proportion of the licence revenue and is forbidden to broadcast advertisements'. However, the fact that 'the BBC derives its revenue through the agency of a government department – the Post Office', 'gives the government a financial hold over the BBC which can be used to hold back development'. Although the government has the power under the BBC's licence to instruct it 'to broadcast or to refrain from broadcasting something specific or some particular class of material', the BBC has an important safeguard against the government using such powers to the detriment of the institution. The BBC is 'authorized to announce publicly that … [it is] broadcasting or refraining from broadcasting something on government instructions. So the government cannot use its powers secretly, and any instruction given by government is open to comment and criticism by parliament and press' (Beadle 1963: 64–7).

Although Williams endorsed the BBC as a public institution that is free and independent of direct state interference and manipulation, he cautioned against any uncritical acceptance of the institution's independence. While direct pressures from the state might be rare, the fact that the government appoints the public authorities that oversee the institution is enough for a certain measure of long-term influence on the part of the government. Attempts to introduce the direct election of the institution's authorities and to bring about 'democratic representation or control by actual producers and broadcasters' within the corporation have continued to be 'very vigorously opposed'. This suggests that the appointed authorities are all part of 'a complicated patronage system on which the real state, as distinct from the formal state, effectively relies' (Williams 1979: 267).

Curran (1988: 300) cites evidence of how the Thatcher administration appointed BBC officials on a partisan basis, and how the government exerted pressure on its board of governors for the suppression of certain programmes of which it disapproved. But according to Williams, no matter what amount of pressure might be brought to bear on the BBC, interference by the government cannot be as rigid as the formal control through a ministry of information as in France. The fact that there is political pluralism (epitomized by 'competitive political parties') makes any rigid or formal control a virtual impossibility (Williams 1979: 267).

Further developments in British broadcasting have revived debates about how the public interest can best be served. In May 1988, for example, the government created a Broadcasting Standards Council (BSC) to monitor 'taste and decency' on radio and television under the chairmanship of Sir William Rees-Mogg. The BSC was, *inter alia*, charged with previewing imported programmes in order to guard against excessive 'sex and violence' on British television. The move attracted criticism, not least from the BBC and the Independent Broadcasting Authority (IBA), who considered the BSC's right to preview as an interference with their traditional 'systems of self-regulation'. Opposition politicians criticised the government for using sex and violence as a pretext to 'inhibit those who dare to criticise' it. In the right to preview is the presupposition that a single group of people appointed by the ruling government can set the moral code for a country of over 56 million people. The Broadcasting Standards Council became part of the Broadcasting Act of 1990.

Proponents of commercial or competitive broadcasting in the West do more than just share Williams's pluralism and his stance against state monopoly over broadcasting institutions. It is their contention that the state must not interfere in any way with the free market forces that shape the broadcasting milieu. They are firmly convinced that when ownership is private, free and open to competition, the audiences who 'are sufficiently sophisticated' are the sole judges of what is good or bad in the television and radio programmes that should be freely available (Wells 1987: 31). Thus, in order to guarantee a free marketplace of entertainment, ideas and serious information, a public-service broadcaster must be viewed as promoting monopolistic tendencies to be guarded against.

For Seiden (1974: 15–16), this goal involves the elimination of public ownership of any kind, which he seems to see as the only real threat to a free and open marketplace. His position is that government-supported media must not be tolerated, for such 'support necessarily goes hand-in-hand with government control'. He argues that it is precisely the absence of government financial support and/or interference in the selection of the persons involved in media operation that has given the American communications system a unique position as a champion of press freedom. He cites France and Britain as states where the government interferes either directly or indirectly with the media.

It is important for the American communications system to reflect the general economic structure of American society, Seiden argues. But this can only happen if government ownership and interference are minimized, given that such involvement inevitably leads to political attempts to conceal and falsify information. Hence the need to maintain a permanent state of tension between the government and the media, making sure that the sharp lines separating their interests are reinforced. He is at the same time somewhat concerned that this ideal might be compromised by a new breed of media practitioners who, to paraphrase him, see themselves as educators rather than informers, thus making the distinction between 'news' and 'editorial' less than watertight.

Seiden makes certain assumptions that others would find to be rather uncritical and therefore difficult to swallow. There is nothing wrong with Seiden's view of the media as watchdogs against political or economic control and manipulation. But one wonders why he should think that such control or manipulation is only possible by the government. Perhaps this attitude is the result of his view of monopoly as possible only when there is state intervention or public control. Finally, if the American communications system is really the free and open marketplace Seiden claims it is, there is apparently no reason why he should be worried about the new breed of journalists who blur the distinction between news and editorials. Given Seiden's premisses, one should assume that audience sovereignty prevails in the long run. After all, who other than the audience can decide what it wants? Seiden thus claims the fear that owners and employees of the mass media possess totalitarian powers over audiences is quite unwarranted in a free-market situation. He maintains that audience sovereignty is assured by means of constant audience polls. Through polls, audiences determine which television and radio programmes survive, and through the circulation figures newspapers and magazines learn the audience's desires.

Yet surely the situation is a little more complex than he suggests? Audience studies are indeed constantly carried out, and they are regularly consulted by journalists and broadcasters, but how sure can Seiden be that, as consumers, the audiences have not come to want only what the media owners and employees have led them to want? Furthermore, Seiden does not say how one should distinguish between audiences that reject a media product because they do not want it, and those that do so because they cannot afford it. For, as far as the argument in favour of commercial broadcasting goes, it seems to imply that in American society the consumer's problem is not that of means, but that of deciding on what to spend the means. This position seems to ignore a number of realities.

Another point made in favour of privately owned media is the importance of using advertising revenue to finance these institutions. According to William G. Harley, communications adviser to the US delegation to the UNESCO general conferences in the 1970s (Wells 1987: 26), such a form of funding is advantageous in that it helps the media to withstand pressures from the government and 'private interest groups'. At the same time it permits the establishment of a plethora of newspapers, magazines and broadcasting stations, which, thanks to their multiplicity, freedom and independence, 'guarantees that no single voice or group of voices can ever achieve predominance'. Motivated by profit though they may be, the private media safeguard the rights of people and act as constructive critics of government.

In a study of the very same American society that has permitted Seiden and others to argue the way they do, Bagdikian (1985) comes out with strikingly different and more critical conclusions. The focus of his argument is that the media, in addition to providing entertainment and selling merchandise, must be in a position to create 'a rich marketplace of ideas and serious information'. Bagdikian considers diversity and richness in the media as the most essential ingredients for the survival of democracy. But, unlike Seiden, he does not think that the absence of government ownership, support or intervention is enough to guarantee this diversity and richness. He is very aware that such desirable ends are much easier to talk about than to bring about. As he remarks, 'public acceptance of a full range of public ideas does not emerge solely from exhortations for tolerance. It comes from experiencing diversity. A public used to a narrow range of ideas will come to regard this narrowness as the only acceptable condition' (1985: 99).

Bagdikian argues that the media in the USA are becoming ever more homogeneous in content and structure even though the population is growing larger, more diverse and confronted with fast-changing circumstances (1985: 98). This, according to him, is a direct consequence of the concentration of control in a relatively small number of corporate hands. If private ownership suffices to ensure richness and diversity in the media, why in a supposedly diverse society such as America are the media so homogeneous in content that 'most newspapers and broadcast programs [are] uniform in basic content, tone and social-political values'? (Bagdikian 1985: 100). Such plurality without diversity is increasing across the world, in the wake of concentrated ownership and globalisation (McChesney 1998, 2001; McChesney and Nichols 2002; Thomas and Nain 2004; BusinessWeek 2004: 36–46; The Economist 2004a: 9, 69–70). As Aggarwala has argued, 'the danger to press freedom inherent in the domination or control of the media by big business may be less obvious than that arising from government subsidy or control of the media but it is not any the less insidious' (1985: 50).

It has been argued that, with few exceptions, most owners who buy or set up private broadcasting institutions are motivated more by the drive to make profit than by a genuine desire to promote richness and diversity in the public mind. The mere fact that commercial broadcasting relies on advertising revenue imposes certain limitations on the type of programmes produced or broadcast. As early as the 1960s, academics were already seriously concerned with the problem of the media's widespread dependence on advertising revenue. This dependence, Halloran argued (1963: 40), reduces broadcasting and the other media to mere profit-making organisations for those whose major purpose is to sell. In such circumstances, the main aim of a newspaper, or of a programme on the radio or television, is 'to get a large audience as quickly as possible so that advertisers may be attracted and held'. These commercial pressures, together with pressures of a political, organisational or professional nature, constitute 'the complex of constraints' to the media's role as 'autonomous "watch-dogs"', with which the media and practitioners must constantly negotiate (Gallagher 1982; Head 1963).

Adkins (1985: 55) sees three major undesirable effects of commercialism in broadcasting. First, the pressure to build up large audiences in order to satisfy advertisers causes programmes that appeal to the smaller interest groups to be squeezed out. 'The complete spectrum of public interests and needs can no longer be served', and the programme types that survive are those that appeal to 'the largest shares of audience and the specific age and socio-economic groups wanted by the advertisers'. Second, the trend is to broadcast not educational and informative programmes but those with 'the strongest appeal to most basic human interests', such as violence and sex, in order to retain the attention of the audience. Third, any programme content likely to bring about a significant drop in audience figures must be avoided. Thus, because emotion is 'more gripping than fact', news programmes tend to focus on the sensational and to displace 'the heavier items involving complicated explanations, little action or comparative numbers'. The stories that are preferred become those with exciting visual content, and 'oversimplification of complex issues seems necessary to avoid the risk of boring and losing the audience'.

However, Adkins fails to consider whether these characteristics are the sole domain of commercial media, or simply tend to be more pronounced in the private sector than in non-commercial state-owned systems. Nevertheless, like Aggarwala, Adkins is equally aware of the shortcomings of a state-dominated broadcasting system, where non-commercialism is not necessarily synonymous with public-service mission or content. This is evidenced in his argument that the optimal composition of a free broadcast system consists neither in exclusive state monopoly nor in total commercialism, but rather in a balance between the two (Adkins 1985: 55). This point is echoed by de Sola Pool (1977: 32), who argues that a country which opts to develop broadcasting either as 'an entertainment medium to serve advertisers' or as 'a propaganda medium for the government' is bound to fail to meet the other needs of its plural society. Although de Sola recognises that a mixed system is probably the best, he still cautions that no single model can suit each and every society. In looking for alternative ways of funding, control and organisation of broadcasting systems, each country must exert itself to determine how broadcasting ought to relate and interact with other social institutions, and what role it must play in propagating the richness, diversity and aspirations of the society.

Since Aggarwala is of the view that press freedom is threatened by government control and by business domination, and that in both cases public interests are relegated to the back seat, he advocates 'free media' independent of big business and/or government control or domination (1985: 50–51). But how these 'free media' can be brought about remains the unanswered question, though Aggarwala does not hide his admiration for the BBC's 'excellent, top-quality television and radio fare'. Concluding his observations on the Italian situation, where there is a mixture of state and private broadcasting, Rando (1986: 39) is less optimistic. Attractive though the ideal of free and unrestricted media might be at a theoretical level, in reality governments are most unlikely to surrender their powers of regulation. In addition, the economics of broadcasting (especially in television) are such that a 'genuine pluralism of content' is out of the question, even where there is a plethora of stations. Rando's grim conclusion is that a truly free media system does not appear feasible with exclusive private control, or under total state monopoly, or even in a dilution of the two. While this extreme position cannot be dismissed summarily, we argue here that for many practical purposes much could be realised in Africa under a careful balance between public and private forms of communication, informed by age-old notions of personhood and domesticated agency that seek coexistence between individual and community interests (Nyamnjoh 2002a; Rowlands 2004).

Blake's Prototype Policy Framework for Africa

I would not want to push the debate any further than I have done or to dampen optimism unduly. The preceding discussion is intended as a mirror against which African scholars, policymakers, investors, NGOs, media practitioners and advocates in the communications industry can examine their projects and schemes, with or without the idea of collective interest or domesticated democracy in mind. I propose, for public scrutiny and enrichment, a prototype policy framework by one of Africa's leading communications scholars, who incidentally has served as minister of information in post-civil-war Sierra Leone.

Cecil Blake, a veteran scholar with a sound knowledge and research experience of the predicament of African media institutions and practitioners, proposes a policy option that could promote the democratisation-driven imperatives of communication in Africa in the twenty-first century. His alternative is predicated upon the argument that the press in a democratic or democratising society needs to be self-regulatory, rather than governed by press laws drawn up by governments, as has been largely the case in Africa. As long as the government arrogates to itself the right to regulate the press, its laws will always tend to limit rather than promote press freedom and exclude rather than broaden access to differ-ent political, cultural and social groups. It is in the light of these considerations that Blake proposes a prototype policy framework of five broad principles:

1. Government will create an environment that will allow for an increased pace of liberalization of the media, and the opening up of ownership of all sub-sectors of the communication sector. Government, in essence, will facilitate the privatization of all media.

2. Government will open access to all who wish to provide information and communication for education, entertainment and development messages consistent with the national vision.

3. In order to ensure that resources will always be available for the successful operation of the sector, government will encourage *investments* and *competition* as the fundamental premises for the running of the communication sector.

4. Government in consultation with the private media and media professional organizations will embark upon the setting up of an *independent* regulatory body in the form of a communications council or communications authority that will, *inter alia*, protect the interests of all citizens who are the ultimate consumers of media content; protect the interest of information providers; handle all issues relating to the issuance and renewal of licenses for all media; develop a professional code of ethics; monitor the adherence and breaches of the ethical codes; set standards for professional practice in the sector; adjudicate grievances not grave enough to warrant litigation through the judiciary; and carry out other functions that will be deemed important by the council or authority.

5. Government and private tertiary level institutions will train media personnel for both the public and private sector on a 'free' basis. Government, concerned about the importance of national integration, social cohesion, peace and the general well-being of all, will ensure that the communications sector receives full support in its efforts to diversify training resources and to contribute towards a well-trained resource pool. (Blake 1997: 262)

The problem with national communications councils, commissions or authorities as they exist in Africa today is their lack of real independence, even when they purport to be autonomous. But, as Blake argues, only a genuinely independent body composed of representatives from government, the private media sector, professional bodies, the churches, the university community and other walks of life can play its part in the democratic transformation of society in Africa. And if current trends at adopting relatively more tolerant constitutions and freedom laws are sustained (Ogbondah 1997), then there is reason to think of such an independent body as feasible. Blake elaborates on the functions of the body as follows:

This body will assist not only in the generation and implementation of the national communication and information policy, but also the monitoring of policy practices across the board – in the private and public sector. It will recommend changes in policy as needed. It is important to point out that this body will not preclude the formation of associations such as associations of broadcasters (private and public), journalists, media owners and so on. It will not usurp the responsibilities of such bodies.

The independent authority/commission will ensure participation by all institutions that operate within the communications sector. It will ease the burden on government, while making certain that information flows in all directions, consistent with democratic transformation and national development plans. It should not be regarded as a 'parallel' body to any department of government. (Blake 1997: 263)

Blake proceeds to propose specific guidelines pertaining to the print media, the electronic media, oramedia, and human resource development, which can be summed up as follows.

Regarding the print media, the independent authority would have to provide guidelines that 'are professionally driven rather than governmentally influenced and structured'. These guidelines would allow for the registration of newspapers, magazines and book publishing houses, based on 'a thorough assessment of all extant press laws, led by professionals in the sector representing the private and public sectors, in consultation with the national bar association or other such legal civil organisation' (1997: 263). Increased freedom for the private press would require media practitioners in this sector 'to adhere strictly to principles such as accuracy, ethical efficacy and fairness'. This adherence requires that the policy commits both government and the private press to 'a common understanding regarding ethical standards' (Blake 1997: 264). Guidelines for the rural press should cover both the public and private sectors, but government should be encouraged to 'strengthen its presence in the rural areas through the use of the rural press in efforts to communicate development messages effectively' (1997: 264).

Blake recognises the importance of the electronic media in a continent with a high degree of illiteracy. He is also very conscious of the danger that their irresponsible and offensive use 'could have more devastating results compared to the print media'. Second, because of their advantage in reaching the widest range of audiences, the electronic media are 'susceptible to massive manipulation', hence the need for special guidelines in their case. He proposes that the issuing of licences and other regulatory concerns be made the responsibility of the independent authority, which should set the rules, standards and enforcement codes, the respecting of which would determine 'the issuance or renewal or non-renewal of licenses to users of the airwaves'. This authority should regulate current monopolisation by government of state radio and television stations, by requiring them 'to expand their coverage to include "news" about competing social forces in society such as opposition parties in a multiparty system'. But all of this would depend on 'the willingness of the government to open up the airwaves without prejudice' (Blake 1997: 265–6).

On oramedia, Blake invites both public and private channels to seek inspiration from the mainstream cultures of Africa for the development and production of local programmes. Such initiatives could serve to preserve cultures and in some instances export African cultures through television programming while still enhancing local production efforts. The independent authority should expect the commitment 'of both the private and public sectors to work towards the production of local programs for entertainment, development messages and social cohesion', and seek to promote synchrony between oramedia, a daily reality of millions of Africans, and the electronic media, which have enormous potential but are often of limited reach. Blake proposes that a unit be provided for within the independent authority that would work 'jointly with indigenous drama and dance troupes, focusing solely on the production of local programs centered on oramedia strategies and content' (Blake 1997: 266–7).

Regarding human resource development, Blake believes that the independent authority should address the central issue of 'the role of the government in the development of human resources for the communication sector as the society becomes democratized'. Blake argues that governments should be made to give up their traditional monopoly over training institutions and their products. The independent authority would have to 'commit the government to open up the human resources development subsector so as to allow competing training institutions from the private sector to participate in the training of personnel for the communications sector. The structure of the training institutions will have to be determined by an interministerial body and the private sector' (Blake 1997: 267).

These measures and their harmonious implementation, regular evaluation and monitoring, Blake believes, 'will help to prevent ugly confrontations not only between the government and the private media, but also between the government and the various forces in civil society' (Blake 1997: 268). It is hoped that with the right communication policies and structures in place, the media would be better able to redefine themselves accordingly, and be of greater service to democratisation as a negotiated process in Africa.

The Future of Democracy and the Media

The overview has indicated that if democratisation requires fundamental changes, as it should, such changes usually entail a challenge to vested interests, be these local, national or foreign, private or public. Contrary to some optimistic accounts (Hyden et al. 2002), media that have facilitated genuine democratisation may appear rare in Africa. It is clear, however, that media which decide in earnest to play an active and positive role in this process will find themselves in a hostile environment if prevailing attitudes and practices are not in tune with the spirit of change. For to democratise means to question basic monolithic assumptions, conventional wisdom about democracy, media, government, power myths and accepted personality cults, and to propose and work for the demystification of the state, custom and society. To democratise in Africa is to provide the missing cultural link to current efforts, links informed by popular ideas of personhood and domesticated agency. To democratise is to negotiate coexistence between competing ideas of how best to provide for the humanity and dignity of all. To democratise is above all to observe and draw from the predicaments of ordinary Africans forced by culture, history and material realities to live their lives as 'subjects' rather than as 'citizens', even as liberal democratic rhetoric claims otherwise.

The mere call for an exploration of alternatives is, as we have seen almost everywhere on the continent, bound to be perceived as a threat. In particular, such a call would receive a hostile hearing from those who have championed the cause of one-dimensionalism nationally and internationally – that is, those who benefit from the maintenance of the status quo, and who stand to lose from any changes. They cannot withstand the challenge, stimulation and provocation that democracy (as the celebration of difference and diversity) promises. They want life to go on without disturbance or fundamental change. And they are well placed to ensure this, thanks to their power to regulate media ownership and control, the power to accord or to deny a voice to individuals and communities. Only well-articulated policies informed by public interest broadly defined to include individual and community expectations, and scrupulously respected, would protect against such abuse of office and privilege.

The future of democracy and the relevance of the media will depend very much on how well African states design policies that negotiate the delicate balance between public interests and private concerns. In the process they must enable interplay between old and new information and communication technologies towards this end. It is a future that could well be bright for communications and democracy in a broad and participatory sense. For, as Alec Russell has aptly observed, one of the enduring mysteries and marvels of Africa is the ability of Africans to pick up again from any setback, including even the most appalling of disasters (Russell 1999: 109). Such determination, demonstrated through the creative appropriation of various world-views, values, influences, and information and communications technologies, implies that Africans have simply refused to celebrate victimhood.

References

Abrahamsen, R. (2000) *Disciplining Democracy: Development Discourse and Good Governance in Africa*, London: Zed Books.

Adkins, G.R. (1985) 'Commercial television: blessing or blight? What commercial TV can mean to a country', *Media Asia* 12(1): 54–5.

Agbor Tabi, P. (1995) 'Address presented by the Minister of Higher Education, Dr. Peter Agbor Tabi, opening ceremony of the Conference on Cameroon literature, 1 December 1994', *The BUN* (Buea University Newsletter) 2(1): 7–9.

Aggarwala, N. (1985) 'NIIO: a hope or a nightmare?', *Media Asia* 12(1): 44–53.

Ahanda, W.A. (1998) 'Exposé sur la déontologie des journalistes', paper presented at the National Seminar on Sports Journalism, ESSTIC, University of Yaoundé II, 27–30 April.

Ahidjo, A. (1964) *Contribution to National Construction*, Paris: Présence Africaine.

Ahidjo, A. (1980) *Anthologie des Discours 1957–1979*, Paris: Nouvelles Editions Africaines.

Ake, C. (2000) *The Feasibility of Democracy in Africa*, Dakar: CODESRIA.

Alabi, N. (ed.) (1996) *L'État de la Presse en Afrique de l'Ouest 1995–1996*, Accra: FES.

Amougou, A.D. (1994) 'La censure administrative de la presse écrite au Cameroun selon la loi de 1990', DSSTIC dissertation, Yaoundé: ASMAC/ESSTIC (mimeo).

Anyakora, G., and Potiskum, S.M. (1996) 'The state of the media in Nigeria', in K. Blay-Amihere and N. Alabi (eds), *State of the Media in West Africa 1995–1996*, Accra: Friedrich-Ebert-Stiftung, pp. 101–8.

Appadurai, A. (1996) *Modernity at Large: Cultural Dimensions of Globalization*, Minneapolis: University of Minnesota Press.

Ardener, E. (1962) 'The Political history of Cameroon', *The World Today* 18(8): 341–50.

Ardener, E. (1967) 'The nature of the reunification of Cameroon', in C. Hazlewood (ed.), *African Integration and Disintegration*, London: Oxford University Press, pp. 285–337.

Arrous, M.B. (2003) *Coaltion, Dispersion: Un Moment Démocratique en Afrique de l'Ouest 'Francophone'*, 1988–1996, Dakar: CODESRIA.

Arthur, A. (1997) 'Media ownership and control in Ghana: past, present and future perspectives', paper presented at the Regional Workshop on Media Ownership and Control in West and Central Africa, Yaoundé, 8–10 September.

Asunkan (1993) Interview, *Cameroon Calling*, 21 February.

Atanga, M.L. (1994) 'The political economy of West Cameroon: a study in the alienation of a linguistic minority', M.Sc. thesis, Ahmadu Bello University, Zaria, Nigeria.

Awake, (1997), 'The Internet: is it for you?', *AWAKE*, 22 July, pp. 3–13.

Awasom, F.N. (2003) 'The vicissitudes of twentieth-century Mankon Fons in Cameroon's changing social order', in W. van Binsbergen (ed.), *The Dynamics of Power and the Rule of Law: Essays on Africa and Beyond*, Hamburg: African Studies Centre Leiden/Lit Verlag, pp. 101–120.

Badu, K.A., and Blay-Amihere, K. (eds) (1995) *State of the Media in Ghana: 1994–1995*, Accra: Friedrich-Ebert-Stiftung.

Bagdikian, B. (1985) 'The US media: supermarket or assembly line?', *Journal of Communication* 35: 97–109.

Bahi, A.A. (1998) 'Les Tambours bâillonnés: contrôle et mainmise du pouvoir sur les médias en Côte d'Ivoire', *Media Development* 45(4): 36–45.

Balandier, G. (1963) *Sociologie Actuelle de l'Afrique Noire*, Paris: Presses Universitaires de France.

Balule, T., and Maripe, B. (2000) *A Quick Guide to Laws and Practices that Inhibit Freedom of Expression in Botswana*, Gaborone: MISA-Botswana.

Barber, K. (1997) 'Introduction', in K. Barber (ed.), *Readings in African Popular Culture*, Oxford: James Currey, pp. 1–12.

Barnett, C. (1998) 'The contradictions of broadcasting reform in post-apartheid South Africa', *Review of African Political Economy* 25(78): 551–70.

Bayart, J.-F. (1973) 'Presse écrite et développement politique au Cameroun', *Revue Française d'Études Politiques Africaines* 88: 48–63.

Bayart, J.-F. (1980) 'One-party government and political development in Cameroon', in Ndiva Kofele-Kale (ed.), *An African Experiment in Nation Building: The Bilingual Cameroon Republic Since Reunification*, Boulder, CO: Westview Press, pp. 159–87.

Bayart, J.-F. (1985) *L'État au Cameroun*, Paris: Presse de la Fondation Nationale des Sciences Politiques.

Bayart, J.-F. (1986) 'Civil society in Africa', in P. Chabal (ed.), *Political Domination in Africa: Reflections on the Limits of Power*, Cambridge: Cambridge University Press, pp. 109–25.

Bayart, J.-F. (1993), *The State in Africa: The Politics of the Belly*, London: Longman.

Bayart, J.-F., Geschiere, P., and Nyamnjoh, F. (2001) 'Autochtonie, démocratie et citoyenneté en Afrique', *Critique Internationale* 10: 177–94.

Beadle, G. (1963) Television: A Critical Review, London: George Allen & Unwin.

Bebey, F. (1963) La Radiodiffusion en Afrique Noire, Seine: Editions Saint-Paul.

Becker, J. (1996) 'The Internet, structural violence and non-communication', Media Development 43(4): 10–12.

Bereng, P.M. (2001) 'Privatisation of the media and national survival in Lesotho', Media Development 48(2): 9–13.

Berger, G. (1998) 'Media and democracy in Southern Africa', Review of African Political Economy 25(78): 599–610.

Berger, G. (2001) 'Deracialisation, democracy and development: transformation of the South African Media, 1994–2000', in K. Tomaselli and H. Dunn (eds), Media, Democracy and Renewal in Southern Africa, Denver: International Academic Publishers.

Berman, F.B. (1998) 'Ethnicity, patronage and the African state: the politics of uncivil nationalism', African Affairs 97(388): 305–10.

Betts, P. (1988) 'French TV soap opera continues to make headlines', Financial Times, 11 October.

Biyitti Bi Essam, J.-P. (1984) 'Une Radio regionale Africaine et son public: analyse d'un divorce', doctorat de 3ème cycle thesis, University of Paris 7 (mimeo).

Blake, C. (1997) 'Democratization: the dominant imperative for national communication policies in Africa in the 21st century', Gazette 59(4/5): 253–69.

Blay-Amihere, K., and Alabi, N. (eds) (1996) State of the Media in West Africa 1995–1996, Accra: Friedrich-Ebert-Stiftung.

Blin, B. (1993) 'Ethical aspects of journalism', International Affairs 9: 39–43.

Boh, H. (1992) Cameroon: State of Human Rights Violations Following October 11 Presidential Elections, Bamenda, 10 November.

Boh, H. (1997) The State of the Media in Cameroon, Yaoundé: Friedrich-Ebert-Stiftung.

Boh, H., and Ntemfac, O. (1991) The Story of Cameroon Calling: Prison Graduate, Bamenda: United News Service.

Bouhafa, M.M. (1997) 'Grassroots media and community empowerment in West Africa', paper presented at the International Conference on Media and Politics, Brussels: Catholic University of Brussels, 27 February–1 March.

Boulaga, F.E. (1997a) La Démocratie de Transit au Cameroun, Paris: L'Harmattan.

Boulaga, F.E. (ed.) (1997b) Democracy in the Throes of Tribalism, Yaoundé: Friedrich-Ebert-Stiftung and Gerddes Cameroun.

Bourgault, L.M. (1995) Mass Media in Sub-Saharan Africa, Bloomington: Indiana University Press.

Boyomo, A.L.C. (1995) 'Mass media et multipartisme en Afrique francophone: Le cas du Cameroun', Fréquence Sud 13: 11–30.

Boyomo, A.L.C., and Nyamnjoh, F.B. (1996) Journalism Training in Cameroon: Curricula Evaluation, Yaoundé: Friedrich-Ebert-Stiftung.

Bridges, W.M. (1933) 'Intelligence report on the Bum Area', Buea Archives.

Browne, D.R. (1963) 'Radio Guinea: a voice of independent Africa', *Journal of Broadcasting* 7: 113–22.

BusinessWeek, (2004) 'Mega Media', 23 February.

Butty, J. (1998) 'The media under attack: the treatment of Liberian journalists since last August gives cause for concern', *West Africa* 4186: 265–6.

Campbell, W.J. (1996) 'Newspapers in emerging democracies: a cross-regional study of the newly independent press in Central Europe and sub-Saharan Africa', paper presented at the Annual Convention for the Association for Education in Journalism and Mass Communication, 10–13 August, Anaheim, CA.

Chabal, P. (1992) *Power in Africa: An Essay in Political Interpretation*, London: Macmillan.

Chabal, P., and Daloz, J.-P. (1999) *Africa Works: Disorder as Political Instrument*, Oxford: James Currey.

Charo, T., and Makali, D. (1998), 'New media and the hate campaign: ethnic conflict brings out the best of hate journalism', *Expression Today* 4, March.

Chiepe, B.D. (1996) 'Reflections from a cartoonist', in M. Leepile (ed.), *Botswana's Media and Democracy: Selected Papers from the Seminar on Media in a Democracy*, Gaborone: Mmegi Publishing House, pp. 31–5.

Chilver, E.M., and Roschenthaler, U. (eds) (2001) *Cameroon's Tycoon: Max Esser's Expedition and Its Consequences*, Oxford: Berghahn Books.

Chimombo, M. (2000) 'Malawi: freedom of speech – freedom of information: the unbalanced equation', paper presented at the Political Economy of the Media in Southern Africa seminar, 25–29 April, Durban: University of Natal.

Chimombo, S. and M. (1996) *The Culture of Democracy: Language, Literature, the Arts and Politics in Malawi, 1992–94*, Zomba: WASI Publications.

Chindji-Kouleu, F. (1997) 'Ethnies, médias et processus démocratique au Cameroun: analyse de contenu de quelques journaux', in D. Zognong and I. Mouiche (eds), *Démocratisation et Rivalités Ethniques au Cameroun*, Yaoundé: IREPE, pp. 63–92.

Chiumbu, S.H. (1997) *Democracy, Human Rights and the Media*, IMK Report no. 23, Department of Media and Communications, University of Oslo.

Chomsky, N. (1999) *Profit over People: Neoliberalism and Global Order*, New York: Seven Stories Press.

Cochrane, J., and Brunner, J. (1998) 'Africa and the Internet: superhighway checkpoints', in P.G. Veit (ed.), *Africa's Valuable Assets: A Reader in Natural Resource Management*, Washington DC: World Resources Institute.

Cole, B. (1995) *Mass Media Freedom and Democracy in Sierra Leone*, Freetown: Premier Publishing House.

Collectif Changer le Cameroun (C3) (1990) *Changer le Cameroun: Pourquoi Pas?*, Yaouonde: Edition C3.

Collectif Changer le Cameroun (1992) *Le Cameroun Eclaté?* Yaoundé: Edition C3.

Collectif Changer le Cameroun (1993) 11 October, 1992, Yaoundé: Edition C3.

Collectif Changer le Cameroun (C3) and Friedrich-Ebert-Stiftung (eds) (1994) *Ethnies et Développement National: Actes du Colloque de Yaoundé 1993*, Yaoundé: Edition C3 and Editions du CRAC.

Comaroff, J., and Comaroff, J. (eds) (1993) *Modernity and Its Malcontents: Ritual and Power in Post Colonial Africa*, Chicago: University of Chicago Press.

Comaroff, J.L., and Comaroff, J. (1999) 'Introduction', in J. Comaroff and J.L. Comaroff (eds), *Civil Society and the Political Imagination in Africa: Critical Perspectives*, Chicago: University of Chicago Press, pp. 1–43.

Comaroff, J., and Comaroff, J.L. (2000) 'Millennial capitalism and the culture of neoliberalism', *Public Culture* 12(2): 291–343.

CPDM (1985) *Bamenda: Fresh Impetus*, Yaoundé: SOPECAM.

CPDM (1991) *Argument for Real Democracy: The Great Provincial Tour of President Paul Biya (August–September–October 1991)*, Yaoundé: SOPECAM.

Crush, J., and McDonald, D. (eds) (2001) 'Evaluating South African immigration policy after apartheid', *Africa Today* 48(3).

Curran, J. (1988) 'Alternative approaches to media reform', in J. Curran and J. Seato, *Power without Responsibility: The Press and Broadcasting in Britain*, Routledge: London.

Dare, O. (1998) 'Democratization in Africa: what role for the media?', paper presented at the 11th Biennial Conference of the African Council for Communication Education, Nairobi, Kenya, 9–15 October.

Datchoua Soupa, C. (1993) 'Des Cas de répressions des délits de presse entre 1990–1993', paper presented at UNESCO seminar, Le Cadre d'Exercise de la Liberté de Presse dans un État de Droit, 6–10 September, Yaoundé.

Department of State (USA) (1993) *Country Reports on Human Rights Practices for 1992*.

De Sola Pool, I., (1977), 'The governance of mass communication: the government, the audience and social groups', in M. Teheranian and V. Hakimzadeh (eds), *Communications Policy for National Development*, London: Routledge & Kegan Paul, pp. 130–48.

Devisch, R. (1995) 'Frenzy, violence, and ethical renewal in Kinshasa', *Public Culture* 7(3): 593–629.

Diamani, J.-P. (1995) 'L'humour politique au Phare du Zaire', *Politique Africaine* 58: 151–7.

Diamond, L. (1994) 'Rethinking civil society: toward democratic consolidation', *Journal of Democracy* 5(3): 4–17.

Dibango, M., (in collaboration with D. Rouard) (1994) *Three Kilos of Coffee: An Autobiography*, Chicago: University of Chicago Press.

Djuidjeu, M. (1988) 'Mass media et développement: les elèves de Yaoundé face à la vidéo-cassette', doctorat de 3ème cycle dissertation, FLSH, University of Yaoundé.

Downing, J.H. (1986) 'Government secrecy and the media in the United States and Britain', in P. Golding, G. Murdock and P. Schlesinger (eds), *Communicating Politics: Mass Communications and the Political Process*, Leicester: Leicester University Press, pp. 153–70.

Downing, J.H. (2001) *Radical Media: Rebellious Communication and Social Movements,* London: Sage Publications.

Duncan, J. (2000) 'Talk left, act right: what constitutes transformation in Southern African media?', *Communications Law in Transition Newsletter* 1(6), 10 June.

Durham, D. (1999) 'Civil lives: leadership and accomplishment in Botswana', in J. Comaroff and J.L. Comaroff (eds), *Civil Society and the Political Imagination in Africa: Critical Perspectives,* Chicago: University of Chicago Press, pp. 192–218.

Economist (2004a), 'Hunting Disney' and 'Disney and Comcast: the battle for the magic kingdom', 14 February.

Economist (2004b), 'I survived' and 'Not guilty: how Lord Hutton cleared the government of "sexing up" its dossier on Iraq's WDM', 31 January.

Ekaney, N. (1976) 'Radio and national development in Cameroon: a descriptive analysis', *Gazette* 22(2): 115–28.

Ela, J.-M. (1974) 'Culture de masse ou opium des masse?', *L'Effort Camerounais,* 26 July: 15–16.

Ellis, S. (1989) 'Tuning in to pavement radio', *African Affairs* 88(352): 321–30.

Ellis, S. (1993) 'Rumour and Power in Togo', *Africa* 63(4): 462–75.

Ellis, S. (1994) 'Democracy and Human Rights in Africa', in R. van den Berg and U. Bosma (eds), *Poverty and Development: Historical Dimension of Development, Change and Conflict in the South,* Ministry of Foreign Affairs: The Hague, pp. 115–24.

Ellis, S. (2000) 'Reporting Africa', *Current History* 99(637): 221–6.

Eneffiok Akpan, A. (1993) *Contemporary Issues in Mass Media and Communication in Nigeria,* Calabar: Vena Educational Consultancy.

Englund, H. (ed.) (2002a) *A Democracy of Chameleons: Politics and Culture in the New Malawi,* Uppsala: Nordiska Afrikainstitutet.

Englund, H. (2002b) 'The village in the city, the city in the village: Migrants in Lilongwe', *Journal of Southern African Studies* 28(1): 137–154.

Englund, H., and Nyamnjoh, F.B. (eds) (2004) *Rights and the Politics of Recognition in Africa,* London: Zed Books.

Eone, T. (1986) *Radio, Publics et Pouvoir au Cameroun: Utilisation Officielles et Besoins Sociaux,* Paris: L'Harmattan.

Eone, T. (1993) 'Role de la presse privée dans un contexte multipartiste au Cameroun', paper presented at UNESCO seminar, Le Cadre d'Exercice de la Liberté de Presse dans un État de Droit, 6–10 September, Yaoundé.

Eone, T. (1994) 'La communication politique aujourd'hui et demain au Cameroun', paper presented at the National Forum on Communication, 29 August–1 September, Yaoundé.

Eribo, F., and Tanjong, E. (eds) (2002) *Journalism and Mass Communication in Africa: Cameroon,* Lanham, MD: Lexington Books/Rowman & Littlefield.

Essang, M.M. (1978) 'La campagne nationale d'alphabitisation au Cameroun: de l'euphorie à l'impasse', B.A. dissertation, ESIJY, Yaoundé (mimeo).

Essono, L.M.O. (1996) 'La démocratie en chansons: les Bikut-si du Cameroun', *Politique Africaine* 64: 52–61.

Etonga, M. (1980) 'An imperial presidency: a study of presidential power in Cameroon', in Ndiva Kofele-Kale (ed.), *An African Experiment in Nation Building: The Bilingual Cameroon Republic Since Reunification*, Boulder, CO: Westview Press, pp. 133–57.

Etta, F.B., and Parvyn-Wamahiu, S. (eds) (2003) *Information and Communication Technologies for Development in Africa: The Experience with Community Telecentres*, Volume 2, Dakar: IDRC/CODESRIA.

Ewumbue-Monono, C. (1992) 'The right to inform and the 1990 Press Law in Cameroon', *Africa Media Review* 6(3): 19–29.

Ewumbue-Monono, C. (2000) 'Anglophone appointees and the anglophone problem: effective anglophone agents', SCNCFORUM, 26 April.

Eyoh, D. (1995) 'From the belly to the ballot: ethnicity and politics in Africa', *Queen's Quarterly* 102(1): 39–51.

Eyoh, D. (1998a) 'Through the prism of a local tragedy: political liberalisation, regionalism and elite struggles for power in Cameroon', *Africa* 68(3): 338–59.

Eyoh, D. (1998b) 'Conflicting narratives of Anglophone protest and the politics of identity in Cameroon', *Journal of Contemporary African Studies* 16(2): 268–71.

Fako, T.T., and Nyamnjoh, F.B. (2000) 'Waiting for Botswana Television: benefits and consequences', *Media Development* 48(3): 37–44.

Fanon, F. (1969) *Pour la Révolution Africaine*, Paris: Maspero.

Fardon, R., and Furniss, G. (eds) (2000) *African Broadcast Cultures*, Oxford: James Currey.

Fauvet, P. and Mosse, M. (2003) *Carlos Cardoso: Telling the Truth in Mozambique*, Cape Town: Double Storey.

Federal Republic of Germany (1996) 'Germany and the global information society: position paper', *Nord–Süd Aktuell* 10(4): 834–7.

Feldmann, T., Graumans, A., and Ukpabi, C. (1998) 'Ethics and media code of practice: African journalists meet Dutch and Western journalists', seminar report, 27 and 28 June, De Balie, Amsterdam, Chudi Communication and Management Consult, Amsterdam.

Feltoe, G. (1996) 'Media Law in Zimbabwe', in Willie Musarurwa Memorial Trust (ed.), *Towards Press Freedom*, Gweru: Superprint, pp. 134–47.

Ferguson, J. (1999) *Expectations of Modernity: Myths and Meanings of Urban Life on the Zambian Copperbelt*, Berkeley: University of California Press.

Findahl, O. (1999) 'Public service broadcasting – a fragile, yet durable construction', *Nordicom Review* 20(1): 13–19.

Fisiy, C.F. (1995) 'Chieftaincy in the modern state: an institution at the crossroads of democratic change', *Paideuma* 41: 49–62.

Fisiy, C.F., and Goheen, M. (1998) 'Power and the quest for recognition: neo-traditional titles among the new elite in Nso, Cameroon', *Africa* 68(3): 383–402.

Fombad, C.M. (1995) 'Freedom of expression in the Cameroon democratic transition', *Journal of Modern African Studies* 33(2): 211–26.

Fombad, C.M. (1999a) 'The constitutional protection of freedom of expression in Cameroon: a comparative appraisal', *SA Public Law* 14(1): 25–45.

Fombad, C.M. (1999b) 'Cameroon', in R. Martin (ed.), *Speaking Freely: Expression and the Law in the Commonwealth*, Toronto: Irwin Law, pp. 87–129.

Fonchingong, T.N. (1998) 'Multipartyism and democratization in Cameroon', *Journal of Third World Studies* 15(2): 119–36.

Fonlon, B. (1964) 'Will we make or mar?', *Abbia* (special) 5: 9–33.

Fonye, H.N. (1973) 'Press freedom in Nigeria and Cameroon: a comparative analysis', B.A. dissertation, University of Lagos (mimeo).

Fonye, H.N. (1988) 'The growth of Radio Cameroon', *Cameroon Tribune*, 2 February.

Fordred, L.J. (1999) 'Narrative, conflict and change: journalism in the new South Africa', PhD thesis, Department of Social Anthropology, University of Cape Town, South Africa.

Franda, M. (2002) *Launching into Cyberspace: Internet Development and Politics in Five World Regions*. Boulder, CO: Lynne Rienner.

Franklin, A., and Love, R. (1998) 'Whose news? Control of the media in Africa', *Review of African Political Economy* 25(78): 546–50.

Friedrich-Ebert-Stiftung (1993a) *Sondage d'Opinion sur le Rôle des Médias dans la Démocratisation au Cameroun*, Yaoundé: FES.

Friedrich-Ebert-Stiftung (1993b) *Le Droit de la Presse au Cameroun: Étude Comparative et Prospective*, Yaoundé: FES.

Friedrich-Ebert-Stiftung (1994) *La Justice des Médias au Cameroun*, Yaoundé: FES.

FES (Friedrich-Ebert-Stiftung) (1996) *La Presse Écrite dans le Paysage Mediatique du Cameroun: Une Analyse Dynamique*, Yaoundé: FES.

Fritz, J.P. (1996) 'Threats to press freedom', in Willie Musarurwa Memorial Trust (ed.), *Towards Press Freedom*, Gweru: Superprint, pp. 81–4.

Gahungu, A. (1981) *Une Stratégie du Développement de la Communication Rurale*, Paris: UNESCO.

Gaillard, P. (1986) 'RFI: "peut mieux faire"', *Jeune Afrique* 1354, 17 December.

Gallagher, M. (1982) 'Negotiation of control in media organizations and occupations', in M. Gurevitch, T. Bennett, J. Curran and J. Woollacott (eds), *Culture, Society and the Media*, London: Methuen, pp. 151–73.

Gallagher, D. (1991) *Public and Private Press in Cameroon: Changing Roles and Issues in the New Pluralism*, Cameroon: University of Yaoundé.

Gardinier, D.E. (1963) *Cameroon: United Nations Challenge to French Policy*, Oxford: Oxford University Press.

Gariyo, Z. (1993) *The Media, Constitutionalism and Democracy in Uganda*, Kampala: Centre for Basic Research.

Garland, E. (1999) 'Developing bushmen: building civil(ized) society in the Kalahari and beyond', in J. Comaroff and J.L. Comaroff (eds), *Civil Society and the Political Imagination in Africa: Critical Perspectives*, Chicago: University of Chicago Press, pp. 72–103.

Garside, C. (1993) 'Newspaper publishing as an enterprise in the West', *International Affairs* 9: 68–71.

Gecau, K. (1997) 'The 1980s background to the popular political songs of the early 1990s in Kenya', in R. Zhuwarara, K. Gecau, and M. Drag (eds), *Media, Democratization and Identity*, Harare: University of Zimbabwe, pp. 149–76.

Geschiere, P. (1997) *The Modernity of Witchcraft: Politics and the Occult in Postcolonial Africa*, Charlottesville: University Press of Virginia.

Geschiere, P., and Gugler, J. (1998) 'Introduction: the urban–rural connection – changing issues of belonging and identification', *Africa* 68(3): 309–19.

Geschiere, P., and Nyamnjoh, F. (1998) 'Witchcraft as an issue in the "politics of belonging": democratization and urban migrants' involvement with the home village', *African Studies Review* 41(3): 69–92.

Geschiere, P., and Nyamnjoh, F. (2000) 'Capitalism and autochthony: the seesaw of mobility and belonging', *Public Culture* 12(2): 423–52.

Gibbons, R.A. (1974) 'Francophone West and Equatorial Africa', in S.W. Head (ed.), *Broadcasting in Africa: A Continental Survey of Radio and Television*, Philadelphia: Temple University Press, pp. 107–24.

Glaser, D. (2000) 'The media inquiry reports of the South African Human Rights Commission: a critique', *African Affairs* 99(396): 373–93.

Gobata, R. (1993) *The Past Tense of Shit (Book One): Contribution of an Uncompromising Critic to the Democratic Process in Cameroon*, Limbe: Nooremac.

Goheen, M. (1992) 'Chiefs, sub-chiefs and local control: negotiations over land, struggles over meaning', *Africa* 62(3): 389–412.

Golding, P. (1974) 'Media role in national development: critique of a theoretical orthodoxy', *Journal of Communication* 24(3): 39–53.

Golding, P. (1977) 'Media professionalism in the Third World: the transfer of an ideology', in J. Curran, M. Gurevitch and J. Woollacott (eds), *Mass Communication and Society*, London: Edward Arnold, pp. 291–308.

Golding, P., and Elliott, P. (1979) *Making the News*, London: Longman.

Golding, P., and Harris, P. (eds) (1997) *Beyond Cultural Imperialism: Globalization, Communication and the New International Order*. London: Sage Publications.

Gooch, C.R. (1997) 'Black journalists in South Africa tread new paths', *Media Development* 44(4): 26–8.

Good, K. (1994) 'Corruption and mismanagement in Botswana: a best-case example?', *Journal of Modern African Studies* 32(3): 499–521.

Good, K. (1999) 'Enduring elite democracy in Botswana', *Democratization* 6(1): 50–66.

Good, K. (2002) *The Liberal Model and Africa: Elites against Democracy*, London: Palgrave.

Gordon, O. (2004) 'Civil society against the state: the independent press and the AFRC–RUF Junta', in I. Abdullah (ed.),, *Between Democracy and Terror: The Sierra Leone Civil War*, Dakar: CODESRIA, pp. 180–96.

Graybill, L. (2000) 'Lingering legacy: apartheid and the South African press', *Current History* 99(637): 227–30.

Gros, J.-G., and Mentan, T. (2003) 'Elections and democratization in Cameroon: Problems and prospects', in J.-G. Gros (ed.), *Cameroon: Politics and Society in Critical Perspectives*, New York: University Press of America, pp. 131–65.

Grossman, L.K. (1994) 'Reflections on life along the electronic superhighway', *Media Studies Journal* 8(1): 27–39.

Guiffo, S.L. (1993) 'Challenge hebdo et le patriote dans la transition démocratique au cameroun: deux approches du traitement de l'information politique nationale du 1er octobre 1990 au 31 octobre 1992', DSSTIC dissertation, ASMAC/ESSTIC Yaoundé (mimeo).

Guyer, J. (1993) 'Wealth in people and self-realization in Equatorial Africa', *Man* (NS), 28(2): 243–65.

Gwellem, J. (1994) 'l'ethique professionnelle et le journaliste Camerounais', paper presented at the National Forum on Communication, Yaoundé, 29 August–1 September.

Hachten, W.A. (1993) *The Growth of Media in the Third World: African Failures, Asian Successes*. Ames: Iowa State University Press.

Halloran, J.D. (1963) *Control or Consent? A Study of the Challenge of Mass Communication*. London: Sheed & Ward.

Halloran, J.D (1993) 'The European image: unity in diversity – myth or reality', presentation at the IAMCR Conference, Dublin, June.

Hamelink, C.J. (1983) *Cultural Autonomy in Global Communications: Planning National Information Policy*, London: Longman.

Hamelink, C.J. (1995) 'The democratic ideal and its enemies', in P. Lee (ed.), *The Democratization of Communication*, Cardiff: University of Wales Press, pp. 15–37.

Hamelink, C.J. (1996) 'Globalisation and human dignity: the case of the Information Superhighway', *Media Development* 43(1): 18–21.

Hamelink, C.J. (1999) 'Introduction: forgetting Africa in the New World equation', in L.U. Uche (ed.), *Mass Communication Democracy and Civil Society in Africa: International Perspectives*, Lagos: UNESCO–NATCOM, pp. 1–8.

Hann, C., and Dunn, E. (eds) (1996) *Civil Society: Challenging Western Models*, London: Routledge.

Harvey, E. (2000), 'Dare to criticise the presidency', *Mail and Guardian*, 7–13 January, p. 22.

Havel, V. (1986) *Living in Truth*, ed. J. Vladislav, London: Faber & Faber.

Head, S.W. (1963) 'Can a journalist be a "professional" in a developing country?', *Journalism Quarterly* 40(4): 594–8.

Head, S.W. (1977) 'Trends in Tropical African Societies', in G. Gerbner (ed.), *Mass Media Policies in Changing Cultures*, London: John Wiley, pp. 83–103.

Hisseini, M.S. (1996) 'Media and professional ethics in Niger', in K. Karikari (ed.), *Ethics in Journalism: Case Studies of Practice in West Africa*, Paris and Accra: Institut Panos, pp. 91–103.

Howard, W.S. (1980) 'Ici on parle français: the journalist and development in Francophone Africa', paper presented at the Twenty-Third Annual Meeting of the African Studies Association, Philadelphia, Pennsylvania, 15–18 October.

Hyden, G., Leslie, M., and Ogundimu, F.F. (eds) (2002) *Media and Democracy in Africa*, Uppsala: Nordiska Afrikainstitutet.

Hyden, G., and Leslie, M. (2002) 'Communications and democratization in Africa', in G. Hyden, M. Leslie and F.F. Ogundimu (eds), *Media and Democracy in Africa*, Uppsala: Nordiska Afrikainstitutet, pp. 1–27.

Hyden, G., and Okigbo, C. (2002) 'The media and the two waves of democracy', in G. Hyden, M. Leslie and F.F. Ogundimu (eds), *Media and Democracy in Africa*, Uppsala: Nordiska Afrikainstitutet, pp. 29–53.

Ibrahim, J. (2003) *Democratic Transition in Anglophone West Africa*, Dakar: CODESRIA.

Ibrahim, Z. (1999) 'What does "community" mean for community radio? Reality check', *Rhodes Journalism Review*, December, p. 15.

IDI (National Democratic Institute for International Affairs) (1993) *An Assessment of the October 11, 1992 Election in Cameroon.*

Jacobs, S. (2000) 'Where the HRC went wrong', *Rhodes Journalism Review*, August: 5.

Jensen, M. (2000), 'Making the connection: Africa and the Internet', *Current History* 99(637): 215–20.

Joseph, R.A. (1977) *Radical Nationalism in Cameroun: Social Origins of the UPC Rebellion*, Oxford: Oxford University Press.

Jua, B.N. (2003) 'Anglophone political struggles and state responses', in J.-G. Gros (ed.), *Cameroon: Politics and Society in Critical Perspectives*, New York: University Press of America, pp. 87–110.

Jua, B.N., and Nyamnjoh, F.B. (2002) 'Scholarship production in Cameroon: interrogating a recession', *African Studies Review* 45(2): 49–71.

Jussawalla, M. (1988) 'The information revolution and its impact on the world economy', in D.I. Riddle (ed.), *Information Economy and Development*, Bonn: Friedrich-Ebert-Stiftung, pp. 11–33.

Kadhi, J.S.M. (1999) 'Anglophone Africa: journalists – puppets of the proprietors?', in M. Kunczik (ed.), *Ethics in Journalism: A Reader on their Perception in the Third World*, Bonn: Friedrich-Ebert-Stiftung, pp. 82–133.

Kale, P.M. (1967) *Political Evolution of the Cameroons*, Buea: Government Printer.

Kandjii, K. (2000) 'De-regulation of the Namibian broadcasting industry: challenges and contradictions', paper presented at the Political Economy of the Media in Southern Africa Seminar, 25–29 April 2000, University of Natal, Durban.

Kapferer, J.-N. (1987) *Rumeurs: Le Plus Vieux Média du Monde*, Paris: Seuil.

Karikari, K. (ed.) (1996a) *Ethics in Journalism: Case Studies of Practice in West Africa*, Paris and Accra: Institut Panos.

Karikari, K. (1996b), 'Media ethics and promotion of democratic culture', in K. Karikari (ed.), *Ethics in Journalism: Case Studies of Practice in West Africa*, Paris and Accra: Institut Panos, pp. 141–52.

Karnik, N.S. (1998) 'Rwanda and the media: imagery, war and refuge', *Review of African Political Economy* 25(78): 611–23.

Kasfir, N. (1998) 'Introduction: the conventional notion of civil society: a critique', in N. Kasfir (ed.), *Civil Society and Democracy in Africa*, London: Frank Cass, pp. 1–20.

Kasoma, F.P. (ed.) (1994) Journalism Ethics in Africa, Nairobi: ACCE.

Kasoma, F.P. (1996) 'The foundations of African ethics (Afriethics) and the professional practice of journalism: the case for society-centred media morality', Africa Media Review 10(3): 93–116.

Kasoma, F.P. (1997a) 'The independent press and politics in Africa', Gazette 59(4–5): 295–310.

Kasoma, F.P. (1997b) 'Communication and press freedom in Zambia', in F. Eribo and W. Jong-Ebot (eds), Press Freedom and Communication in Africa, Trenton: Africa World Press, pp. 135–56.

Kasoma, F.P. (1999) 'Independent media, professionalism and ethics in journalism education', in L.U. Uche (ed.), Mass Communication Democracy and Civil Society in Africa: International Perspectives, Lagos: UNESCO–NATCOM, pp. 445–59.

Katz, E. (1977) 'Cultural continuity and change: the role of mass media', in M. Teheranian and V. Hakimzadeh (eds), Communications Policy for National Development, London: Routledge & Kegan Paul, pp. 109–29.

Katz, E., and Wedell, G. (1978) Broadcasting in the Third World, London: Macmillan.

Khan, A.W. (1998) 'Journalism and armed conflict in Africa: the civil war in Sierra Leone', Review of African Political Economy 25(78): 585–97.

Kofele-Kale, N. (1980) 'Reconciling the dual heritage: reflections on the "Kamerun Idea"', in N. Kofele-Kale (ed.), An African Experiment in Nation Building: the Bilingual Cameroon Republic Since Reunification, Boulder, CO: Westview Press, pp. 3–23.

Konings, P. (2003) 'Religious Revival in the Roman Catholic Church and the Autochthony–Allochthony Conflict in Cameroon', Africa 73(1): 31–56.

Konings, P., and Nyamnjoh, F.B. (1997) 'The anglophone problem in Cameroon', Journal of Modern African Studies 35(2): 207–29.

Konings, P., and Nyamnjoh, F.B. (2003) Negotiating an Anglophone Identity: A Study of the Politics of Recognition and Representation in Cameroon, Leiden: Brill.

Koomson, A.K.B. (1996) 'A Survey of ethical violations by Ghanaian journalists', K. Karikari (ed.), Ethics in Journalism: Case Studies of Practice in West Africa, Paris, Accra: Institut Panos, pp. 36–68.

Kunczik, M. (1988) Concepts of Journalism: North and South, Bonn: FES.

Kunczik, M. (ed.) (1999) Ethics in Journalism: A Reader on Their Perception in the Third World, Bonn: Friedrich-Ebert-Stiftung.

Kupe, T. (1999) 'Cultures of secrecy', Rhodes Journalism Review, December.

Kurian, G.T. (ed.) (1982) World Press Encyclopedia, London: Mansell Publishing.

Kymlicka, W. (ed.) (1995) The Rights of Minority Cultures, Oxford: Oxford University Press.

Land, M. (1992) 'Ivoirian television, willing vector of cultural imperialism', Howard Journal of Communications 4(1–2): 10–27.

Land, M. (1994) 'Cultural imperialism in Côte d'Ivoire: who's to blame', Faculty Papers: Midwestern State University, Series 3, 12 (1992–1994): 71–94.

Land, M. (1995) 'Reggae, resistance and the state: television and popular music in the Côte d'Ivoire', Critical Studies in Mass Communication 12(4): 438–54.

Land, M. (1997) *The Partisan Press in Cameroon and Democratic Change*, paper presented at the 47th Annual Conference of the International Communication Association, 22–26 May, Montreal.

Lardner, T. (1993) 'Democratization and forces in the African media', *Journal of International Affairs* 47(1): 89–93.

Lee, P. (1995) 'Introduction: the illusion of democracy', in P. Lee (ed.), *The Democratization of Communication*, Cardiff: University of Wales Press, pp. 1–14.

Lele, J.K. (1995) *Tribalisme et Exclusions au Cameroun: Le Cas des Bamiléké*, Yaoundé: Les Editions du CRAC.

Lent, J.A. (1997) 'Rebirth of cartooning in the South', *Media Development* 44(4): 3–7.

Lent, J.A. (2001) 'Cartooning and democratisation world-wide', *Media Development* 48(2): 54–8.

Lerner, D. (1964 [1958]) *The Passing of Traditional Society: Modernizing the Middle East*, New York: Free Press.

Leslie, M. (2002) 'The Internet and Democratization', in G. Hyden, M. Leslie and F.F. Ogundimu (eds), *Media and Democracy in Africa*, Uppsala: Nordiska Afrikainstitutet, pp. 107–28.

Le Vine, V.T. (1964) *The Cameroons: From Mandate to Independence*, Berkeley: University of California Press.

Lightfoot, D.A. (1965) 'The Zambia broadcasting corporation', *EBU Review* 89B: 27–9.

Linden, A. (1998) *Communication Policies and Human Rights in Third-World Countries*, Nijmegen: University of Amsterdam.

Lloyd, P.C. (1965) 'The political structure of African kingdoms: an exploratory model', *Political Systems and the Distribution of Power*, ASA Monographs 2, London: Tavistock, pp. 63–112.

Lootvoet, B., and Ecoutin, J.-M. (1993) 'Les maux de la presse écrite guinéenne', *Politique Africaine* 51: 153–60.

Lukong, P.N. (1987) 'Public feedback in Cameroon tribune: the case of the English semi–weekly', B.A. dissertation, ASMAC/ESSTI, Yaoundé (mimeo).

Lush, D. (1998) 'The role of the African media in the promotion of democracy and human rights', in S. Kayizzi-Mungerwa, A.O. Olukoshi, and L. Wohlgemuth (eds), *Towards a New Partnership with Africa: Challenges and Opportunities*, Uppsala: Nordiska Afrikainstitutet, pp. 42–65.

Lwanda, J.L. (1993) *Kamuzu Banda of Malawi: A Study in Promise, Power and Paralysis*, Scotland: Dudu Nsomba Publications.

Lynch, M.D. (1997/98) 'Information highways', in *World Information Report*, Paris: UNESCO, pp. 285–303.

Lyon, D., (1986) 'From "post-industrialism" to "information society": a new social transformation?', *Sociology* 20(4): 577–88.

Makali, D. (1998) 'The ugly face of media corruption: Samuel Gichuru buys out Dispatch Edition', *Expression Today* 8, September, pp. 1–3.

Mamdani, M. (1990) 'State and civil society in contemporary Africa: reconceptualizing the birth of state nationalism and the defeat of popular movements', *Africa Development* 15(3/4): 47–70.

Mamdani, M. (1996) *Citizen and Subject: Contemporary Africa and the Legacy of Late Colonialism*, Cape Town: David Philip.

Mamdani, M. (ed.) (2000) *Beyond Rights Talk and Culture Talk*, Cape Town: David Philip.

Manhando-Makore, S. (2001) 'Free for all? The case of Zimbabwe's media', *Media Development* 48(2): 14–18.

Martin, R. (ed.) (1999) *Speaking Freely: Expression and the Law in the Commonwealth*, Toronto: Irwin Law.

Mason, A. (2001) 'Cartoon journalism in Africa puts political power into perspective', *Media Development* 48(2): 50–53.

Mattelart, A., Delcourt, X., and Mattelart, M. (1984) *International Image Markets: In Search of an Alternative Perspective*, London: Comedia.

Mayer, W. (1993) 'The rights and responsibilities of journalists and the means of upholding them in the West', *International Affairs* 9: 56–62.

Mazonde, I. (ed.) (2002) *Minorities in the Millennium: Perspectives from Botswana*, Gaborone: Lightbooks.

Mbassi-Manga, F. (1964) 'Cameroon: a marriage of three cultures', *Abbia* (special) 5, March: 131–44.

M'Bayo, R.T., Onwumechili, C., and Nwanko, N.R. (eds) (2000) *Press and Politics in Africa*, Lewiston, NY: Edwin Mellen Press.

Mbembe, A. (1984) *Ruben um Nyobe, Le Problème National Kamerunais*, Paris: L'Harmattan.

Mbembe, A. (1992) 'Provisional notes on the postcolony', *Africa* 62(1): 3–37.

Mbembe, A. (2001) *On the Postcolony*, Berkeley: University of California Press.

Mbida, A. (1995) 'La censure administrative de la presse au Cameroun', *Frequence Sud* 13(77–89).

Mbock, C.G. (ed.) (1996) *Cameroun Pluralisme Culturel et Convivialité*, Ivry: L'Edition Nouvelles du Sud.

Mbougueng, V., 1998, 'Côte d'Ivoire. Entre les marteau et... la plume', *Jeune Afrique l'Intelligent* 1976, 24–30 November: 2425.

McChesney, R.W. (1998) 'The political economy of global media', *Media Development* 45(4): 3–8.

McChesney, R.W. (2001) 'Global media, neoliberalism, and imperialism', *Monthly Review* 52: 10; www.monthlyreview.org/301rwm.htm.

McChesney, R.W., and Nichols, J. (2002) *Our Media Not Theirs: The Democratic Struggle against Corporate Media*, New York: Seven Stories Press.

McDowell, S., and Pashupati, K. (1998) 'India's Internet policies: ownership, control, and purposes', *Media Development* 45(4): 18–24.

McQuail, D., and Siune, K. (eds) (1998) *Media Policy: Convergence, Concentration and Commerce*, London: Sage.

Medard, J.-F. (1978) 'L'état sous-développé au Cameroun', *Année Africaine*, pp. 35–84.

Media Development (2000) 'Okinawa Charter on Global Information Society', 47(4): 47–50.

Medubi, O. (2000) 'Leadership stereotypes and lexical choices: an example of Nigerian cartoons', International Journal of Comic Art 2(1): 198–206.

Mehler, A. (1997) 'Cameroun: une transition qui n'a pas eu lieu', in J.-F. Daloz and Quantin (eds), Transistions Démocratiques Africaines: Dynamiques et Contraintes (1990–1994), Paris: Karthala.

Melody, W.H. (1987) 'The Information Society: implications for economic institutions and market theory', in Jörg Becker (ed.), Transborder Data Flow and Development, Bonn: Friedrich-Ebert-Stiftung, pp. 15–28.

Menang, T. (1996) 'A Survey of Cameroon's new English language newspaper', Epasa Moto 1(3): 320–28.

Mendo Ze, G. (1990) Pour un Multipartisme Réfléchi en Afrique Noire: Le Cas du Cameroun, Yaoundé: Editions Gaps/Gideppe.

Mentan, E.T. (1996) 'Constitutionalism, press, and factional politics: coverage of SAWA minority agitations in Cameroon', in S. Melone, A.M. She and L. Sindjoun (eds), La Réforme Constitutionnelle du 18 Janvier 1996 au Cameroun: Aspects Juridiques et Politiques, Yaoundé: Friedrich-Ebert-Stiftung/GRAP, pp. 182–98.

Mentan, E.T. (1997) 'Colonial legacies, democratisation and the ethnic question in Cameroon', in D. Zognong and I. Mouiche (eds), Démocratisation et Rivalités Ethniques au Cameroun, Yaoundé: CIREPE, pp. 33–61.

Mercer, C. (2002) Towards Cultural Citizenship: Tools for Cultural Policy and Development, Stockholm: Bank of Sweden Tercentenary Foundation/Gidlunds Forlag.

Merrill Lynch (2002) Wireless Matrix – 4Q01: Quarterly Update on Global Wireless Industry Metrics, New York: Merrill Lynch.

Meyer, R. (1994) 'Démocratie et développement: le rôle des médias en Afrique', Développement et Coopération 6: 18–21.

Miller, D., and Slater, D. (2000) The Internet: An Ethnographic Approach, Oxford: Berg.

Ministry of Communication (ed.) (1993) Human Rights in Cameroon: White Paper Published by the Government of the Republic of Cameroon, Yaoundé: Les Éditions de L'Imprimerie Nationale.

Minnie, J. (1999) 'The Winds of Windhoek', Rhodes Journalism Review, December: 12–13.

MISA, (1994) Media in Angola: Report of the MISA Task Force to Angola December 1–8 1993 Organised in Conjunction with the Sindicato dos Jornalistas Angolanos (SJA), Windhoek: Media Institute of South Africa.

MISA (1999) So This Is Democracy? State of the Media in Southern Africa 1998, Windhoek: MISA.

Mkandawire, T., and Olukoshi, A. (eds) (1995) Between Liberalisation and Repression: The Politics of Structural Adjustment in Africa, Dakar: CODESRIA Books.

Mnangagwa, E.D. (1996) 'Press freedom: the Zimbabwe experience – 2', Willie Musarurwa Memorial Trust (ed.), Towards Press Freedom, Gweru: Superprint, pp. 112–18.

Moemeka, A.A. (1997) 'Communalistic societies: community and self-respect as African values', in C. Christians and M. Traber (eds), *Communication Ethics and Universal Values*, London: Sage, pp. 170–93.

Mogekwu, M. (2001) 'The politics of press freedom and the national economy in Swaziland', *Media Development* 48(2): 19–24.

Monga, C. (1992) *La Recomposition du Marche Politique au Cameroun* (1991–1992): *De la Nécessité d'un Aménagement du Monitoring Electoral*, Forum Démocratique: Fondation Friedrich-Ebert-Stiftung.

Monga, C. (1995) 'Civil society and democratisation in francophone Africa', *Journal of Modern African Studies* 33(3): 359–79.

Monga, C. (1996) *The Anthropology of Anger: Civil Society and Democracy in Africa*, Boulder, CO: Lynne Rienner.

Monga, C. (1997) 'Cartoons in Cameroon: anger and political derision under monocracy', in K. Anyidoho (ed.), *The Word Behind Bars and the Paradox of Exile*, Evanston, IL: Northwestern University Press, pp. 146–69.

Monga, Y. (2000) '"Au Village!": Space, Culture, and Politics in Cameroon', *Cahiers d'Etudes Africaines*, 40(160): 723–49.

Mono Ndjana, H. (1997a) *Les Proverbes de Paul Biya*, Yaoundé: Edition du Carrefour.

Mono Ndjana, H., (1997b), 'Anti-plaidoyer pour les ethnies', in F.E. Boulaga (ed.), *La Démocratie à l'Epreuve du Tribalisme*, Yaoundé: Friedrich-Ebert-Stiftung and Gerddes, pp. 95–105.

Morris, A., and Bouillon, A. (eds) (2001) *African Immigration to South Africa: Francophone Migration of the 1990s*, Protea and IFAS: Pretoria.

Mpe, P. (2001) *Welcome to Our Hillbrow*, University of Natal Press: Pietermaritzburg.

Mukasa, S.G. (1998) 'Towards a global knowledge for environmentally sustainable development agenda in 21st century Southern Africa', *Communicatio* 17(1): 1–27.

Mukong, A. (1985) *Prisoner without a Crime*, Limbe: Alfresco.

Mulcahy, K.V., and Widoff, J. (1986) 'The administrative foundations of American public broadcasting', *Journal of Arts Management and Law* 15(4): 31–58.

Munzu, S. (1993) 'Le droit pénal et la communication de masse dans un état de droit: perspectives et orientations', paper presented at the UNESCO seminar on 'Le Cadre d'Exercice de la Liberté de Presse dans un Etat de Droit', 6–10 September, Yaoundé.

Murdock, G. (1994) 'The new mogul empires: media concentration and control in the age of divergence', *Media Development* 41(4): 3–6.

Mwampembwa (Gado), G. (1997) 'African cartoonists take risks', *Media Development* 44(4): 17–18.

Mytton, G. (1983) *Mass Communication in Africa*, London: Edward Arnold.

Ndao, M., (1996) 'Media and professional ethics in Senegal', in K. Karikari (ed.), *Ethics in Journalism: Case Studies of Practice in West Africa*, Paris and Accra: Institut Panos, pp. 120–40.

Ndembiyembe, P.C., (1997) 'Média, tribalisme et démocratie', in F.E. Boulaga.

(ed.), *La Démocratie à l'Epreuve du Tribalisme*, Yaoundé: Friedrich-Ebert-Stiftung and Gerddes, pp. 49–57.

Ndogo, K. (1980) 'La presse privée au Cameroun depuis l'indépendance: thermomètre zéro', B.A. dissertation, ESIJY, Yaoundé (mimeo).

Ndongo, C. (1997) *Paul Biya: Un Nouvel Élan*, Yaoundé: Editions Africa MultiMédia.

Ndongo, J.F. (1985) 'La responsabilité du journaliste du renouveau', *L'Unité* (special issue) 663: 29–30.

Ndongo, V.N. (1987) *Information et Démocratie en Afrique: L'Expérience Camerounaise*, Yaoundé: SOPECAM.

Ndongo, V.N. (1993) *Les Médias au Cameroun: Mythes et Délires d'une Société en Crise*. Paris: L'Harmattan.

Ngah, A. (1998) 'Journalisme et considerations déontologiques au Cameroun', M.A. dissertation, FSSG, Institute Catholique de Yaoundé (mimeo).

Ngenge, T.S. (2003) 'The institutional roots of the "Anglophone Problem" in Cameroon', in J.-G. Gros (ed.), *Cameroon: Politics and Society in Critical Perspectives*, New York: University Press of America, pp. 61–86.

Ngniman, Z. (1993) *Cameroun: La Démocratie Emballée*. Yaoundé: Editions CLE.

Ngugi, C.M. (1995) 'The mass media and democratisation in Africa', *Media Development* 42(4): 49–52.

Ngwainmbi, K.E. (1995) *Communication Efficiency and Rural Development in Africa*, Lanham, MD: Rowman & Littlefield.

Ngwane, G. (1997) 'Cameroon: nation at a crossroads', *West Africa*, 20–26 October, pp. 1678–80.

Nji, R.Y. (1985) 'Effects of censorship on Cameroon press: (a 19 years experience 1966–1985)', B.A. dissertation, ASMAC/ESSTI, Yaoundé (mimeo).

Nkwi, P.N. (1979) 'Cameroon grassfield chiefs and modern politics', *Paideuma* 25: 99–115.

Nkwi, P.N., and Nyamnjoh, F.B. (eds) (1997) *Regional Balance and National Integration in Cameroon: Lessons Learned and the Uncertain Future*, Yaoundé: ASC/ICASSR.

Nkwi, P.N., and Warnier, J.-P. (1982) *Elements for a History of the Western Grassfields*. Yaoundé: University of Yaoundé.

Nkwo, T.Z. (1975) 'Broadcasting in English-speaking Cameroon: a general survey', B.A. dissertation, ESIJY, Yaoundé (mimeo).

Nlandu-Tsasa, C. (1997) *La Rumeur au Zaire de Mobutu: Radio-Trottoir à Kinshasa*, Paris: L'Harmattan.

Ntemfac, O. (1993) 'Ethnicity and power in the newsroom: a statistical presentation of staff recruitment and deployment in CRTV in 1993', DSSTIC dissertation, ASMAC/ESSTIC, Yaoundé (mimeo).

N'thepe, G.N. (1993) 'Aspects pratiques de la loi relative à la liberté de communication sociale', paper presented at the UNESCO seminar on 'Le Cadre d'Exercice de la Liberté de Presse dans un État de Droit', 6–10 September, Yaoundé.

Ntiyanogeye, A. (1994) *Répertoire de la Presse d'Information au Burundi: Des Origines à nos Jours*, Bujumbura: Editions Intore.

Ntumazah, N. (2001) Ndeh Ntumazah: A Conversational Autobiography, Bamenda: Patron Publishing House.

Nyahunzvi, T., (1996), 'Journalism training: opportunities, limitations, institutions and funding', in Willie Musarurwa Memorial Trust (ed.), Towards Press Freedom, Gweru: Superprint, pp. 155–64.

Nyahunzvi, T.M. (2001) 'The Zimbabwe Mass Media Trust: an experiment that failed', Media Development 48(2): 31–6.

Nyamnjoh, F.B. (1985) 'Change in the concept of power amongst the Bum', M.A. dissertation, FLSS, Yaoundé, University of Yaoundé (mimeo).

Nyamnjoh, F.B. (1989) 'Broadcasting for nation-building in Cameroon: development and constraints', Ph.D. thesis, Centre for Mass Communication Research (CMCR), University of Leicester.

Nyamnjoh, F.B. (1996a) 'Africa and the information superhighway: silent majorities in search of a footpath', Africa Media Review 10(2): 1–21.

Nyamnjoh, F.B. (1996b) Mass Media and Democratisation in Cameroon, Yaoundé: Friedrich-Ebert-Stiftung.

Nyamnjoh F.B. (1996c) 'Media and multi-party politics in transitional Cameroon', Nord–Süd Aktuell 10(4): 738–52.

Nyamnjoh, F.B. (1996d) The Cameroon GCE Crisis: A Test of Anglophone Solidarity, Limbe: Nooremac.

Nyamnjoh, F.B. (1996e) 'Protest journalism as a literary genre: the case of Anglophone Cameroon journalism today', Epasa Moto 1(3): 350–57.

Nyamnjoh, F.B. (1999) 'Cameroon: a country united by ethnic ambition and difference', African Affairs 98(390): 101–18.

Nyamnjoh, F.B. (2000a) '"For many are called but few are chosen": globalisation and popular disenchantment in Africa', African Sociological Review 4(2): 1–45.

Nyamnjoh, F.B. (2000b) 'Zapiro and South African political cartooning', International Journal of Comic Art 2(2): 54–76.

Nyamnjoh, F.B. (2001a) 'Review article: expectations of modernity in Africa or a future in the rear-view mirror?', Journal of Southern African Studies 27(2): 363–9.

Nyamnjoh, F.B. (2001b) 'Delusions of development and the enrichment of witchcraft discourses in Cameroon', in H.L. Moore and T. Sanders (eds),, Magical Interpretations, Material Realities: Modernity,Witchcraft and the Occult in Postcolonial Africa, London: Routledge, pp. 28–49.

Nyamnjoh, F.B. (2002a) '"A child is one person's only in the womb": domestication, agency and subjectivity in the Cameroonian grassfields', in R. Werbner (ed.), Postcolonial Subjectivities in Africa, London: Zed, pp. 111–38.

Nyamnjoh, F.B. (2002b) 'Local attitudes towards citizenship and foreigners in Botswana: an appraisal of recent press stories', Journal of Southern African Studies 28(4): 755–75.

Nyamnjoh, F.B. (2002c) 'Cameroon: over twelve years of cosmetic democracy', News from the Nordic Africa Institute 3: 5–8; www.nai.uu.se.

Nyamnjoh, F.B. (2003) 'Might and right: chieftaincy and democracy in

Cameroon and Botswana', in W. van Binsbergen (ed.), The Dynamics of Power and the Rule of Law: Essays on Africa and Beyond, Leiden: African Studies Centre Leiden/Hamburg: Lit Verlag, pp. 121–49.

Nyamnjoh, F.B., and Fokwang, J. (2003) 'Politics and music in Cameroon', in J.-G. Gros (ed.), Cameroon: Politics and Society in Critical Perspectives, New York: University Press of America, pp. 185–209.

Nyamnjoh, F.B., and Jua, N.B. (2002) 'African universities in crisis: the political economy of violence in African educational systems', African Studies Review 45(2): 1–26.

Nyamnjoh, F.B., and Rowlands, M. (1998) 'Elite associations and the politics of belonging in Cameroon', Africa 68(3): 320–37.

Nyamongo, I.K., (1999) 'Burying the dead, culture and economics: an assessment of two Kenyan cases', International Social Science Journal 160: 255–61.

Nyati-Ramahobo, L. (2002) 'From a phone call to the high court: Wayeyi visibility and the Kamanakao Association's campaign for linguistic and cultural rights in Botswana', Journal of Southern African Studies 28(4): 685–709.

OAU, (1995), 'OAU paper presented at ICC workshop on New Information Technology and Standardization of Communication Equipment in Africa', ICC's Seminar on New Information Technologies in Africa, Yaoundé, 29–31 May.

Ochieng, P. (1992) I Accuse the Press: An Insider's View of the Media and Politics in Africa, Nairobi: Initiatives Publishers and Acts Press.

Ogbondah, C.W. (1997) 'Communication and democratization in Africa: constitutional changes, prospects and persistent problems for the media', Gazette 59(4–5): 271–94.

Ogbondah, C.W. (2002) 'Media Laws in Political Transition', in G. Hyden, M. Leslie and F.F. Ogundimu (eds), Media and Democracy in Africa, Uppsala: Nordiska Afrikainstitutet, pp. 55–80.

Ogundimu, F.F. (2002) 'Media and democracy in twenty-first-century Africa', in G. Hyden, M. Leslie and F.F. Ogundimu (eds), Media and Democracy in Africa, Uppsala: Nordiska Afrikainstitutet, pp. 207–38.

Okigbo, C. (1995) 'National images in the age of the information superhighway: African perspectives', Africa Media Review 9(2): 105–21.

Okunnor, A. (1998) 'Freedom of the press: legal codes governing the operation of Africa's press industry', West Africa 4186: 269–70.

Olorunnisola, A.A. (2000) 'African media, information providers and emigrants as collaborative nodes in virtual social networks', African Sociological Review 4(2): 46–71.

Oloyede, B. (1996) Press Freedom in Nigeria: A Critical Analysis of Salient Issues, Abeokuta: Kunle Alayande.

Onadipe, A. (1998) 'The media in Africa: in the eye of the storm', West Africa 4186: 262–5.

Onomo, J.P.O. (1997) 'Symétries hégémoniques Beti–Bamiléké et rivalités politiques', in D. Zognong and I. Mouiche (eds), Démocratisation et Rivalités Ethniques au Cameroun, Yaoundé: CIREPE, pp. 93–122.

Owens, B., and Land M. (1999) 'Dissent and beyond: the independent press in two post-authoritarian systems', in J. Biberman and A.F. Alkhafaji (eds), *Business Research Yearbook: Global Business Perspectives* 6: 565–9.

Owona, G. (1995) *Un Bateau dans la Tourmente? Cameroun: Des Raisons d'Espérer*, Douala: Editions Intermedia.

Palmer, A.W. (1997) 'Reinventing the democratic press of Benin', in F. Eribo and W. Jong-Ebot (eds), *Press Freedom and Communication in Africa*, Trenton, NJ: Africa World Press, pp. 243–62.

Paterson, C.A. (1998) 'Reform or re-colonisation? The overhaul of African television', *Review of African Political Economy* 25(78): 571–83.

Phiri, B., and Powers, D. (2001) 'Plurality and power relations in Zambian broadcasting', *Media Development* 48(2): 25–30.

Piot, C. (1999) *Remotely Global: Village Modernity in West Africa*, Chicago: University of Chicago Press.

Pityana, N.B. (2000) 'South Africa's inquiry into racism in the media: the role of national institutions in the promotion and protection of human rights', *African Affairs* 99(397): 525–32.

Pollock, J.H.H. (1927) 'An assessment report on the Bum area', Buea Archives, unpublished.

Pratt C.B. (1994) 'Journalism ethics and the new communication', in P.F. Kasoma (ed.), *Journalism Ethics in Africa*, Nairobi: ACCE, pp. 51–70.

Quenum, A.J. (1996) 'Journalists and professional ethics in Benin', in K. Karikari (ed.), *Ethics in Journalism: Case Studies of Practice in West Africa*, Paris and Accra: Institut Panos, pp. 10–24.

Ramose, M.B. (1999) *African Philosophy through Ubuntu*, Harare: Mond Books.

Ramphele, M. (1999) 'When good people are silent...', Vice Chancellor's address, graduating ceremony, Faculty of Humanities, University of Cape Town, December, *Mail and Guardian*, 10–16 December, p. 13.

Rando, G. (1986) 'Broadcasting in Italy: democracy and monopoly of the airwaves', *Media Information Australia* 40: 39–48.

Randrianja, S. (1998) 'Ethnonationalisme et représentations de l'histoire à travers Feon'ny Merina et Masova', paper presented at ASC Leiden seminar on 'The Role of Media in Africa', Leiden, 8 October.

Ras-Work, T. (ed.) (1998) *Tam Tam to Internet*, Johannesburg: Mafube.

Rhodes Journalism Review (1999) 'African Media Debates', Department of Journalism and Media Studies, Rhodes University, December.

Rhodes Journalism Review (2000) 'Racism in the Media', Department of Journalism and Media Studies, Rhodes University, August.

Ronning, H. (1994) *Media and Democracy: Theories and Principles with Reference to an African Context*, Harare: Sapes Books.

Rowlands, M. (2004) 'Cultural rights and wrongs: uses of the concept of property', in K. Verderey and C. Humphrey (eds), *Property in Question: Value Transformations in the Global Economy*, Oxford: Berg, pp. 302–19.

Rowlands, M., and Warnier, J.-P. (1988) 'Sorcery, power and the modern state in Cameroon', *Man* 23(1): 118–32.

294   Africa's Media, Democracy and the Politics of Belonging

Rudin, H.R. (1938) Germans in the Cameroons 1884–1914: A Case Study in Modern Imperialism, London: Jonathan Cape.

Rueschemeyer, D., Stephen, E.H., and Stephens, J.D. (1992) Capitalist Development and Democracy, Cambridge: Polity Press.

Russell, A. (1999) Big Men, Little People: Encounters in Africa, London: Macmillan.

Rutten, M. (1998) 'The media in multiparty Kenya: a look at the watchdogs', paper presented at ASC Leiden seminar on 'The Role of Media in Africa', Leiden, 8 October.

Rwomire, A. (1992) 'The mass media and cultural imperialism in Southern Africa', Peace Research: The Canadian Journal of Peace Studies 24(3): 33–50.

Rying, C.-A. (1994) 'Entre libération et survie', Cahiers pour Croire Aujourd'hui 143: 17–21.

Sangho, O.S. (1996) 'Problems of ethics in the media of Mali', in K. Karikari (ed.), Ethics in Journalism: Case Studies of Practice in West Africa, Paris and Accra: Institut Panos, pp. 69–90.

Schlesinger, P. (1978) Putting 'Reality' Together: BBC News, London: Constable.

Schramm, W. (1964) Mass Media and National Development: The Role of Information in the Developing Countries, Stanford: Standford University Press.

SDLP/UJAO (1994) L'État de la Presse en Afrique de l'Ouest: Rapport 1993, Dakar: GIA.

SDLP/UJAO (1995) Média, Legislation et Déontologie en Afrique de l'Ouest, Dakar: La Senegalaise de l'Imprimerie.

Seaton, J. (1988) 'Broadcasting and the theory of public service', in J. Curran and J. Seaton, Power without Responsibility: The Press and Broadcasting in Britain, London: Routledge.

Seibert, G. (1999) Comrades, Clients and Cousins: Colonialism, Socialism and Democratization in Sao Tomé and Príncipe, Leiden: Leiden University Press.

Seiden, M.H. (1974) Who Controls the Mass Media?, New York: Basic Books.

Senghor, D. (1996) 'Introduction: the emergence of information ethics', in K. Karikari (ed.), Ethics in Journalism: Case Studies of Practice in West Africa, Paris and Accra: Institut Panos, pp. 1–9.

Sesay, S.K. (1998) 'Press on the cross: reports on how the press is faring in Sierra Leone', West Africa 4186: 266–8.

Shanda-Tonme (1995) Crise du SDF et Problème Bamiléké: Les Clarifications, Bafoussam: Editions Les Montagnes.

Shapiro, J. (1996) Zapiro: The Madiba Years, Cape Town: David Philip.

Shapiro, J. (1997) Zapiro: The Hole Truth, Cape Town: David Philip.

Sindjoun, L. (ed.) (2004) Comment Peut-on Être Opposant au Cameroun? Politique Parlementaire et Politique Autoritaire, Dakar: CODESRIA.

Socpa, A. (2002) Democratisation et Autochtonie au Cameroun: Trajectoires Regionales Divergentes, Leiden: Leiden University Press.

Søndergaard, H. (1999) 'Some reflections on public service broadcasting', Nordicom Review 20(1): 21–8.

Sonnè, W. (1997) 'De la dynamique de la qualité d'autochtone dans la démocratisation au Cameroun: cas de la région de Douala', in D. Zognong and I. Mouiche (eds), *Démocratisation et Rivalités Ethniques au Cameroun*, Yaoundé: CIREPE, pp. 179–99.

Soola, E.O. (1996) 'Cases of unethical practice in some Nigerian media', K. Karikari, *Ethics in Journalism: Case Studies of Practice in West Africa*, Paris and Accra: Institut Panos, pp. 104–19.

SOPECAM (1991) *Cameroon: Rights and Freedoms: Collection of Recent Texts*, Yaoundé: SOPECAM.

Soyinka, W. (1996) 'Address', in Willie Musarurwa Memorial Trust (ed.), *Towards Press Freedom*, Gweru: Superprint, pp. 10–12.

Spitulnik, D. (2002) 'Alternative small media and communicative spaces', in G. Hyden, M. Leslie and F.F. Ogundimu (eds), *Media and Democracy in Africa*, Uppsala: Nordiska Afrikainstitutet, pp. 177–205.

Syvertsen, T. (1999) 'The many uses of the "public service" concept', *Nordicom Review* 20(1): 5–12.

Tabapssi, F.T. (1999) *Le Modèle Migratoire Bamiléké (Cameroun) et Sa Crise Actuelle: Perspectives Économique et Culturelle*, Leiden: Leiden University Press.

Tabi, E.M. (1994) 'Impact of interpersonal communication on the efficiency and productivity of an organisation: the case of CRTV', dissertation, Institut International de Jeunesse et Sport (IIJS), Yaoundé (mimeo).

Takougang, J. (1997) 'Cameroon: Biya and incremental reform', in J.F. Clark and D.E. Gardinier (eds), *Political Reform in Francophone Africa*, Boulder: Westview Press, pp. 162–81.

Takougang, J. (2003) 'The 2002 legislative election in Cameroon: a retrospective on Cameroon's stalled democracy movement', *Journal of Modern African Studies* 41(3): 421–35.

Takougang, J., and Krieger, M. (1998) *African State and Society in the 1990s: Cameroon's Political Crossroads*, Boulder: Westview Press.

Tanjong, E., and Ngwa, G.A. (2002) 'Public perceptions of Cameroonian journalists', in F. Eribo, and E. Tanjong (eds), *Journalism and Mass Communication in Africa: Cameroon*, Lanham, MD: Lexington Books/Rowman & Littlefield, pp. 17–24.

Tataw, E.E. (1984) 'The English language private press in the South West Province: problem and promise', B.A. dissertation, ASMAC/ESSTI, Yaoundé (mimeo).

Taylor, C. (1994) 'The politics of recognition', in A. Gutmann (ed.), *Multiculturalism: Examining the Politics of Recognition*, Princeton: Princeton University Press.

Tchindji, P.-P. (1996) *Le Régime Camerounais de Répression Judiciaire des Infractions de Presse: Analyse Critique du Système Contenu dans la Loi 90/052 du 19 Décembre 1990*, Yaoundé: Friedrich-Ebert-Stiftung.

Tchop Tchop (1997) *Candidat Unique de l'Opposition*, vol. 1 (audio sketch), Douala.

Teer-Tomaselli, R. (2001) 'Transformation, nation-building and the South African media, 1993–1999', in K. Tomaselli and H. Dunn (eds), *Media, Democracy and Renewal in Southern Africa*, Denver: International Academic Publishers.

Teer-Tomaselli, R., and Tomaselli, K. (1996) 'Reconstituting public service broadcasting: media and democracy during transition in South Africa', in M.B. Anderson (ed.), Media and Democracy, Oslo: University of Oslo Press, pp. 217–42.

Thioune, R.M. (ed.) (2003) Information and Communication Technologies for Development in Africa: Opportunities and Challenges for Community Development, vol. 1, Dakar: IDRC/CODESRIA.

Thoka, M.D. (2001) 'Cellphones, ancestors and rural/urban connections. report of research conducted in Monwabisi Park in November 2000', paper presented at Joint Conference of AASA and SASCA, UNISA, Pretoria, 9–11 April.

Thomas, P., and Lee, P. (1994) 'Editorial: public communication – superhighway or one-way street', Media Development 41(4): 2.

Thomas, P.N., and Lee, P. (1997) 'Editorial', Media Development 44(4): 2.

Thomas, P.N., and Lee, P. (1998) 'Editorial', Media Development 45(4): 2.

Thomas, P.N., and Nain, Z. (eds) (2004) Who Owns the Media? Global Trends and Local Resistances, Southbound/WACC/Zed Books: London.

Todd, P., and Bloch, J. (2003) Global Intelligence: The World's Secret Services Today, London: Zed Books.

Tolen, A. (1997) The Electoral Process in Cameroon, Yaoundé: FEMEC.

Tomaselli, K. (2002) 'Media ownership and democratization', in G. Hyden, M. Leslie and F.F. Ogundimu (eds), Media and Democracy in Africa, Uppsala: Nordiska Afrikainstitutet, pp. 129–55.

Tomaselli, K., and Dunn, H. (2001) 'Reform and outreach: analysing Southern African media', Media Development 48(2): 3–8.

Toulabor, C.-M. (1981) 'Jeu de mots, jeu de vilains', Politique Africaine 1(3): 55–71.

Toure, A. Jr. (1996) 'A survey of media and ethics in la Côte d'Ivoire', in K. Karikari (ed.), Ethics in Journalism: Case Studies of Practice in West Africa, Paris and Accra: Institut Panos, pp. 25–35.

Tudesq, A.-J. (1992) L'Afrique Noire et ses Televisions, Paris: Antropos/INA.

Tudesq, A.-J. (1995) Feuilles d'Afrique: Étude de la Presse de l'Afrique Sub-Saharienne. Talence: MSHA.

Tudesq, A.-J. (1997) 'Problems of press freedom in Côte d'Ivoire', in F. Eribo and W. Jong-Ebot, (eds), Press Freedom and Communication in Africa, Trenton: Africa World Press, pp. 291–302.

Tueno Tagne, R.B. (1996) 'Le quatrième pouvoir sous l'emprise du capital: le phénomène du 'GOMBO' à la CRTV', B.A. dissertation, ASMAC/ESSTIC, Yaoundé (mimeo).

Tumi, C.C. (2000) 'Open letter to the Minister of Territorial Administration, Yaounde', The Post 222, 10 November; also http://wagne.net/messager/messager/forum/forum162a.html.

Uche L.U. (1985) 'The politics of Nigeria's radio broadcast industry: 1932–1983', Gazette 35(1): 19–29.

Uche, L.U. (ed.) (1996) North–South Information Culture: Trends in Global Communications and Research Paradigms, Lagos: Longman.

Uche, L.U. (1999a) 'Economic and emancipative potentials of the information superhighway regime for Africa south of the Sahara', in L.U. Uche (ed.), Mass Communication Democracy and Civil Society in Africa: International Perspectives, Lagos: UNESCO–NATCOM, pp. 191–203.

Uche, L.U. (ed.) (1999b) Mass Communication Democracy and Civil Society in Africa: International Perspectives, Lagos: UNESCO–NATCOM.

Ugboajah, F.O. (1985) '"Oramedia" in Africa', F.O. Ugboajah (ed.), Mass Communication, Culture and Society in West Africa, London: Hans Zell, pp. 165–76.

Ukpabi, C. (ed.) (2001) Handbook on Journalism Ethics: Journalism Practice and Training African Case Studies, Windhoek: MISA.

UNESCO, (1980) Intergovernmental Conference on Communication Policies in Africa, Yaoundé (Cameroon) 22–31 July 1980: Final Report, Paris: UNESCO.

UNJCI (1997) Écrire Parler Montrer: Être Journaliste, Abidjan: Friedrich-Ebert-Stiftung and Union Nationale des Journalistes de Côte d'Ivoire.

van Audenhove, L. (1998) 'The African information society: rhetoric and practice', Communicatio 24(1): 76–84.

van Binsbergen, W. (2004) 'Can ICT belong in Africa, or is ICT owned by the North Atlantic region?', in W. van Binsbergen and R. van Dijk (eds), Situating Globality: African Agency in the Appropriation of Global Culture, Leiden: Brill, pp. 107–46.

van de Veur, P.R. (2002) 'Broadcasting and political reform', in G. Hyden, M. Leslie and F.F. Ogundimu (eds), Media and Democracy in Africa, Uppsala: Nordiska Afrikainstitutet, pp. 81–105.

van Kessel, I. (1998) 'Mass media in South Africa: from liberation to black empowerment', paper presented at African Studies Centre seminar on 'The Role of Media in Africa', Leiden, 8 October.

Vladislav, J., (ed), (1986) Václav Havel or Living in Truth, London: Faber & Faber.

Vogt, A. (1996) 'Medienentwicklung, regionale Journalistenverbände und Medienkommissionen in Westafrika', Nord–Süd Aktuell 10(4): 727–37.

WAJA (1996) Accra Declaration on Media and Democracy in West Africa, Accra, 29 March.

Waldon, J. (1995) 'Minority cultures and the cosmopolitan alternative', in W. Kymlicka (ed.), The Rights of Minority Cultures, Oxford: Oxford University Press, pp. 93–119.

Washburn, P.C. (1985) 'International radio broadcasting: some considerations for political sociology', Journal of Political and Military Sociology 13(1): 33–51.

Wells, C. (1987) The UN, UNESCO and the Politics of Knowledge, London: Macmillan.

Werbner, R. (1996) 'Introduction: multiple identities, plural arenas', in R. Werbner and T. Ranger (eds), Postcolonial Identities in Africa, London: Zed Books, pp. 1–27.

Werbner, R. (2002) 'Introduction: postcolonial subjectivities: the personal, the political and the moral', in Richard Werbner (ed.), Postcolonial Subjectivities in Africa, London: Zed Books, pp. 1–21.

298   Africa's Media, Democracy and the Politics of Belonging

Werbner, R., and Gaitskell, D. (eds) (2002) 'Minorities and citizenship in Botswana', *Journal of Southern African Studies* 28(4).

Williams, R. (1979) 'Institutions of the technology', in A. Mattelart and S. Siegelaub (eds), *Communication and Class Struggle: Capitalism, Imperialism*, New York: International General, pp. 265–7.

Windseck, D. (1997) 'Contradictions in the democratization of international communication', *Media, Culture and Society* 19(2): 219–46.

Wiredu, K. (1997) 'Democracy and consensus in African traditional politics: a plea for a non-party polity', in E.C. Eze (ed.), *Postcolonial African Philosophy: A Critical Reader*, Oxford: Blackwell Publishers, pp. 303–12.

Wriston, W.B. (1994) 'The inevitable global conversation', *Media Studies Journal* 8(1): 17–25.

Wongibe E.F. (1987) 'Professional solidarity among Cameroon journalists', B.A. dissertation, ASMAC/ESSTI, Yaoundé (mimeo).

Wongo, A.A. (1977) 'Cameroun: la presse écrite malade', B.A. dissertation, ESIJY, Yaoundé (mimeo).

Yenshu, E. (1998) 'The discourse and politics of indigenous/minority peoples rights in some metropolitan areas of Cameroon', *Journal of Applied Social Sciences* 1(1): 59–76.

Yenshu, E. (2003) 'Levels of historical awareness: the development of identity and ethnicity in Cameroon', *Cahiers d'Études Africaines* 43(3) 171: 591–628.

Young, C. (1994) 'In search of civil society', in J.W. Harbeson, D. Rothchild and N. Chazan (eds), *Civil Society and the State in Africa*, Boulder: Lynne Rienner, pp. 33–50.

Zaffiro, J.J. (1993) 'Mass media, politics and society in Botswana: the 1990s and beyond', *Africa Today* 40(1): 7–25.

Zaffiro, J. (2000) 'Broadcasting reform and democratization in Botswana', *Africa Today* 47(1): 87–102.

Zeleza, P.T. (2003) *Rethinking Africa's Globalization, Volume 1: The Intellectual Challenges*, Trenton: Africa World Press.

Zhuwarara, R., Gecau, K., and Drag, M. (eds) (1997) *Media, Democratization and Identity*. Harare: University of Zimbabwe.

Ziegler, D., and Asante, M.K. (1992) *Thunder and Silence: The Mass Media in Africa*, Trenton: Africa World Press.

Zognong, D. (1997) 'La question Bamiléké pendant l'overture démocratique au Cameroun', in D. Zognong and I. Mouiche (eds), *Démocratisation et Rivalités Ethniques au Cameroun*, Yaoundé: CIREPE, pp. 123–55.

Index

308   *Africa's Media, Democracy and the Politics of Belonging*

Northern Michigan University

3 1854 008 082 235